Churchill's Black Dog

Churchill's Black Dog
and other phenomena of the human mind

Anthony Storr

COLLINS
8 Grafton Street, London W1, 1989

William Collins Sons and Co. Ltd
London · Glasgow · Sydney · Auckland
Toronto · Johannesburg

BRITISH LIBRARY CATALOGUING IN PUBLICATION DATA
Storr, Anthony, *1920-*
    Churchill's black dog: and other phenomena of the
    human mind.
    1. Creativity
    I. Title
    153.3′5

ISBN 0 00 215126 X

Printed and bound in Great Britain by
William Collins Sons and Co. Ltd, Glasgow

Contents

Preface

Freud defined psychological health as being able to love and work. The majority of the essays included in this collection are more concerned with the latter activity than with the former. I have long been interested in the psychology of the creative imagination. What internal dynamic forces impel men and women to devote so much time and energy to creative invention, whether in the arts or in the sciences? Although success may eventually bring the conventional rewards of fame and money, many artists and scientists struggle for years without attaining either, and some win recognition only posthumously. For example, Gregor Mendel's experiments laid the foundation for the science of genetics. Yet it was not until sixteen years after his death that the value of his work became widely appreciated. Creative work must be inspired by drives which have nothing to do with worldly success.

Freud considered that imaginative activity originated from dissatisfaction.

> We may lay it down that a happy person never phantasies, only an unsatisfied one. The motive forces of phantasies are unsatisfied wishes, and every single phantasy is the fulfilment of a wish, a correction of an unsatisfying reality. (*Standard Edition,* 9:146)

Freud tended to dismiss fantasy as illusory, escapist wish fulfillment, along with dreams and play; a view which I regard as profoundly mistaken, and which is dealt with at some length in the essay "Psychoanalysis and Creativity." The great creative achievements of mankind are not to be equated with idle daydreams. Nor, as Freud claimed, is the creativity of the artist quite different from that of the scientist, an assumption which is examined in "Why Psychoanalysis Is Not a Science."

Yet there is a sense in which Freud was right to derive imagination from dissatisfaction. For is it not part of human destiny never to be content with what is, but always to be seeking something better? This "hunger of imagination," as Dr. Johnson called it, operates at every level, from mundane desires for more food or money to utopian visions of universal harmony, whether on earth or in heaven. It is surely this hunger which accounts for man's supremacy as a species. If man, like some insects, was preprogrammed to be more or less perfectly adapted to his environment, he would live a stereotyped life with neither the need to look for anything better nor the capacity to imagine it. But man is extremely flexible. Because he is not specifically adapted to one particular environment, he can adapt to many. Because he only has a few inbuilt responses, he is capable of learning, of invention, of assimilating novelty, and of creating symbols, a capacity considered in the essay "The Psychology of Symbols." Man's creative adaptability paradoxically derives from his primary lack of adaptation.

Moreover, the life-span of both men and women extends far beyond the period of life during which reproduction is a prime concern. "Aspects of Adult Development" explores some of the changes which take place during the mid-life period and afterward, and underlines the fact that some of the works of art which we most treasure have been created by those past middle age.

Creative imagination is not, as Freud would have it, an

escape from reality, but an integral part of human nature which finds every variety of expression from gardening to poetry, from athletics to composing music. We are never content with what is; we must always strive after something better.

If discontent is the spur to imagination, we might expect to find that the most creative human beings were the most discontented. Although this is far too simple a view of a complex problem, there is some truth in it. Discontent is not the same as neurosis. The inner disharmony which makes particular human beings accomplish marvels is often alleviated by their achievements. It is those who can find no way of expressing or resolving their conflicts who become neurotic. The connection between creativity and mental illness is explored in "Sanity of True Genius."

As the essays on Churchill, Kafka, and Newton demonstrate, though dissimilar in temperament and creative in quite different fields, they were all driven men. However, during the greater part of their lives, their creative gifts protected them against breakdown. The same is true of C. G. Jung, who, in mid-life, admitted being threatened by psychosis.

No one reading the novels of William Golding can fail to recognize his preoccupation with the darker depths of human nature; but friendship, as well as ignorance, bars me from further speculation. The same considerations apply to my essay on C. P. Snow, which is a tribute to a warm and generous friend rather than a detailed exploration of either his novels or his personality.

The opposite of creativity is destructiveness; and so I have included the essay "Why Human Beings Become Violent." Murder, the ultimate act of violence, is briefly referred to as predominantly a domestic crime, a reflection which is explored in more detail in "Othello and the Psychology of Sexual Jealousy."

The last essay, "Psychiatric Responsibility in the Open

Society," may seem anomalous. During the course of my professional life, I have been very little involved with public affairs. But the employment of doctors, and more particularly of psychiatrists, in the interrogation of prisoners, aroused my wrath; and the first article which I wrote for a weekly paper was a protest against this infringement of the Hippocratic oath. I was particularly concerned about the use of sensory deprivation as a means of breaking down detainees in Northern Ireland. It might justifiably be said that this latter abuse was a perversion of creativity, which tenuously links this essay with the others in the book. The Ulster interrogators took research into brain function out of the laboratory, and transformed it into a method of extracting information by causing acute mental distress amounting to torture. I was shocked, not only by the cruelty involved, but by the misuse of scientific investigation.

hiatrists who attempt biographical studies of grea
are apt to allow theory to outrun discretion: with th
lt that many so-called psychoanalytic biographies ha
both bad biography and bad psychoanalysis. Th
strous study of Woodrow Wilson by Freud and Bullitt
se in point.

n this chapter, I advance a hypothesis about Church
ch I think is warranted by the facts. But what I have
must be regarded as tentative, for the possibilities
or in this complicated field are very great. Althoug
urchill himself provided many autobiographical detai
ecially in *My Early Life,* these are not the kind of deta
ich are of much service to the psychiatrist. For Church
owed as little interest in the complexities of his own p
ology as he did in the psychology of others; and wou
ve been the first to dismiss this essay as both futile a
pertinent. Moreover, as C. P. Snow remarks in his essay
riety of Men, Churchill's character was "abnormally imp
rable to most kinds of insight."[1] His deeds, speeches, a
reer have been lavishly and repeatedly recorded, but v
tle of what has been written about him reveals anything
s inner life. Although Churchill can be rated as an art
oth as writer and painter, he was not, like many arti
trospective or concerned with his own motives. Indeed
e had been, he could scarcely have achieved what he c
or introspection is the accomplice of self-distrust and
nemy of action.

Winston Churchill is still idolized, not only by those o
ho remember his speeches in 1940, and who believe,
o, that it was to his courage that we owe our escape fr
Nazi tyranny; but by men and women all over the world
vhom he has become a symbol, a personification of va
But Churchill was also a human being, with the same nee
nstincts, hopes, and fears which pertain to all of us. It i
disservice to a great man to draw attention to his huma
nor to point out that, like other men, he had imperfecti

Churchill's Black Dog

1

Churchill: The Man

THE PSYCHIATRIST WHO takes it upon himsel
character study of an individual whom he ha
engaged upon a project which is full of risk. I
of his profession, the psychiatrist has an unr
tunity for the appraisal of character, and may
that he knows more persons deeply and int
most of his fellows. But, when considering some
died, he is deprived of those special insights wh
be attained in the consulting room, and is, like t
obliged to rely upon what written evidence ha
available. In the analytical treatment of a patie
chiatrist is able to check the validity of the
which he proffers by the patient's response,
changes which occur in the patient as a re
increased comprehension of himself. The psych
often be wrong or premature in his interpreta
patient's behavior and character; but, as the long
analysis continues, errors will gradually be elimi
the truth recognized by both parties in the analyt
action. Deprived of this constant appraisal and re

and flaws. Churchill, in spite of his aristocratic birth and social position, started life with disadvantages which he never wholly conquered, although his whole career was an effort to overcome them. Without these disadvantages he would have been a happier, more ordinary, better-balanced, and lesser human being. But had he been a stable and equable man, he could never have inspired the nation. In 1940, when all the odds were against Britain, a leader of sober judgment might well have concluded that we were finished. Political leaders are accustomed to dissimulation. Even when defeat at the polls is imminent, or the policies which they support have been shown to be futile, they will, until the eleventh hour, continue to issue messages of hope to their supporters. In 1940, any political leader might have tried to rally Britain with brave words, although his heart was full of despair. But only a man who had known and faced despair within himself could carry conviction at such a moment. Only a man who knew what it was to discern a gleam of hope in a hopeless situation, whose courage was beyond reason, and whose aggressive spirit burned at its fiercest when he was hemmed in and surrounded by enemies, could have given emotional reality to the words of defiance which rallied and sustained us in the menacing summer of 1940. Churchill was such a man: and it was because, all his life, he had conducted a battle with his own despair that he could convey to others that despair can be overcome.

For Winston Churchill, like his ancestor the first Duke of Marlborough, suffered from prolonged and recurrent fits of depression; and no understanding of his character is possible unless this central fact is taken into account. His own name for depression was "Black Dog": and the fact that he had a nickname for it argues that it was all too familiar a companion. For great sections of his life, Churchill was successful in conquering his depression; but old age and the narrowing of his cerebral arteries in the end undermined his resistance. The last five years of his protracted existence were so melancholy that even Lord Moran draws a veil over them. It was a cruel fate which ordained that Churchill should survive till the age of ninety; for the "Black Dog" which he had controlled and largely mastered in earlier years at last overcame his fighting spirit.

Churchill is, of course, not a lone example of a great man suffering from recurrent depression. Goethe was of similar temperament; so were Schumann, Hugo Wolf, Luther, Tolstoy, and many others. The relation between great achievement and the depressive temperament has yet to be determined in detail, but there can be little doubt that, in some natures, depression acts as a spur. When depression is overwhelming, the sufferer relapses into gloom and an inactivity which may be so profound as to render him immobile. To avoid this state of misery is of prime importance; and so the depressive, before his disorder becomes too severe, may recurrently force himself into activity, deny himself rest or relaxation, and accomplish more than most men are capable of, just because he cannot afford to stop. We do not know how many men of exceptional achievement have this tendency towards depression, for it may often be well concealed. That some do, and that Churchill was one of them, admits of no possible doubt.

There is still dispute as to how far the tendency to suffer from recurrent depression is the product of heredity, and how much it is the result of early conditioning. Until the science of genetics is further advanced than it is at present, we shall not be able to answer this question fully. In Churchill's case, it is safe to assume that both factors played their part. For we know that at least two of Churchill's most distinguished ancestors were afflicted by swings of mood of some severity; and there is some evidence to suggest that they were not the only members of the family to be afflicted in this way. A. L. Rowse, writing of the first Duke of Marlborough, says:

Marlborough was *sensible* in the French sense, a most sensitive register of all the impressions that came to him. An artist by temperament in his ups and downs— the depression he got before the precipitant of action, the headaches that racked him at all the obstructions he had to put up with, and the self-control he exercised so habitually that it became second nature to him. It exacted its price.[2]

In 1705, the Duke wrote: "I have for these last ten days been so troubled by the many disappointments I have had that I think if it were possible to vex me so for a fortnight longer it would make an end of me. In short, I am weary of my life."[3] This weariness is a recurrent theme in his letters: "I am extremely out of heart," "My dearest soul, pity me and love me."[4] Although it may be argued that many men might write like this in times of stress, Rowse is not the only historian to observe that the first Duke of Marlborough alternated between optimism and depression in a way which some people would not expect in one of England's most famous military commanders. Winston Churchill himself observed, "Sometimes he was overdaring and sometimes overprudent; but they were separate states of mind, and he changed from one to the other in quite definite phases."[5]

The other Churchill forebear who exhibited the same kind of temperament was Lord Randolph, Winston's father. A. L. Rowse writes of him:

Though a very quick and piercing judge of a situation, his judgement was not really reliable. He was self-willed and impulsive, above all impatient. If he had only had patience all the rest would have come into line. But he had the defect of the artistic temperament, what we in our day of psychological jargon diagnose as the manic-depressive alternation—tremendous high spirits and racing energy on the upward bound, depression and discouragement on the down. This rhythm is present in a more or less marked degree with all persons of creative capacity, particularly in the arts. And clearly this strongly artistic strain we have observed in the stock came out in him, as it has done again in his son.[6]

Rowse is wrong in thinking that the manic-depressive alternation is present in all creative persons, some of whom belong to a very different temperamental group; but he is obviously right in his diagnosis of the Churchill family.

One other member deserves mention in this connection: the Winston Churchill who was father of the first Duke of Marlborough. An ardent Royalist, he retired to his country seat in East Devon after the King's forces had been defeated in the Civil War. Here he occupied himself by writing history: *Divi Brittanici: Being a Remark upon the Lives of all the Kings of this Isle.* Although we are not informed in detail of his temperamental constitution, A. L. Rowse describes him as follows: "Sunk in glum resentment, he had, at any rate, the consolation that intelligent people have who are defeated and out of favour: reading and writing. . . . His spirit was not defeated: it burns with unquenched ardour in what he wrote."[7] The later and more famous Winston adopted the same policy when he was out of office; and we may be thankful that creative activity can and does provide an effective defense against the depression which threatens to overwhelm those who possess this temperament when they are neither occupied nor sustained by holding a position of consequence.

Brendan Bracken says five of the last seven Dukes of Marlborough suffered from melancholia;[8] but it is difficult to confirm this even from Rowse's books, which Bracken alleges are the source of his information. There seems little doubt, however, that the cyclothymic temperament, that is, the tendency to rather extreme swings of mood, was part of the Churchill inheritance.

Before leaving the question of Churchill's heredity, we must take a glance at his physical endowment. It is probable, though not certain, that physique and character are intimately connected, and that the structure and shape of the body reflect genetic rather than environmental influences. A man's cast of mind is largely influenced by the way he is brought up and educated. His physical endowment, though modifiable to some extent, is more likely to be a datum of heredity.

It is clear that Churchill was possessed of enormous vitality. He survived to the age of ninety; and, by the age of eighty, he had surmounted a heart attack, three attacks of pneumonia, two strokes, and two operations. He habitually ate, drank, and smoked as much as he wanted, and this much was a great deal. Until he was seventy, he hardly ever complained of fatigue. Yet, this extraordinary constitution was not based upon natural physical strength of a conventional kind. Indeed, he started life with considerable physical disadvantages. As Lord Moran puts it: "I could see this sensitive boy, bullied and beaten at his school, grow up into a man, small in stature, with thin, unmuscular limbs, and the white delicate hands of a woman; there was no hair on his chest, and he spoke with a lisp and a slight stutter."[9]

Winston Churchill himself, in a letter from Sandhurst written in 1893, claimed, "I am cursed with so feeble a body, that I can scarcely support the fatigues of the day; but I suppose I shall get stronger during my stay here."[10] His height was only five feet six and a half inches; and his chest measured but thirty-one inches, which, by Sandhurst standards, was quite inadequate. When the poet Wilfred Scawen Blunt met Churchill in 1903, he described him as "a little square-headed fellow of no very striking appearance."[11] The physical courage which he consistently, and sometimes rashly, displayed was not based upon any natural superiority of physique, but rather upon his determination to be tough in spite of lack of height and muscle. His search for physical danger in early youth, and his reckless self-exposure in France, even though his behavior put others in danger, bear witness to the fact that his courage was not something that he himself took for granted, but rather something which he had to prove to himself; a compensation for inner doubts about his own bravery.

No man is immune from fear; but those who have been endowed by nature with exceptionally powerful physiques are generally less disturbed by physical danger than most of us. Churchill was uncommonly brave; but his courage was of a more remarkable and admirable variety than that which is based upon an innate superiority of physical endowment. He never forgot that, at his second preparatory school, he had been frightened by other boys throwing cricket balls at him, and had taken refuge behind some trees. This, to him, was a shameful memory; and, very early in life, he determined that he would be as tough as anybody could be. When he was eighteen, he nearly killed himself when being chased by his cousin and brother by jumping from a bridge to avoid capture. He fell twenty-nine feet, ruptured a kidney, remained unconscious for three days and unable to work for nearly two months. There is no doubt whatever that Churchill's physical courage was immense; but it rested upon his determination to conquer his initial physical disadvantages, much as Demosthenes' skill in oratory is said to have been the consequence of his will to overcome an impediment in his speech.

There have been many attempts to discern a relationship between physique and character, of which W. H. Sheldon's is both the most detailed and the most successful.[12] Sheldon claimed that he could discern three main components in a man's physical makeup, to which he gave the somewhat awkward names of endomorphy, mesomorphy, and ectomorphy. He also constructed a scale of temperament comprising three sets of twenty basic traits which were generally closely allied to the subject's physique. The three main varieties of temperament are known as viscerotonia, somatotonia, and cerebrotonia.

When one comes to examine Churchill, it is obvious that his physique was predominantly endomorphic. His massive head, the small size of his chest compared with his abdomen, the rounded contours of his body, and the small size of his extremities were all characteristic. So was his smooth, soft skin, which was so delicate that he always wore specially obtained silk underwear. One would expect a man with this physique to be predominantly viscerotonic in temperament: earthy, unhurried, deliberate, and predictable. Churchill actually does rate high on eleven out of the twenty viscerotonic traits; but he also scores almost equally high on somatotonia––that is, the temperament which is allied to the powerful and athletic frame of the mesomorph. According to Sheldon, men whose temperament differs widely from that which accords with their physique are particularly subject to psychological conflict, since they are at odds with their own emotional constitution.

Churchill was a very much more aggressive and dominant individual than one would expect from his basic physique. His love of risk, of physical adventure, his energy and assertiveness are traits which one would expect to find in a heavily muscled mesomorph, but which are unexpected in a man of Churchill's endomorphic structure.

In other words, we have a picture of a man who was, to a marked extent, forcing himself to go against his own inner nature: a man who was neither naturally strong, nor naturally particularly courageous, but who made himself both in spite of his temperamental and physical endowment. The more one examines Winston Churchill as a person, the more one is forced to the conclusion that his aggressiveness, his courage, and his dominance were not rooted in his inheritance, but were the product of deliberate decision and iron will. "I can look very fierce when I like," he said to his doctor.[13] But the expression of bulldog defiance which appears in his most popular photographs was not evident upon his face before the war, and, as Moran hints, is likely to have been assumed when declaiming speeches in front of the looking glass, and thenceforth used on appropriate public occasions.

Before turning from the question of inherited physical and psychological characteristics to consideration of the environmental influences which shaped Churchill's character, it is worth glancing at one more typology. The Swiss psychiatrist C. G. Jung was responsible for introducing the terms "extravert" and "introvert" into psychology; most people are familiar with the broad outlines of what is meant by these two terms. The extravert is a person whose chief orientation is toward the events and features of the external world. The recesses of his own soul are not of much concern to the predominantly extraverted person, nor is he much concerned with abstractions, ideas, or the subtleties of philosophy. The main interest of the extraverted person is in action, not in thought, and when troubled, he seeks to do things to distract himself rather than to explore his inner life to determine the cause of his distress. Churchill was undoubtedly highly extraverted. He showed little interest in philosophy and none in religion, and he dismissed psychology as irrelevant.

Jung's further subdivision of types into thinking, feeling, sensation, and intuition has not been widely accepted; but his delineation of the extraverted intuitive in *Psychological Types* fits Churchill so accurately that it ought to persuade people to take another look at the book. Jung writes:

> Wherever intuition predominates, a particular and unmistakeable psychology presents itself. . . . The intuitive is never to be found among the generally recognized reality values, but is always present where possibilities exist. He has a keen nose for things in the bud pregnant with future promise. . . . Thinking and feeling, the indispensable components of conviction, are, with him, inferior functions, possessing no decisive weight: hence they lack the power to offer any lasting resistance to the force of intuition.[14]

Hence, according to Jung, the intuitive's lack of judgment, and also his "weak consideration for the welfare of his neighbours." The intuitive is "not infrequently put down as a ruthless and immoral adventurer," terms often applied to Churchill in his youth, and yet "his capacity to inspire his fellow-men with courage, or to kindle enthusiasm for something new, is unrivalled."[15]

In his extremely interesting essay on Churchill, C. P. Snow refers to his lack of judgment. In fact, he says that it was "seriously defective." He goes on:

> Judgment is a fine thing: but it is not all that uncommon. Deep insight is much rarer. Churchill had flashes of that kind of insight, dug up from his own nature, independent of influences, owing nothing to anyone outside himself. Sometimes it was a better guide than judgment: in the ultimate crisis when he came to power, there were times when judgment itself could, though it did not need to, become a source of weakness.
>
> When Hitler came to power Churchill did not use judgment but one of his deep insights. This was absolute danger, there was no easy way round. *That* was what we needed. It was an unique occasion in our history. It had to be grasped by a nationalist leader. Plenty of people on the left could see the danger: but they did not know how the country had to be seized and unified.[16]

I think that the kind of insight to which C. P. Snow is referring might equally well be called intuition. Intuition is in many respects an unreliable guide, and some of Churchill's intuitions were badly wrong. In the First World War, his major strategic conception, the invasion of Gallipoli, was a failure, but his idea of the development of the tank, although it was not properly used at the time, was certainly a success. It is worth noting that as early as 1917 he described a project for making landing craft for tanks and also for

something very like the transportable harbors used in the
1944 invasion of France. His intuition was at least as often
right as it was wrong, and in his anticipation of the menace
of Hitler, and later of the threat of Russian domination of
Europe, he was intuitively right where others, who had
better judgment than he, failed to see the important point.
Jung's description of the extraverted intuitive has much
which applies to Churchill. As Jung points out, this type is
lacking in judgment. Churchill could never think for long at
a time. Although he had brilliant ideas, he was hardly susceptible to reason and could not follow a consecutive argument when presented to him by others. His famous demand
that all ideas should be presented to him on a half sheet of
paper is an illustration of this point. Alanbrooke, in his
wartime diary, wrote of him: "Planned strategy was not his
strong card. He preferred to work by intuition and by
impulse. . . . He was never good at looking at all the implications of any course he favoured. In fact, he frequently
refused to look at them."[17] It is also true that he was, in
many respects, deficient in feeling. He had little appreciation of the feelings of others. On three separate occasions,
Churchill had promised Alanbrooke the supreme command
of the Allied forces. Yet, when it was finally decided that the
invasion of Europe should be entrusted to the command of
an American, Churchill showed little appreciation of the
bitter disappointment which Alanbrooke experienced: "Not
for one moment did he realize what this meant to me. He
offered no sympathy, no regrets at having had to change his
mind, and dealt with the matter as if it were one of minor
importance."[18] As Jung writes, "Consideration for the welfare of others is weak."[19]

All those who worked with Churchill paid tribute to the
enormous fertility of his new ideas, the inexhaustible stream
of invention which poured from him, both when he was
Home Secretary, and later when he was Prime Minister and
director of the war effort. All those who worked with him

also agreed that he needed the most severe restraint put
upon him, and that many of his ideas, if they had been put
into practice, would have been utterly disastrous.

In Jungian terminology, Churchill was an extraverted
intuitive. In W. H. Sheldon's classification, he was predominantly endomorphic, with a strong secondary mesomorphic
component. In terms of classical, descriptive psychiatry, he
was of cyclothymic temperament, with a pronounced tendency to depression. These descriptive classifications,
though overloaded with jargon, are still valuable as an
approach to character, but they reveal very little about the
dynamics of a person's inner life. What follows will be an
attempt, necessarily speculative, to examine something of
Churchill's psychological structure insofar as this is possible.

Let us begin with a further consideration of Churchill's
"Black Dog." Lord Moran, who, more than most people,
realized the importance of depression in Churchill's psychology, first mentions this in the following passage from his
book:

> August 14th 1944.
> The P.M. was in a speculative mood today.
> "When I was young," he ruminated, "for two or three
> years the light faded out of the picture. I did my work. I
> sat in the House of Commons, but black depression
> settled on me. It helped me to talk to Clemmie about it.
> I don't like standing near the edge of a platform when
> an express train is passing through. I like to stand right
> back and if possible to get a pillar between me and the
> train. I don't like to stand by the side of a ship and look
> down into the water. A second's action would end every-
> thing. A few drops of desperation. And yet I don't want
> to go out of the world at all in such moments. Is much
> known about worry, Charles? It helps me to write down
> half a dozen things which are worrying me. Two of
> them, say, disappear, about two nothing can be done, so

it's no use worrying, and two perhaps can be settled. I
read an American book on the nerves, *The Philosophy of
Fate;* it interested me a great deal."

I said: "Your trouble—I mean the Black Dog business—you got from your forebears. You have fought
against it all your life. That is why you dislike visiting
hospitals. You always avoid anything that is depress-
ing."

Winston stared at me as if I knew too much.[20]

Later in the book, Lord Moran quotes a conversation with
the dying Brendan Bracken:

"You and I think of Winston as self-indulgent; he has
never denied himself anything, but when a mere boy
he deliberately set out to change his nature, to be tough
and full of rude spirits.

"It has not been easy for him. You see, Charles,
Winston has always been a 'despairer.' Orpen, who
painted him after the Dardanelles, used to speak of the
misery in his face. He called him the man of misery.
Winston was so sure then that he would take no further
part in public life. There seemed nothing left to live for.
It made him very sad. Then, in his years in the wilderness, before the Second War, he kept saying: 'I'm finished.' He said that about twice a day. He was quite
certain that he would never get back to office, for everyone seemed to regard him as a wild man. And he
missed the red boxes awfully. Winston has always been
wretched unless he was occupied. You know what he
has been like since he resigned. Why, he told me that he
prays every day for death."[21]

Many depressives deny themselves rest or relaxation
because they cannot afford to stop. If they are forced by
circumstances to do so, the black cloud comes down upon
them. This happened to Churchill when he left the Admiralty in May 1915, when he was out of office during the

thirties, when he was defeated in the election of 1945, and after his final resignation. He invented various methods of coping with the depression which descended when he was no longer fully occupied by affairs of state, including painting, writing, and bricklaying; but none of these were wholly successful. In order to understand why, we must venture some way into the cloudy and treacherous waters of psychoanalytic theory.

It is widely appreciated that psychoanalysis is chiefly concerned with the effect of environment, especially the very early environment, upon adult character. It is less generally realized that the psychoanalytic standpoint is not incompatible with the typological or constitutional approaches which we have hitherto adopted in our psychiatric scrutiny of Churchill. The two viewpoints are complementary, rather than contradictory. A man's genetic inheritance may predispose him to depression, but whether he actually suffers from it or not is likely to depend upon his early experiences within the family. Psychoanalysis does not assume that all individuals are born alike and would react in precisely the same way to the influences of the environment. There is no blueprint for an ideal upbringing, since no two individuals are the same. What psychoanalysis does assume, however, is that the psychological disturbances from which people suffer are related to the whole emotional climate in which they were reared, and that neurosis and psychosis in adult life are explicable in terms of a failure of the environment to meet the needs of the particular individual under scrutiny, at a time when those needs were paramount.

One salient characteristic of adults who suffer from depression is their dependence on external sources to maintain self-esteem. Of course, we are all dependent on externals to some extent. If a perfectly normal man is taken suddenly from his family, his job, and his social circle, and put into a situation of uncertainty and fear, he will become profoundly depressed. The Russian secret police know this well: which is why they arrest a suspect in the middle of the night without warning, place him in solitary confinement, and refuse him any communication with the outside world or any information about his future. It takes but a few weeks of solitary imprisonment in these circumstances to reduce most people to a state of profound dejection, an apathetic stupor in which both hope and pride disappear. We all need some support from the external world to maintain our sense of our own value.

Nevertheless, most of us can tolerate disappointments in one sphere of our existence without getting deeply depressed, provided the other spheres remain undamaged. Normal people may mourn, or experience disappointment, but because they have an inner source of self-esteem, they do not become or remain severely depressed for long in the face of misadventure, and are fairly easily consoled by what remains to them.

Depressives, in contrast to these normal folk, are much more vulnerable. If one thing in the external world goes wrong, they are apt to be thrown into despair. Even if people attempt to comfort them, they are likely to dismiss such efforts as futile. Disappointment, rejection, bereavement may all, in a depressive, pull a trigger which fires a reaction of total hopelessness: for such people do not possess an inner source of self-esteem to which they can turn in trouble, or which can easily be renewed by the ministrations of others. If, at a deep internal level, a person feels himself to be predominantly bad or unlovable, an actual rejection in the external world will bring this depressive belief to the surface; and no amount of reassurance from wellwishers will, for a time, persuade him of his real worth.

Psychoanalysis assumes that this vulnerability is the result of a rather early failure in the relationship between the child and his parents. In the ordinary course of events, a child takes in love with his mother's milk. A child who is wanted, loved, played with, cuddled, will incorporate within himself a lively sense of his own value; and will therefore surmount the inevitable setbacks and disappointments of childhood with no more than temporary sorrow, secure in the belief that the world is predominantly a happy place, and that he has a favored place in it. And this pattern will generally persist throughout his life.

A child, on the other hand, who is unwanted, rejected, or disapproved of will gain no such conviction. Although such a child may experience periods of both success and happiness, these will neither convince him that he is lovable nor finally prove to him that life is worthwhile. A whole career may be dedicated to the pursuit of power, the conquest of women, or the gaining of wealth, only in the end to leave the person face to face with despair and a sense of futility, since he has never incorporated within himself a sense of his value as a person; and no amount of external success can ultimately compensate him for this.

> On one of his birthdays a few years before, in answer to my sister Diana's exclamation of wonderment at all the things he had done in his life, he said: "I have achieved a great deal to achieve nothing in the end." We were listening to the radio and reading the always generous newspaper eulogies. "How can you say that?" she said. He was silent. "There are your books," I said. "And your paintings," Diana followed. "Oh yes, yes, there are those." "And after all, there is us," we continued. "Poor comfort we know at times: and there are other children who are grateful that they are alive." He acknowledged us with a smile. . . .[22]

Sarah Churchill, in her book *A Thread in the Tapestry,* begins her portrait of her father with these sentences; and it is surely percipient of her to do so. For she, and other members of the family, must have realized, in those last sad years, that in spite of the eulogies, the accolades, the honors, Winston Churchill still had a void at the heart of his being which no achievement or honor could ever completely fill.

It is interesting to compare this passage with another

written by Churchill himself, emanating not from his old age, but from his early manhood. *Savrola*, Winston Churchill's only novel, was the first book upon which he embarked, though it was actually the third to be published. Though half completed in 1897, it was not in print till 1900, since *The Story of the Malakand Field Force* and *The River War* intervened. Savrola, the orator and revolutionary, is, it has often been observed, a picture of Churchill himself. We are introduced to him in his study, surrounded by Gibbon, Macaulay, Plato, and Saint-Simon.

> There were still some papers and telegrams lying unopened on the table, but Savrola was tired; they could, or at any rate, should wait till the morning. He dropped into his chair. Yes, it had been a long day, and a gloomy day. He was a young man, only thirty-two, but already he felt the effects of work and worry. His nervous temperament could not fail to be excited by the vivid scenes through which he had lately passed, and the repression of his emotion only heated the inward fire. Was it worth it? The struggle, the labour, the constant rush of affairs, the sacrifice of so many things that make life easy, or pleasant—for what? A people's good! That, he could not disguise from himself, was rather the direction than the cause of his efforts. Ambition was the motive force and he was powerless to resist it.[23]

"Was it worth it?" The question recurs again and again in the lives of people who suffer from depression. At the end of *Savrola,* the query is reiterated. The revolution has been successful, but "a sense of weariness, of disgust with struggling, of desire for peace filled his soul. The object for which he had toiled so long was now nearly attained and it seemed of little worth. . . ."[24] Savrola has to go into exile, and looks back on the city he has liberated, now partially destroyed by shell fire:

The smoke of other burning houses rose slowly to join the black, overhanging cloud against which the bursting shells showed white with yellow flashes.

"And that," said Savrola after prolonged contemplation, "is my life's work."[25]

Even more interesting is the passage in which Savrola, "weary of men and their works," ascends into his observatory to "watch the stars for the sake of their mysteries." He contemplates the beauty of Jupiter:

> Another world, a world more beautiful, a world of boundless possibilities, enthralled his imagination. He thought of the future of Jupiter, of the incomprehensible periods of time that would elapse before the cooling process would render life possible on its surface, of the slow steady march of evolution, merciless, inexorable. How far would it carry them, the unborn inhabitants of an embryo world? Perhaps only to some vague distortion of the vital essence; perhaps further than he could dream of. All the problems would be solved; all the obstacles overcome; life would attain perfect development. And this fancy, overleaping space and time, carried the story to periods still more remote. The cooling process would continue; the perfect development of life would end in death; the whole solar system, the whole universe itself would one day be cold and lifeless as a burnt-out firework.
>
> It was a mournful conclusion. He locked up the observatory and descended the stairs, hoping that his dreams would contradict his thoughts.[26]

The underlying despair, so characteristic of the depressive temperament, could hardly be better demonstrated. However successful Savrola is, he is still left uncertain as to the value of his achievement. His fantasy of life attaining "perfect development" in some far-distant future is automatically cancelled by his belief that the universe must finally cool to a lifeless stop. The man who, a few years before his death, said to his daughter, "I have achieved a great deal to achieve nothing in the end," is displaying an absolutely consistent emotional pattern, already evident in early manhood.

What were the childhood origins of Churchill's depressive disposition? Any answer must necessarily be partly a matter of guesswork, but certain obvious factors present themselves for consideration, of which parental neglect is the most striking.

Winston Churchill was a premature child, born two months before he was expected. No one can say with certainty whether prematurity has an adverse effect upon future emotional development, but we do know that the way in which a baby is nursed and handled affects the rate of its physical and mental progress, and that even the youngest child is sensitive to the environment. A premature child is unexpected and, therefore, something of an embarrassment. We know that preparations for Winston Churchill's appearance were incomplete, for there was a lack of baby clothes; and a first child, in any case, is apt to be somewhat of an anxiety to an inexperienced mother. How was Churchill handled as a baby? All we know is that, in accordance with the custom of those days, he was not fed by his mother, but handed over to a wet nurse about whom we know nothing.

His mother, Lady Randolph, was only twenty when Winston was born. She was a girl of exceptional beauty, far too engaged in the fashionable social life of the time to be much concerned about her infant son. Lord Randolph, deeply involved in politics, would not have been expected to take more than a remote interest in his son and heir, and he more than fulfilled this expectation. In fact, Churchill received remarkably little affection or support from either parent in the vital years of early childhood. The person who saved him from emotional starvation was, of course, Mrs. Everest, the nanny who was engaged early in 1875 within a few months of his birth, and who remained his chief support and confidante until her death when Churchill was twenty. Her photograph hung in his room until the end of his own life. She is immortalized as the housekeeper in *Savrola,* and although Randolph Churchill makes use of the same quotation in his biography of his father, it is worth repeating here, since it reveals something of Winston Churchill's attitude to love:

> His thoughts were interrupted by the entrance of the old woman with a tray. He was tired, but the decencies of life had to be observed; he rose, and passed into the inner room to change his clothes and make his toilet. When he returned, the table was laid; the soup he had asked for had been expanded by the care of his housekeeper into a more elaborate meal. She waited on him, plying him the while with questions and watching his appetite with anxious pleasure. She had nursed him from his birth with a devotion and care which knew no break. It is a strange thing, the love of these women. Perhaps it is the only disinterested affection in the world. The mother loves her child; that is maternal nature. The youth loves his sweetheart; that too may be explained. The dog loves his master; he feeds him; a man loves his friend; he has stood by him perhaps at doubtful moments. In all there are reasons, but the love of a foster-mother for her charge appears absolutely irrational. It is one of the few proofs, not to be explained even by the association of ideas, that the nature of mankind is superior to mere utilitarianism, and that his destinies are high.[27]

Churchill's concept of "disinterested affection" is worth comment. For it is surely not as astonishing as he implies that a nurse should love her charge. A nanny is a woman without children of her own, and without a husband. What could be more natural than that she should devote herself to the child who is placed in her care, and give him all the affection and love for which she has no other outlet? In the passage quoted above, Churchill is showing surprise at being loved, as if he had never felt that he was entitled to it. In the ordinary course of events, a small child receives from his mother and father love which he neither questions nor doubts. And he will generally extend his expectation of love to nannies, relatives, and other members of the family circle. As he grows up, he will find that not everyone loves him as he has come to expect; and this may surprise and disappoint him. But his surprise will surely be evoked by the discovery that some people do *not* love him, rather than by the fact that people other than his parents *do* love him.

Happy children do not ask *why* their mothers or anybody else love them; they merely accept it as a fact of existence. It is those who have received less than their early due of love who are surprised that anyone should be fond of them, and who seek for explanation of the love which more fortunate children take for granted. People who suffer from depression are always asking themselves why anyone should love them. They often feel entitled to respect, to awe, or to admiration; but as for love, that is too much to expect. Many depressives only feel lovable insofar as they have some achievement to their credit, or have given another person so much that they feel entitled to a return. The idea that anyone might give him love just because he is himself is foreign to the person of depressive temperament. In showing astonishment at Mrs. Everest's disinterested love, Churchill is surely revealing what one would expect from his emotional disposition, that he had not experienced from his parents that total, irrational acceptance which we all need, and which is given by most mothers to a wanted baby. And although Mrs. Everest's affection made up for what was missing to some extent, it could not replace the love of parents.

We cannot now obtain as much information as we would like about Churchill's very early childhood, but that his parents were neglectful is undoubted. As Randolph Churchill says in his biography:

> The neglect and lack of interest in him shown by his parents were remarkable, even judged by the standards of late Victorian and Edwardian days. His letters to his mother from his various schools abound in pathetic requests for letters and for visits, if not from her, from Mrs Everest and his brother Jack. Lord Randolph was a busy politician with his whole interest absorbed in politics; Lady Randolph was caught up in the whirl of fashionable society and seems to have taken very little interest in her son until he began to make his name resound through the world. It will later be seen how neglectful she was in writing to him when he was for three years a subaltern in India and when his father and Mrs Everest were dead. His brother Jack, more than five years younger, could not be a satisfactory correspondent and Winston was to feel exceptionally lonely and abandoned.[28]

We are, I believe, entitled to assume that Winston Churchill was deprived by parental neglect of that inner source of self-esteem upon which most predominantly happy persons rely, and which serves to carry them through the inevitable disappointments and reverses of human existence. What were the ways in which he endeavored to make up for this early lack and to sustain his self-esteem in spite of lack of parental affection?

The first and most obvious trait of character which he developed as a response to his deprivation was ambition. As he himself wrote of Savrola, "Ambition was the motive force and he was powerless to resist it." And in a letter to his mother, written in 1899 in India, he writes: "What an awful thing it will be if I don't come off. It will break my heart for I have nothing else but ambition to cling to. . . ."[29] Children who have been more loved and appreciated than Winston Churchill do have something other than ambition to cling to. Ambition is, of course, a perfectly "normal" trait, to be expected in any young man reared in the competitive climate of Western civilization. But Churchill's ambition was certainly inordinate; and it made him unpopular when he was young. Sir Charles Dilke is reported as writing that Rosebery was the most ambitious man he had ever met; but later he amended this opinion by writing alongside it, "I have since known Winston Churchill."[30] Ambition, when, as in Churchill's case, it is a compulsive drive, is the direct result of early deprivation. For if a child has but little inner conviction of his own value, he will be drawn to seek the recognition and acclaim which accrue from external achievement. In youth, especially, success, or even the hope of success, whether financial, political, or artistic, can be effective in staving off depression in those who are liable to this disorder. It is the inevitable decay of hope as a man gets older which accounts for the fact that severe attacks of depression become more common in middle age. It may be argued that very able people are always ambitious, since it is natural enough for a gifted man to require scope for his abilities and to want those ambitions to be recognized. In Lord Reith's phrase, to be "fully stretched" is a pleasure in itself.[31] But the compensatory quality of Churchill's ambition is not difficult to discern. Even his famous remark to Lady Violet Bonham Carter, "We are all worms. But I do believe that I am a glow-worm,"[32] is revealing, in that it combines self-abasement and self-glorification in a single phrase.

Extreme ambition, of the Churchillian variety, is not based upon sober appraisal of the reality of one's gifts and deficiencies. There is always an element of fantasy, unrelated to actual achievement. This may, as it did with Churchill, take the form of a conviction that one is being reserved for a special purpose, if not by the Deity, then at least by fate. One of the most remarkable features of Churchill's psychology is that this conviction persisted throughout the greater part of his life, until, at the age of sixty-five, his fantasy found expression in reality. As he said to Moran, "This cannot be accident, it must be design. I was kept for this job."[33] If Churchill had died in 1939, he would have been regarded as a failure. Moran is undoubtedly right when he writes of "the inner world of make-believe in which Winston found reality."[34] It is probable that England owed her survival in 1940 to this inner world of make-believe. The kind of inspiration with which Churchill sustained the nation is not based on judgment, but on an irrational conviction independent of factual reality. Only a man convinced that he had an heroic mission, who believed that, in spite of all evidence to the contrary, he could yet triumph, and who could identify himself with a nation's destiny could have conveyed his inspiration to others. The miracle had much in common with that achieved by a great actor, who, by his art, exalts us and convinces us that his passions are beyond the common run of human feeling. We do not know, and we shall never know, the details of Churchill's world of make-believe. But that it was there, and that he played an heroic part in it, cannot be gainsaid. Before the invention of nuclear weapons, many a schoolboy had dreams of military glory which are hardly possible today. To be a great commander, to lead forces in battle against overwhelming odds, to make an heroic last stand, to win the Victoria Cross, are ambitions which have inspired many generations in the past. Churchill was born in an age when such dreams were still translatable into reality; and he sought to realize them in his early career as a soldier. But, unlike many soldiers, he did not become disillusioned. Even as an old man, it was difficult to restrain him from deliberately exposing himself to risk when he went out to France after the second front had been embarked upon. The schoolboy's daydream persisted: and his search for danger was not simply a desire to prove his physical courage, a motive which was undoubtedly operative in early youth. It also rested upon a conviction that he would be preserved, that nothing could happen to a man of destiny—a belief which he shared with General Gordon, who likewise, throughout his life, exposed himself deliberately to death, and who inspired others by his total disregard of danger.

The conviction of being "special" is, in psychoanalytic jargon, a reflection of what is called "infantile omnipotence." Psychoanalysis postulates, with good reason, that the infant has little appreciation of his realistic stature in the world into which he is born. Although a human infant embarks on life in a notably helpless state, requiring constant care and attention in order to preserve him, his very helplessness creates the illusion that he is powerful. For the demands of a baby are imperious. A baby must be fed, cleaned, clothed, and preserved from injury, and, in the normal course of events, these demands are met by a number of willing slaves who hasten to fulfill them. As the child matures, he will gradually learn that his desires are not always paramount, and that the needs of others must sometimes take precedence. This is especially so in a family where there are other children. The hard lesson that one is not the center of the universe is more quickly learned in the rough and tumble of competition with brothers and sisters. Only children may fail to outgrow this early stage of emotional development; and, although Winston Churchill was not an only child, his brother Jack, born in 1880, was sufficiently younger for Winston to have retained his solitary position during five crucial years. Paradoxically, it is children who are deprived as well as solitary who retain the sense of omnipotence. A failure to meet a child's need for total care and total acceptance during the earliest part of his existence leaves him with a sense of something missing and something longed for; and he may, in later life, try to create conditions in which his slightest whim is immediately attended to, and resent the fact that this is not always possible.

In Churchill, this characteristic was evident. During one

of his illnesses he required two nurses. His wife told Lord Moran: "Winston is a pasha. If he cannot clap his hands for a servant he calls for Walter as he enters the house. If it were left to him he'd have the nurses for the rest of his life. He would like two in his room, two in the passage. He is never so happy, Charles, as he is when one of the nurses is doing something for him while Walter puts on his socks."35 Churchill's arrogance, impatience, and lack of consideration for others must have made him extremely difficult to live with; but these traits were softened by his magnanimity. How did so egocentric a man inspire devotion in those who served him, whose immediate needs he seldom considered, who might have to stay up till all hours to suit his own peculiar timetable, and who were often exposed to his formidable temper? It is not an easy question to answer; but it is often true that men who demand and need a great deal of attention from others are manifesting a kind of childlike helplessness which evokes an appropriate response, however difficult they may be. His wife recorded that the only time he had been on the Underground was during the general strike. "He went round and round, not knowing where to get out and had to be rescued eventually."36 As with a small child, omnipotence and helplessness went hand in hand. There are a good many characters in public life who would be totally nonplussed if they had to get their own meals, darn their own socks, or even write their own letters.

The fact that Churchill was an aristocrat must have been of considerable service to him. However neglected he was by his parents, there was Mrs. Everest to minister to him: and she was later succeeded by his wife, his valet, his doctor, and innumerable attendants and servants. Those of us who are old enough to remember the days in which the aristocracy and the upper middle class took it for granted that the ordinary details of living, food, clothes, travel, and so on would be taken care of by some minion or other, and who have since adapted to fending for ourselves, can without difficulty recall that the existence of servants did minister to our sense of self-esteem. Churchill was not rich in early life. He had to make his living by his pen. But he knew nothing of the lives of ordinary people, and, like other members of his class, grew up with the assumption that he was a good many cuts above the general run of the population. This assumption has stood many of his ilk in good stead. The English upper class have been notorious for handing over their children to the care of servants, and, in the case of boys, disposed to send them to boarding schools at an absurdly early age. The sense of belonging to a privileged class is some mitigation for the feeling of early rejection; and the Churchill family was, of course, of particular distinction within that privileged class. The young Winston Churchill may have felt lonely and unloved, but it cannot have been long before he became conscious that he was "special" in another, less personal sense: the scion of a famous house with a long line of distinguished ancestors behind him. The fact that he chose to write biographies both of his father and of the first Duke of Marlborough shows how important this was to him.

When a child's emotional needs are not met, or only partially met, by his parents, he will generally react to this frustration by hostility. The most "difficult," badly behaved children are those who are unloved; and they tend to treat all authority as hostile. Winston Churchill was no exception. But even the most rebellious and intransigent child retains, in imagination, a picture of the parents he would have liked to have. The negative image of authority as rejecting, cruel, and neglectful is balanced by a positive image of idealized parents who are invariably loving, tender, and understanding. And the less a child knows or has intimate contact with his real parents, the more will this double image persist. Real parents are real people: sometimes loving, sometimes impatient; sometimes understanding, sometimes imperceptive. The child reared in the intimacy of an ordinary family soon amalgamates the images of "good" and "bad," and comes to realize that, in other human beings as in himself, love and hate, goodness and badness, are inextricably intermingled. Psychiatrists have often observed that delinquent and emotionally disturbed children who have parents who are actually neglectful or cruel still maintain that these "bad" parents are really "good," and blame themselves for the parents' faults. This idealization of parents serves a defensive and protective function. A small child, being weak and defenseless, finds it unbearable to believe that there are no adults who love, support, and guide him; and if there are not, he invents them.

Winston Churchill showed this idealization very clearly. Of his mother, he wrote: "She shone for me like the Evening Star. I loved her dearly—but at a distance."[37] This romantic view of his mother gave way to a more realistic appraisal of her, when, as a young man of twenty-three, he was compelled to recognize her financial irresponsibility, and to write to her about her extravagances. But the images formed in childhood are not so easily dispelled; and Churchill, at least in his early years, retained a romantic view of women which was derived from his idealization of his beautiful mother. Violet Bonham Carter draws attention to this:

> This inner circle of friends contained no women. They had their own place in his life. His approach to women was essentially romantic. He had a lively susceptibility to beauty, glamour, radiance, and those who possessed these qualities were not subjected to analysis. Their possession of all the cardinal virtues was assumed as a matter of course. I remember his taking umbrage when I once commented on the "innocence" of his approach to women. He was affronted by this epithet as applied to himself. Yet to me he would certainly have applied it as a term of praise.[38]

Like many another romantic, Churchill was in youth somewhat awkward in his approach to women, although he was emotionally involved with at least three girls before he married. In his latter years he took little notice of women, and indeed would hardly speak to them. But the romantic ' vision persisted, attaching itself to the figure of Queen Elizabeth II. When contemplating the Queen's photograph, he is reported as saying: "Lovely, inspiring. All the film people in the world, if they had scoured the globe, could not have found anyone so suited to the part."39 Royalty never lost its magic for him; and, like his ancestor in the time of the Civil War, he remained an ardent Royalist throughout his life, despite the declining popularity of the monarchical principle among the sophisticated. When Churchill spoke of himself as a servant of the Queen, he undoubtedly felt that he was. His idealization of the monarchy, which extended itself to the kings and queens of other states besides Britain, meant that he seldom saw royalty as creatures of flesh and blood, any more than he saw his parents as human beings. It is a characteristic that he shared with many others in Great Britain.

Winston Churchill's idealization of his father was even more remarkable. It is not surprising that a small boy should see so beautiful and elegant a young mother as a fairy princess. But his father, though a notable public figure and a highly gifted man, was so consistently disapproving of, or uninterested in, his small son, that Churchill's hero worship of him can only be explained in terms of the psychological mechanism outlined above. As Violet Bonham Carter writes: "The image remained upon its pedestal, intact and glorious. Until the end he worshipped at the altar of his Unknown Father."40 And his father remained entirely unknown to him, never talked intimately with him, and seldom wrote to him except to reprove him. After Lord Randolph's death from general paralysis of the insane, when Winston Churchill was twenty, he learned large portions of his father's speeches by heart, and, in 1906, published a two-volume biography of him. Filial devotion could hardly go further; but it was devotion to an image, not to a real father whose life he had shared.

Children whose emotional needs have been insufficiently satisfied by their parents react to the lack by idealization on the one hand, and hostility on the other. Winston Churchill's obstinacy, resentment of authority, and willfulness were manifest very early in his life. He was sent to boarding school before his eighth birthday; and it is evident from his earliest reports that the school authorities became the recipients of the hostility which he must have felt towards his parents, but which was never manifested because of his idealization of them. He was repeatedly late: "No. of times late. 20. very disgraceful." From being described as "a regular pickle" in his earliest report, he is later designated as "troublesome," "very bad," "careless," "a constant trouble to everybody," and "very naughty."[41] He remained at this school from November 1882 till the summer of 1884, and himself recorded how much he hated it. It is likely that he was removed because of the severe beatings he received, for the headmaster was a sadistic clergyman who would inflict as many as twenty strokes of the birch upon the bare buttocks of the little boys under his care, and who clearly enjoyed this exercise of his authority. But savage punishment failed to cow Winston Churchill, and probably served to increase his intolerance towards authority.

It is interesting to note that, in his early letters from school, he did not complain, but reported himself as happy; although, as he later admitted, this was the very opposite of the truth. Small boys who are miserable at boarding school very frequently conceal the fact from their parents. Ignorance of what the world is really like may lead them to suppose that ill-treatment and lack of sympathetic understanding is the expected lot of boys; and that, if they are unhappy, it is a sign of weakness and their own fault. This is especially true of those with a depressive tendency, for the hostility they feel towards parents and other authorities easily becomes turned inward against themselves. They therefore report themselves as happy because they feel they ought to be so, and easily deceive imperceptive parents who are not concerned to discover the truth.

There is, indeed, an intimate connection between depression and hostility, which was not understood until Freud had unraveled it. The emotionally deprived child who later becomes prey to depression has enormous difficulty in the disposal of his hostility. He resents those who have deprived him, but he cannot afford to show this resentment, since he needs the very people he resents; and any hostility he does manifest results in still further deprivation of the approval and affection he so much requires. In periods of depression, this hostility becomes turned inward against the self, with the result that the depressive undervalues himself or even alleges that he is worthless. "I have achieved a great deal to achieve nothing in the end."

It is this difficulty in disposing of hostility which drives some depressives to seek out opponents in the external world. It is a great relief to find an enemy on whom it is justifiable to lavish wrath. Winston Churchill was often accused of being a warmonger, which he was not. But there is no doubt that fighting enemies held a strong emotional appeal for him, and that, when he was finally confronted by an enemy whom he felt to be wholly evil, it was a release which gave him enormous vitality. Hitler was such an enemy; and it is probable that Churchill was never happier than when he was fully engaged in bringing about Hitler's destruction. For here, at last, was an opportunity to employ the full force of his enormous aggressiveness. Here was a monstrous tyranny, presided over by an archdemon who deserved no mercy, and whom he could attack with an unsullied conscience. If all depressives could constantly be engaged in fighting wicked enemies, they would never suf-

fer from depression. But, in day-to-day existence, antago-
nists are not wicked enough, and depressives suffer from
pangs of conscience about their own hostility.

It is not decrying Churchill to state that his magnanimity
and generosity to his many enemies rested upon this basis.
People with Churchill's kind of early background know
what it is to be insulted and injured; and, in spite of their
internal store of hostility, they retain a capacity to identify
with the underdog. It is unlikely that Churchill would have
ever felt anything but hatred for Hitler, had the latter survived. But he showed an unusual compassion for the other
enemies he defeated. Brendan Bracken reports that when
Churchill sued Lord Alfred Douglas for making defama-
tory statements about him, he was not elated when he won
the case. Indeed, he appeared depressed; and this was
because he could not bear the thought of his defeated opponent being sent to prison.[42] Although Churchill relished
being in action against the enemies of England, compassion
for them was equally in evidence, and he did not hesitate, at
the age of twenty-three, to criticize Kitchener for the "inhu-
man slaughter of the wounded" at Omdurman and to attack
him in print for having desecrated the Mahdi's tomb.[43]

This alternation between aggression and compassion is
characteristic of persons with Churchill's character structure. No one could have had more pride in the British
Empire; and yet, when Churchill was twenty-seven, he was
writing of "our unbridled Imperialists who have no thought
but to pile up armaments, taxation and territory."[44] This
criticism was prompted by his reading of Seebohm Rown-
tree's book *Poverty,* which engaged his compassion for the
underfed working class, neglected by Imperialist politicians.
Churchill was highly aggressive, and in many ways insensitive, but he was far from ruthless, and when he could imag-
inatively enter into the distress of others he was genuinely
concerned. This was especially so in the case of prisoners,
with whom he could closely identify himself. Churchill's

period of office as Home Secretary was notable for the improvements which he introduced in the treatment of "political" prisoners, in his day the suffragettes; for the reform which allowed "time to pay" in the case of those who would otherwise have been imprisoned for the nonpayment of fines; and for the introduction of measures which reduced the number of young offenders sent to prison. He also advocated the introduction of lectures and concerts to prisoners, and insisted upon the provision of books for them.

Churchill's compassionate concern with prisoners originated in part with his generalized capacity to identify himself with the underdog, which we have already discussed. It also had a more particular root which sprang from his personal experience. During the Boer War he was captured by the Boers and incarcerated as a prisoner of war. Although his period of imprisonment was very brief, for he was caught on November 15 and escaped on December 12, this experience made an ineradicable impression upon him. In *My Early Life* he writes of his imprisonment as follows:

> Prisoner of War! That is the least unfortunate kind of prisoner to be, but it is nevertheless a melancholy state. You are in the power of your enemy. You owe your life to his humanity, and your daily bread to his compassion. You must obey his orders, go where he tells you, stay where you are bid, await his pleasure, possess your soul in patience. Meanwhile the war is going on, great events are in progress, fine opportunities for action and adventure are slipping away. Also the days are very long. Hours crawl like paralytic centipedes. Nothing amuses you. Reading is difficult; writing impossible. Life is one long boredom from dawn till slumber.
>
> Moreover, the whole atmosphere of prison, even the most easy and best regulated prison, is odious. Companions in this kind of misfortune quarrel about trifles and get the least possible pleasure from each other's society. If you have never been under restraint before and never known what it was to be a captive, you feel a

sense of constant humiliation in being confined to a narrow space, fenced in by railings and wire, watched by armed men, and webbed about with a tangle of regulations and restrictions. I certainly hated every minute of my captivity more than I have ever hated any other period in my whole life. . . . Looking back on those days, I have always felt the keenest pity for prisoners and captives. What it must mean for any man, especially an educated man, to be confined for years in a modern convict prison, strains my imagination. Each day exactly like the one before, with the barren ashes of wasted life behind, and all the long years of bondage stretching out ahead. . . .

Dark moods come easily across the mind of a prisoner. . . .[45]

Not all persons react to imprisonment like this. There are some who actively seek prison as a refuge from the troubles of this world. Others spend their time more or less contentedly reading or engaged in solitary reflection. It is those who are liable to depression who most suffer pangs of the kind that Churchill described; for, deprived of the outside sources of stimulation which sustain them and the opportunity for adventure and excitement which is a defense against their innate tendency, they relapse into that state above all which they most fear.

Churchill was never happy unless he was fully occupied, asleep, or holding the floor. He had no small talk. It is impossible to imagine him being cozily relaxed. He had to be perpetually active, or else he relapsed into "dark moments of impatience and frustration," as Violet Bonham Carter describes his moods.[46] As early as 1895 he was writing to his mother from Aldershot:

I find I am getting into a state of mental stagnation when even letter writing becomes an effort and when any reading but that of monthly magazines is impossible. This is of course quite in accordance with the

> spirit of the army. It is indeed the result of mental
> forces called into being by discipline and routine. It is a
> state of mind into which all, or nearly all, soldiers fall.
> From this slough of despond I try to raise myself by
> reading and re-reading Papa's speeches, many of
> which I know almost by heart. But I really cannot find
> the energy to read any other serious work.[47]

Army discipline and routine had a constraining effect upon
him, not unlike that of prison; and the realization that he
became depressed as a result may have contributed to his
decision to seek political, rather than further military, glory.

  We have already mentioned Churchill's dislike of standing
near the edge of a railway platform. He also admitted to
Moran, while staying at Claridges, that he disliked sleeping
near a balcony. "I've no desire to quit this world," he said
with a grin, "but thoughts, desperate thoughts come into the
head."[48] He was also apprehensive about traveling by air,
and was fond of quoting Dr. Johnson on sea travel: "Being in
a ship is being in a jail, with the chance of being drowned."
An underlying preoccupation with death, so characteristic
of the depressive temperament, is easily detectable. In early
youth, he was convinced that he would die young, as his
father had. We can attribute this in part to an identification
with his idealized father; but a conviction that time is short
and an early realization of the ephemeral nature of human
life is typical. His dislike of visiting hospitals belongs in this
category of preoccupation, and so does his early tendency to
hypochondriasis. Lucy Masterman reports of him in 1910,
"He thought he had got every mortal disease under heaven,
and was very much inclined to dine off slops and think
about the latter end." When Admiral Pound died, Churchill
said, "Death is the greatest gift God has made to us."[49] It is
not argued here that Churchill was ever suicidal—there is
no evidence on that point. But it seems likely that death had
a kind of fascination for him against which he had to defend
himself. Men who have to be hyperactive in order to protect

themselves against depression generally have a secret long-
ing for total peace and relaxation; and the garden of Proser-
pina, "where even the weariest river winds somewhere safe
to sea," has a special appeal which has to be fought against.

Churchill at first reacted to authority by intransigent disobedience. This rebelliousness was not only a way of discharging his hostility, but a means of self-assertion—
probably the only way of self-assertion available to a boy
who, at that stage, felt himself to be weak physically, and
who showed no disposition to excel in any school subject
except history. Soon, however, another means of preserving,
or rather gaining, self-esteem presented itself. Although he
continued to perform inadequately in most school subjects,
certainly far less well than his intelligence warranted, he
discovered that he had a gift for words, a gift which became
his principal asset, and which stood him in good stead
throughout his life.

Before the use of words became his chief vehicle of self-
expression, he had, at the age of eleven, shown a desire
to learn the cello. Had this desire been granted, it is possible that music might have become important to him;
for, as many musicians know, the world of sound can be
a never-ending source of solace, and the ability to play an
instrument is both a means of self-expression and a source
of self-esteem. But Churchill's early interest in music was
not encouraged, and soon died out; and his musical taste
remained at the level of Sullivan and music-hall songs.

Churchill's attitude to words and the use of them is of
interest psychologically. When he first met Violet Bonham
Carter, he asked her whether she thought that words had a
magic and a music quite independent of their meaning. For
Churchill, they undoubtedly did. The magic of words
became part of his inner world of make-believe. Sartre, in
his autobiography, has recorded a similar process:

> A Platonist by condition, I moved from knowledge to its
> object; I found ideas more real than things, because
> they were the first to give themselves to me and because
> they gave themselves like things. I met the universe in
> books: assimilated, classified, labelled and studied, but
> still impressive; and I confused the chaos of my experi-
> ence through books with the hazardous course of real
> events. Hence my idealism which it took me thirty years
> to undo.[50]

All through his life Churchill was a voluble fount of ideas.
Smuts said of him: "That is why Winston is indispensable.
He has ideas." His imagination was really creative; and it
expressed itself in rhetoric, in an ornate phraseology which
soon soared above the sober and often intransigent facts of
reality. This was why he was always having to be restrained
by his advisers; by his civil servants when he was Home
Secretary; by his chiefs of staff, especially Alanbrooke,
when he was Prime Minister.

The literary style which first attracted him was that of
Gibbon, whom he frankly imitated: and he also owed much
to Macaulay. It is not surprising that these authors appealed
to him. Of the two, Gibbon is the wittier, the more realistic,
and the better balanced. His sentences, beautifully constructed, have a strong appeal to the musical ear. The
remarkable thing is that Gibbon did not abuse his literary
gift to distort history or advance his own prejudices, with the
possible exception of his intolerance towards Christianity.
Gibbon's *Decline and Fall* remained a standard work for
many years. The same cannot be said of Macaulay, who used
the magic of words to persuade his readers of views which
were often highly subjective.

Churchill knew that his imagination could mislead him
into false appraisals, but he could always be brought back to
reality, although it might take hours of argument to do so.
Churchill's grasp of military strategy was considerable, but
it was liable to be interfered with by his romantic imagina-

tion, which often led him to disregard the logic of the possible. And the fact that he could clothe his ideas in magnificent language must have made those ideas even more convincing to him. He was able to inspire himself as well as others by the magic of words, which indeed can take on a life of their own.

Artists and philosophers create worlds which may be, and often are, substitutes for the disappointing and stubborn facts of human existence. Had Churchill not been born into an aristocratic and political family, he might have become a writer of a different kind. Since his interest in other human beings was minimal, and his grasp of human psychology negligible, it is unlikely that he would have ever been a novelist of character. But he could have written good adventure stories, and did so in *My Early Life,* which, although true autobiography, has in places the pace and dash of a thriller. But Churchill's imagination was captured by dreams of military glory and of political power; and so, although he can be rated as a literary artist, his creativity also found expression in imaginative schemes of social reform, in military inventions like the tank, and in strategic conceptions like Gallipoli, for the failure of which he was made a scapegoat.

Even as an orator, Churchill remained essentially literary. As he said of himself: "I am not an orator, an orator is spontaneous."[51] In youth, his chief ambition was to be master of the spoken word, but it was an ambition which he never completely realized. Although some of his phrases, especially in his 1940 speeches, have become immortal, his was a literary rather than an oratorical talent. His speeches were carefully written out, and often learned by heart; and, in youth, he was extremely nervous before delivering them. He lacked the common touch which great orators like Lloyd George possessed: and his diligence in preparing his speeches is another example of his extraordinary determination to conquer his natural disadvantages, and to succeed in spite of, rather than because of, his native endowment.

One of the most successful of modern writers, Georges Simenon, says, "Writing is not a profession, but a vocation of unhappiness."[52] Not all artists are depressive by temperament; but those that are habitually use their skill to ward off the "Black Dog," and commonly go through a period of depression directly they have completed a new work. During this interval, before they can get started again, they often believe that they are finished, and that they will never have another original idea; but, in time, the creative impulse generally reasserts itself. It is likely that Churchill used his writing as a defense against the depression which invariably descended upon him when he was forced to be inactive. This psychological mechanism is clearly evident when we come to consider his painting. He did not start to paint until he was forty, and what initiated this new departure was a period of despair. Several observers have attested to the severity of Churchill's depression after the failure of the Dardanelles expedition which he had initiated, and which led to his resignation from the Admiralty in 1915. Violet Bonham Carter records: "He took me into his room and sat down on a chair—silent, despairing—as I have never seen him. He seemed to have no rebellion or even anger left. He did not even abuse Fisher, but simply said, 'I'm finished.' "[53] Churchill himself wrote of this period:

> I had long hours of utterly unwonted leisure in which to contemplate the frightful unfolding of the war. At a moment when every fibre of my being was inflamed to action, I was forced to remain a spectator of the tragedy, placed cruelly in a front seat. And then it was that the Muse of Painting came to my rescue—out of charity and out of chivalry, because after all she had nothing to do with me—and said, "Are these toys any good to you? They amuse some people."[54]

And from that time onward, painting became a great resource to Winston Churchill: something to which he could always turn in time of trouble, something which would invariably engage his interest and provide a perpetual challenge.

Psychoanalysis has long recognized the relation between aggression and depression, and the difficulty which the depressed person has in the disposal of his aggressive impulses. Although creative activity frequently contains an aggressive component, this is not always easy to discern; nor do we habitually think of painting a picture or composing a symphony as an aggressive activity. Those who find my thesis unconvincing should turn to Churchill's own account of his approach to a canvas in his book *Painting as a Pastime:*

> Very gingerly I mixed a little blue paint on the palette with a very small brush, and then with infinite precaution made a mark about as big as a bean upon the affronted snow-white shield. It was a challenge, a deliberate challenge, but so subdued, so halting, indeed so cataleptic, that it deserved no response. At that moment the loud approaching sound of a motor-car was heard in the drive. From this chariot there stepped swiftly and lightly none other than the gifted wife of Sir John Lavery. "Painting! But what are you hesitating about? Let me have a brush—the big one." Splash into the turpentine, wallop into the blue and the white, frantic flourish on the palette—clean no longer—and then several large, fierce strokes and slashes of blue on the absolutely cowering canvas. Anyone could see that it could not hit back. No evil fate avenged the jaunty violence. The canvas grinned in helplessness before me. The spell was broken. The sickly inhibitions rolled away. I seized the largest brush and fell upon my victim with berserk fury. I have never felt any awe of a canvas since.55

He later compares painting a picture to fighting a battle. Indeed, this little book is one of the most revealing things he ever wrote about himself.

Churchill's predilection for rather grandiose, highly colored language was related to the need of his romantic imagination to lighten the gloom into which he was apt to descend. His choice of color in painting is strictly analogous:

> I must say I like bright colours. . . . I cannot pretend to feel impartial about the colours. I rejoice with the brilliant ones, and am genuinely sorry for the poor browns. When I get to heaven I mean to spend a considerable portion of my first million years in painting, and so get to the bottom of the subject. But then I shall require a still gayer palette than I get here below. I expect orange and vermilion will be the darkest, dullest colours upon it, and beyond them there will be a whole range of wonderful new colours which will delight the celestial eye.[56]

In psychoanalytic jargon, this is a "manic defense." The counterpart to the gloomy, subfusc world of the depressive is a realm of perpetual excitement and action in which colors are richer and brighter, gallant deeds are accomplished by heroes, and ideas are expressed in language replete with simile, ornamented with epithet, and sparkling with mellifluous turns of phrase. In his book on painting, Churchill gives us a delightful glimpse into his inner world of make-believe: a world where every prospect pleases, but which is just as remote from reality as is the downcast, hopeless hell of the man who feels useless and "finished."

Churchill's need of this manic realm is equally reflected in his choice of friends. Holders of the Victoria Cross were immediately attractive to him, irrespective of their personalities; for they were all real live heroes who coincided with those in his inner world. So were ebullient, energetic adventurers, like Lord Birkenhead and Lord Beaverbrook. Churchill was a poor judge of character. The sober, steadfast, and reliable seldom appealed to him. What he wanted were people who would stimulate, amuse, and arouse him.

Lord Moran notes that he was unimpressed by many of the quietly distinguished doctors who were sent to see him, but easily fell for the near-charlatans, the men with the gift of the gab who were unrestrained by scientific caution. The flamboyant extravert is life-enhancing, although exhausting; he brings zest and vitality to life. Men like Birkenhead helped Churchill to find and sustain the manic side of his own personality.

In an earlier passage we have taken note of the fact that persons with Churchill's type of psychological structure find it hard to learn that they are not the center of the universe. Because of the lack of intimate relations, first with parents and later with other people, they remain egocentrically oriented: narcissistic. Every baby starts life in a predominantly solipsistic state; most progress to a more mature emotional condition in which it is realized not only that other people have desires and needs, but also that one's own desires and needs interact with them in such a way that one can both satisfy and be satisfied simultaneously. The child who is early deprived forms no such conception; with the result that he makes inordinate demands on other people, but has little idea of being able to give them much. Churchill was generous to defeated enemies, but remained extremely demanding and insensitive to the requirements of others. His principal love object remained himself, because that self had never, in childhood, been satisfied.

Psychoanalysts describe such a character as "oral," because it is through the mouth that the baby's earliest needs are met; and, when they are not met, oral traits of character persist, both literally and metaphorically. It is interesting that, in one of his earliest school reports, Churchill is described as greedy; and it is also recorded that he was beaten for stealing sugar. All through his life, he needed feeding at frequent intervals; he was dependent on, though not necessarily addicted to, alcohol, and was a heavy smoker of cigars. He was also greedy for approval. His intimates knew that, if he showed them a manuscript of what he was writing, what he wanted was praise unadulterated with any tinge of criticism. "You are not on my side" was the reproach levelled at friends who ventured any adverse comment upon his ideas or his creations. The part of him which still demanded the total and uncritical acceptance which he had never had as a child still divided the world into black and white, so that friendship and disagreement were regarded as incompatible. Because of this characteristic, his own relationship to friends was also uncritical. He was intensely loyal. As Brendan Bracken said, "He would go to the stake for a friend";[57] and this was what he expected from his own friends. He remained hungry—hungry for fame, for adulation, for success, and for power; and although he gained all these in full measure, the end of his life showed that he never assimilated them into himself, but remained unsatisfied.

It is often said of Churchill that he "lacked antennae"; that is, that he was insensitive where other people were concerned. There are several anecdotes which reveal that, quite unwittingly, he gave offense to other people on social occasions by neglecting them or taking no notice of them. This imperviousness to atmosphere is characteristic of the narcissistic person, who, like a small child, is still living in a private world which takes little account of other people except insofar as they provide what the child wants. We expect that small children will be "selfish," intent on their own satisfaction, with little regard for what others are feeling. Churchill retained this characteristic in adult life; and it was directly related to his early deprivation. For the "selfish" are those who have never had enough. It is only the child whose emotional needs have been satisfied who is later able to give as much as he takes. Churchill said of himself, quite accurately, "I have devoted more time to self-expression than to self-discipline." Had he been less egocentric he would not have achieved so much; had he been more self-disciplined, he would have been less inspiring.

We have discussed in some detail the methods which
Churchill employed to prevent himself from relapsing into
the depression which dogged him, and against which, as
Lord Moran said, he was fighting all his life. Perhaps the
most remarkable feature of Churchill's psychology is that,
on the whole, the defenses he employed against depression
proved so successful. Although in youth he suffered long
periods of depression, his various methods of dealing with
this disability seem to have had the result that, in later life,
he could generally extricate himself from the slough of
despond and never let himself be overwhelmed by it until
his old age. Those who knew him intimately during his
years in the political wilderness may report differently.
There are some hints that he drank more heavily during this
period. But on the written evidence at present available, the
success with which he dealt with his own temperament is
quite extraordinary. Indeed, it is quite likely that some of
those who were comparatively close to him never realized
that he was liable to depression at all.

At the beginning of this chapter, I suggested that the
relation between great achievement and the depressive temperament was worth more attention than has yet been
bestowed upon it. In psychiatric practice, it is not at all
uncommon to come across men of great ability and dynamic
force who have achieved far more than the common run of
success, and who are generally supposed by their contemporaries to be, if not necessarily happy, at least free from any
kind of neurotic disability. On the surface, such men appear
to be more confident than the average. They often inspire
those who serve them, set an example by their own enormous
appetite for work, and appear to possess inexhaustible vitality. Those who follow in their wake regard such leaders as
being superhuman, and merely envy their energy without
stopping to inquire what it is that drives them. Yet, anyone
who has himself ventured along the corridors of power
knows that the extremely ambitious are often highly vulner-

able, that the tycoon may be lost if his luck deserts him, and that the personal and emotional relationships of those who pursue power are often sadly inadequate. Ambition, taken in isolation, may be a trait of character which merely reflects a man's desire to find adequate scope for his abilities. It can also be a demonic force, driving the subject to achieve more and more, yet never bringing contentment and peace, however great the achievement. The degree to which the highly successful are able to conceal, both from themselves and from others, that they are tormented beings, is extraordinary; and it is often only in the consulting room that the truth emerges. Alanbrooke, weary of the war and the enormous responsibility he carried, was content to lay down his burden and retire to domestic happiness and bird watching. Churchill, on the other hand, was extremely reluctant to abandon power, although, as early as 1949, after his first stroke, some medical opinion considered that he should no longer pursue high office. There is no doubt in my mind as to which of the two men was the happier and the better balanced. Yet Alanbrooke, as he would himself have been the first to admit, could never have inspired the nation as did Churchill.

The end of Churchill's long life makes melancholy reading. It is indeed a tragedy that he survived into old age. Moran records that, after his retirement in April 1955, "Winston made little effort to hide his distaste for what was left to him of life," and adds that "the historian might conclude that this reveals a certain weakness in moral fibre." Any historian who does so conclude will merely reveal his ignorance of medicine. For cerebral arteriosclerosis, with which Churchill was seriously affected, not only saps the will, as Lord Moran says. It also makes impossible the mechanisms of defense with which a man copes with his temperamental difficulties. In old age, most people become to some extent caricatures of themselves. The suspicious become paranoid, the intolerant more irritable, and the depressives less able to rouse themselves from the slough of despond.

Moran brings his story to a close five years before Churchill's death because he "thought it proper to omit the painful details of the state of apathy and indifference into which he sank after his resignation." I think he was right, as a doctor, to do so. He records that Churchill gave up reading, seldom spoke, and sat for hours before the fire in what must have amounted to a depressive stupor. To dwell upon the medical and psychiatric details of Churchill's end would have exposed Moran to even more criticism from his medical colleagues than he received in any case. But the fact that the "Black Dog" finally overcame an old man whose brain could, because of an impaired blood supply, no longer function efficiently, merely increases our admiration for the way in which, earlier in life, he fought his own disability. For he carried a temperamental load which was indeed an exceptionally heavy burden.

It is at this point that psychoanalytic insight reveals its inadequacy. For, although I believe that the evidence shows that the conclusions reached in this chapter are justified, we are still at a loss to explain Churchill's remarkable courage. In the course of his life he experienced many reverses: disappointments which might have embittered and defeated even a man who was not afflicted by the "Black Dog." Yet his dogged determination, his resilience, and his courage enabled him, until old age, to conquer his own inner enemy, just as he defeated the foes of the country he loved so well.

We have often had occasion to comment upon Churchill's "inner world of make-believe" in which, as Moran says, he found reality. At one period in his life, he was fortunate. For, in 1940, his inner world of make-believe coincided with the facts of external reality in a way which very rarely happens to any man. It is an experience not unlike that of passionate love, when, for a time, the object of a man's desire seems to coincide exactly with the image of woman he carries within him. In 1940, Churchill became the hero that he had always dreamed of being. It was his finest hour. In that dark time, what England needed was not a shrewd, equable, balanced leader. She needed a prophet, a heroic visionary, a man who could dream dreams of victory when all seemed lost. Winston Churchill was such a man; and his inspirational quality owed its dynamic force to the romantic world of fantasy in which he had his true being.

NOTES

1. C. P. Snow, *Variety of Men* (London: Macmillan, 1967), p. 120.

2. A. L. Rowse, *The Early Churchills* (London: Macmillan, 1956), pp. 227–28.

3. Quoted in ibid., pp. 251–52.

4. Quoted in ibid., pp. 241, 252.

5. Quoted in ibid., p. 252.

6. A. L. Rowse, *The Later Churchills* (London: Macmillan, 1958), pp. 287–88.

7. Rowse, *The Early Churchills*, p. 29.

8. Quoted in Lord Moran, *Churchill: The Struggle for Survival 1940–1965* (London: Constable, 1966), p. 745.

9. Ibid., p. 621.

10. Quoted in Randolph S. Churchill, *Winston S. Churchill*, vol. 1 (London: Heinemann, 1966), p. 212.

11. Quoted in ibid., 2:69.

12. W. H. Sheldon, *The Varieties of Human Physique* (New York: Harper, 1940); and *The Varieties of Temperament* (New York, Harper, 1942).

13. Quoted in Moran, *Churchill*, p. 621.

14. C. G. Jung, *Psychological Types*, vol. 6 of *Collected Works*, 20 vols., trans. R. F. C. Hull (London: Routledge and Kegan Paul, 1953–79), vol. 6, para. 613.

15. Ibid., paras. 613, 614.

16. Snow, *Variety of Men*, p. 125.

17. Quoted in Arthur Bryant, *The Turn of the Tide* (London: Collins, 1957), p. 25.

18. Quoted in ibid., p. 707.

19. Jung, *Psychological Types*, para. 613.

20. Moran, *Churchill*, p. 167.

21. Ibid., p. 745.

22. Sarah Churchill, *A Thread in the Tapestry* (London: Deutsch, 1967), p. 17.

23. Winston S. Churchill, *Savrola* (Bath: Cedric Chivers, 1973), pp. 39–40.

24. Ibid., pp. 253–54.

25. Ibid., p. 259.

26. Ibid., pp. 42–43.

27. Ibid., p. 41.

28. R. Churchill, *Winston S. Churchill*, 1:45.

29. Quoted in ibid., p. 441.

30. Quoted in ibid., p. 53.

31. Lord Reith, television interview on BBC's *Face to Face*.

32. Quoted in Violet Bonham Carter, *Winston Churchill As I Knew Him* (London: Pan, 1967), p. 16.

33. Quoted in Moran, *Churchill*, p. 776.

34. Ibid., p. 778.

35. Quoted in ibid., p. 433.

36. Quoted in ibid., p. 247.

37. Winston S. Churchill, *My Early Life* (London: Collins, 1959), p. 13.

38. Carter, *Churchill As I Knew Him*, p. 152.

39. Quoted in Moran, *Churchill*, p. 203.

40. Carter, *Churchill As I Knew Him*, p. 28.

41. R. Churchill, *Winston S. Churchill*, 1:50–52.

42. Moran, *Churchill*, pp. 744–45.

43. W. Churchill, *My Early Life*, p. 234.

44. Ibid.

45. Ibid., p. 265.

46. Carter, *Churchill As I Knew Him*, p. 23.

47. Quoted in R. Churchill, *Winston S. Churchill*, 1:260.

48. Quoted in Moran, *Churchill*, p. 167.

49. Quoted in ibid., p. 122.

50. Jean-Paul Sartre, *Words*, trans. Irene Clephane (London: Hamish Hamilton, 1964), p. 37.

51. Quoted in Moran, *Churchill*, p. 429.

52. Georges Simenon, in *Writers at Work*, Paris Review Interviews, vol. 1, (London: Secker and Warburg, 1958), p. 132.

53. Carter, *Churchill As I Knew Him*, p. 427.

54. Winston S. Churchill, *Painting as a Pastime* (Harmondsworth: Penguin, 1964), p. 20.

55. Ibid., p. 21.

56. Ibid., p. 29.

57. Quoted in Moran, *Churchill*, p. 746.

2

Kafka's Sense of Identity

I MUST BEGIN by saying that I approach the study of Kafka from the point of view of a psychiatrist rather than from that of a literary scholar. Because Kafka was both a great writer and also scrupulously honest, he is able, in a unique way, to illumine an area of psychological experience which, though not infrequently encountered in certain kinds of psychiatric patient, is remote from that of the ordinary person.

I have called this chapter "Kafka's Sense of Identity." What do I mean by "identity"? In *A Critical Dictionary of Psychoanalysis,* Charles Rycroft defines identity as "The sense of one's continuous being as an entity distinguishable from all others."[1] Erik Erikson, the psychiatrist who has written most extensively on the subject, refers to "a subjective sense of invigorating sameness and continuity." (I note in passing that a photographic reproduction of Michelangelo's *David* adorns the dustjacket of the English edition of Erikson's book *Identity.* I shall return to why that particular image is associated with the notion of identity at a later point.) Erikson goes on to quote from a letter written by

William James to his wife: "A man's character is discernible in the mental or moral attitude in which, when it came upon him, he felt himself most deeply and intensely active and alive. At such moments there is a voice inside which speaks and says: '*This* is the real me.' "² Jung is surely referring to the same phenomenon when he writes:

> Personality is the supreme realization of the innate idiosyncrasy of a living being. It is an act of high courage flung in the face of life, the absolute affirmation of all that constitutes the individual, the most successful adaptation to the universal conditions of existence, coupled with the greatest possible freedom for self-determination.³

Although William James uses the word "character" and Jung uses the word "personality," they and Erik Erikson are referring to the same experience: that of being positively, fully oneself, without equivocation or pretense, and they are affirming that this experience is fulfilling and life-enhancing.

Contrast these statements with the words which Kafka puts into the mouth of the supplicant in one of the two versions of "Conversation with the Supplicant" in his early story "Description of a Struggle": "There's never been a time in which I have been convinced from within myself that I am alive. You see, I have only such a fugitive awareness of things around me that I always feel they were once real and are now fleeting away."⁴ So little is the young supplicant convinced of the validity of his own existence that he has to draw attention to himself in church by his eccentric behavior. In one version of the story he says, "It is the aim of my life to get people to look at me."⁵ In the other version, he refers to "a need to let myself be nailed down for a brief hour by those eyes,"⁶ as if being stared at convinced him, for the moment, of the reality of his own existence.

Although Kafka was writing fiction, I think that we can be

sure that these passages refer to his own experience, and I agree with Ronald Hayman, who, in his recent biography of Kafka, writes that the characters in this story are "transparent self-projections."[7]

It may, at first sight, seem paradoxical that a writer who is so unlike any other, who is so uniquely himself as Kafka, should entertain doubts about his own identity. When he was actually writing, and when he read and reread what he had written, I think his doubts about himself diminished or disappeared. But, once away from his writing desk, when in the company of others, those doubts constantly recurred. Many of those who knew Kafka were clearly deeply fond of him, and some, like Gustav Janouch, made him the object of hero worship. With those he knew, Kafka could be at times a lively and humorous companion. But, one must recall, Kafka himself said that even with Max Brod, his closest friend, he had never been able to hold a prolonged conversation in which he really revealed himself.

With strangers, he was always ill at ease. In a letter to Felice Bauer dated June 1913, Kafka writes: "But if I am in an unfamiliar place, among a number of strange people, or people whom I feel to be strangers, then the whole room presses on my chest and I am unable to move, my whole personality seems virtually to get under their skins, and everything becomes hopeless."[8]

Kafka is not the only writer to describe such feelings. In a letter to Richard Woodhouse written in October 1818, John Keats writes, "A Poet is the most unpoetical of any thing in existence; because he has no identity." He goes on, "When I am in a room with People if ever I am free from speculating on creations of my own brain, then not myself goes home to myself: but the identity of every one in the room begins to press upon me that I am in a very little time annihilated—not only among Men; it would be the same in a Nursery of children."[9]

For most people, interaction is a recurrent and necessary affirmation of identity. Indeed, without any kind of interaction with others, the term "identity" has no meaning. For identity depends upon contrast, and contrast demands that there should be at least one other person with whom the one can be contrasted. Just as the size of an object cannot be determined without reference to other objects, so the qualities of a person cannot be described without comparison with the qualities of other persons. One cannot be "kind" or "clever" or "ironical" or "self-effacing" in a vacuum. Because of the nature of thought and language, our descriptive statements are bound to imply an opposite.

Since identity implies difference, it follows that the affirmation of identity requires a modicum of self-esteem. If a person is to hold his own in the company of others, he must have some sense of being himself worthwhile. We all know people who have no such sense of their own worth; who never put forward opinions of their own, but who always anxiously agree with the opinions of others. We rightly refer to such people as "nonentities" because their true identities are not made manifest. These are the people who seem constantly to be apologizing for their own existence, as if they felt that they had no right to be alive. Often, these people are intermittently or permanently depressed. From time to time they may assert themselves in explosive outbursts of aggression against those to whom they too closely strive to conform; but after such outbursts are over, they revert to their habitual overadaptation to the other.

There are others who have even greater difficulty in affirming, or even in preserving, identity. Instead of welcoming interaction with others as a life-enhancing opportunity for self-affirmation, they treat people as a threat; as potential enemies who might, at any time, attack and destroy them. R. D. Laing describes how, in the course of an analytic group session, an argument occurred between two patients: "Suddenly, one of the protagonists broke off the argument to say, 'I can't go on. You are arguing to have the pleasure of triumphing over me. At best you win an argument. At worst you lose an argument. *I am arguing in order to preserve my existence.'* " Laing comments: "A firm sense of one's own autonomous identity is required in order that one may be related as one human being to another. Otherwise, any and every relationship threatens the individual with loss of identity."[10]

On what does a firm sense of one's autonomous identity depend? First, there is the question of the individual's relation with his own body. It seems probable that, to start with, the human infant has little idea of where he begins and ends. Having, for nine months, been incorporated within someone else, he needs time to discover that his own limbs belong to him, and that his skin is an envelope which constitutes a boundary between him and the rest of the world. He probably makes these discoveries by coming up against objects in the external world; the side of his crib, his mother's body, and so on. It is easy to understand why Freud referred to the pristine ego as a *bodily* ego.[11] The sense of "I"-ness, of identity, is for most people rooted in the body, although of course it comes to include much else in the course of time. This, no doubt, is why the publishers chose to put Michelangelo's *David* on the dust jacket of Erikson's book *Identity*. The *David* is a paean of praise to the beauty of the male body, and one cannot imagine David's identity as not being rooted in his physical existence. However, not everyone feels like this. Some people feel that the body is a kind of appendage to their true self; almost an object in the external world with which they are connected, but with which they do not identify. Some such people actively dislike or despise their bodies.

This was certainly true of Kafka. We know, from his "Letter to His Father," that he regarded his own body with distaste, and that he compared it unfavorably with that of his father.

> For instance, I remember how we often undressed together in the same bathing-hut. There I was, skinny,

weakly, slight, you strong, tall, broad. Even inside the
hut I felt myself a miserable specimen, and what's
more, not only in your eyes, but in the eyes of the
whole world, for you were for me the measure of all
things.[12]

It is not until August 15, 1911, when he was twenty-eight
years old, that Kafka is able to record in his diary, "The time
which has just gone by and in which I haven't written a word
has been so important for me because I have stopped being
ashamed of my body in the swimming pools in Prague,
Königssaal and Czernoschitz."[13] However, later in the same
year he reverts to his former attitude: "It is certain that a
major obstacle to my progress is my physical condition.
Nothing can be accomplished with such a body. I shall have
to get used to its perpetual balking."[14]

Kafka is writing about his body as if it were an object in
the external world quite separate from himself. It is of
course true that all human beings are capable of temporary
detachment of this kind, and this is particularly true of
intellectuals. Indeed, conceptual thought demands this
degree of abstraction. However, even dedicated scholars
generally find that, after a spell of concentrated work, they
abandon their books and return to the life of the senses, to
identification with the body. Kafka and others like him seem
habitually more alienated than this. This alienation, in
Kafka's case, was not related to his later ill health. Although
Kafka died of laryngeal and pulmonary tuberculosis in
1924, his first hemoptysis did not occur until August 1917.
We cannot be sure when the disease took sufficient hold to
interfere with his general health and vitality, but it certainly
did not do so in his early years. Although, throughout his
life, Kafka was concerned about his physical health and
suffered from all manner of psychosomatic symptoms, he
was able to swim, to row, and to go for long hikes in the
country when he was in his twenties. His feeling of physical
inferiority dated from childhood, and was emotionally

determined, not based upon reality. A well-known photo-graph of Kafka, taken when he was about five, shows him as a skinny, frightened waif. Although a later portrait, taken at the age of eleven, shows a handsome boy who might justifiably have been proud of his looks, it is evidently the earlier image which impressed itself upon his mind, and which persisted, unmodified by later developments. There is a good example in his early fragment of a novel, *Wedding Preparations in the Country,* which demonstrates that Kafka was familiar with the experience of being dissociated from his body. Raban is hesitating about whether or not to travel to the country to meet his fiancée:

> And besides, can't I do it the way I always used to as a child in matters that were dangerous? I don't even need to go to the country myself, it isn't necessary. I'll send my clothed body. If it staggers out of the door of my room, the staggering will not indicate fear, but its noth-ingness. Nor is it a sign of excitement if it stumbles on the stairs, if it travels into the country, sobbing as it goes, and there eats its supper in tears. For I myself am meanwhile lying in my bed, smoothly covered over with the yellow-brown blanket, exposed to the breeze that is wafted through that seldom-aired room.[15]

The dissociation between his body and what Raban feels as himself could scarcely be more complete. Later, Raban interestingly anticipates "Metamorphosis" by fantasizing that, as he lies in bed, he assumes the shape of a big beetle.

We all start life as helpless infants, totally dependent upon, and at the mercy of, those who are supposed to care for us. Some people, of whom Kafka was one, never grow out of this stage of helplessness. Those who are alienated from the body cannot feel the potentialities of the body. Their inner picture of themselves as powerless persists even though they become grown men and women who could, if they had a realistic notion of their own powers, stand up for themselves.

Melanie Klein postulated that the human infant, because of its early helplessness, reacts to frustration as if it were persecution and fears its own destruction by the powerful persons on whom it depends. According to her account, the infant, and especially the neglected infant, harbors within itself intensely destructive impulses which it tends to attribute to (project upon) those who care for it. In later life, any kind of suffering is liable to resuscitate these early feelings and is therefore conceived as an attack upon the self. This account, improbable as it may seem at first sight, is certainly borne out by Kafka's self-scrutiny. In a letter to Max Brod he wrote:

> If for example—this is purely an example—if my stomach hurts, it is no longer really my stomach but something that is basically indistinguishable from a stranger who has taken it into his head to club me. But that is so with everything. I am nothing but a mass of spikes going through me; if I try to defend myself and use force, the spikes only press in the deeper.[16]

It is by no means certain, and in any case unprovable, that all infants suffer the persecutory fears that Melanie Klein postulates. Even if they do so, the majority of infants pass through this "paranoid-schizoid" stage to one in which they can trust others, and in which the expectation of loving care outweighs the anxieties consequent upon being helpless. A minority, like Kafka, do not. How far this is dependent upon the quality of care actually given to the infant, and how far it is the consequence of inherited differences in constitution, is impossible to say; but it is certainly the case that the circumstances of Kafka's infancy were somewhat unfavorable. We know that very soon after Kafka's birth, his mother was summoned back to work in his father's shop, and that the nurse to whom he was first entrusted was replaced by another within a year or two. We know, from his own account, that Kafka never felt he saw enough of his mother, and that he never became reconciled to her absence. In his diary for October 24, 1911 Kafka recalls that when he was ill as a child, his mother would come back from the business to look after him, and that this was comforting. He wishes that he was ill enough to have to go to bed in order to recapture that experience.[17] Even by the standards of the day, Kafka saw uncommonly little of his parents during infancy. In addition, his childhood was unsettled by five moves of home: one before he was two years old, another seven months later, and a third when he was about four years old, in 1877. Two further moves occurred, in 1888 and 1889. Another disturbing factor was the deaths of both his younger brothers. One, born in 1885, when Kafka was two, died less than two years later, of measles. A second brother, born in 1887, survived for only six months. These factors alone are certainly not enough to account for Kafka's persistent ontological insecurity, but may have contributed something toward it. What appears certain is that Kafka carried with him into adult life the sense of being at the mercy of other people and events; of being a victim, rather than of being someone who could act upon the world by exercising his own volition. This seems to me to be a theme which runs through nearly everything that he wrote, perhaps reaching its acme in *The Trial*.

Once I knew a man who graphically illustrated similar feelings. He drew a picture of a circle surrounded by arrows, all of which pointed inward toward the center. He himself was the circle; the arrows represented the hostile impingement of the actual world upon him, against which he felt himself to be defenseless.

Another man, whose lack of early maternal care could be proven, remained terrified of any situation in which he was helpless in the hands of others. The notion of having to submit to a surgical operation, for example, so frightened him that he said he would prefer to die rather than to submit to such an ordeal.

We live in a world in which thousands of people find themselves, in reality, in the hands of malignant persecutors. It has often been suggested that Kafka was prescient in anticipating the horrors of the concentration camps, in which Milena and three of his sisters died. I do not believe this. What Kafka was able to do, in a way equaled by no one else, was to articulate fears which lurk in the recesses of the mind in all of us, but which, in the ordinary course of events, only become manifest in those whom we label "psychiatric patients."

Together with the fear of being injured or annihilated goes the fear of being ignored, or treated as being of no account. Swift, writing of Gulliver in the hands of the giants of Brobdingnag, records, "That which gave me the most Uneasiness among those Maids of Honour, when my Nurse carried me to visit them, was to see them use me without any Manner of Ceremony like a Creature who has no sort of Consequence."[18]

To gain a sense of one's own validity as a person, one has to be treated as actually being there, as counting for something. In his "Letter to His Father," Kafka writes of this "sense of nothingness that often dominates me,"[19] which, he says, comes largely from his father's influence. He recalls with particular horror an occasion on which, when he was whimpering for water at night, his father picked him up and left him outside on the balcony: "Even years afterwards I suffered from the tormenting fancy that the huge man, my father, the ultimate authority, would come almost for no reason at all and take me out of bed in the night and carry me out on to the *pavlatche* [balcony], and that therefore I was a mere nothing for him."[20] For Kafka, this particular incident seems to have been of immense significance. It may be compared with the experience of the seven-year-old Proust, who never forgot that, because she was entertaining a guest at dinner, his mother once failed to give him her usual good-night kiss. George Painter, author of the standard biography of Proust, refers to this incident as the most important event in Proust's life, because "it told him that love is doomed and happiness does not exist."[21]

The importance of both incidents is, of course, not their actual occurrence, but what they epitomize in the lives of these great writers. Proust's *Weltanschauung* is dominated by the impossibility of love, Kafka's by the sense of helplessness.

To be treated as if one hardly existed, as if one counted for nothing, is to live in a world in which, since power is in the hands of others, there is no way of predicting what is going to happen. Although the human infant is entirely dependent upon those who care for him, he is equipped with means for indicating his needs. If those needs are met in a way that is rational and considerate, he will grow up to conceive of the world as likely to be rational and considerate. Thus, if he is fed when he is hungry, allowed to sleep when he is tired, played with when he is lively, and cleaned when he is wet and dirty, there will appear to be a firm connection between what goes on in the external world and what he himself is feeling. But suppose that the infant's feelings are not considered; that he is fed when adults happen to think of it; that he is kept awake when he wishes to sleep, and put down to sleep when he wishes to be played with; that he is picked up and moved around at the whim of adults, without reference to his protests. For such a child the world will seem incomprehensible and unpredictable. Because what actually happens is unrelated to his feelings, it will appear to him that the world is ruled by capricious giants whom he cannot influence. Moreover, one can see that such a dislocation between the inner and outer worlds of the child must lead to an intensified preoccupation with fantasy and a sense of despair. If one can neither understand the world nor gain any satisfaction for one's needs from it, one is bound to be driven in upon oneself.

The capriciousness and unpredictability of authority is a

central theme in both *The Trial* and *The Castle*. Even the giants make a brief appearance when, in *The Trial*, Josef K. listens to the manufacturer and the deputy manager discussing the former's business scheme: "Then, as the two of them leaned against his desk, and the manufacturer set out to win the newcomer's approval for his scheme, it seemed to K. as if two giants of enormous size were bargaining above his head for himself."[22] This is surely a child's-eye view. Cannot most of us recall our parents, or other adults, discussing what should be done with us, perhaps to which school we should be sent, as if we had no say in the matter, as if we hardly existed?

I do not believe or suggest that Kafka's treatment by his father entirely accounted for the way in which he viewed authority, nor did Kafka himself think so. But his "Letter to His Father" does illustrate the fact that injudicious handling can damage sensitive natures. Hermann Kafka seems to have been a dogmatic, hearty bully who could tolerate no disagreement with his views, and who was subject to fits of rage which terrified his son. In addition he was inconsistent. He insisted on good table manners but was constantly infringing his own injunctions. Even if he himself had no firm opinion about a particular subject, he would confidently assert that anyone who did so was wrong. Hermann Kafka sounds as if he belonged to that not inconsiderable number of persons who can only maintain their own self-esteem by putting others down. It is an effective technique for undermining the sensitive and those who cannot stand up for themselves. Kafka wrote:

> You were capable, for instance, of running down the Czechs, and then the Germans, and then the Jews, and what is more, not only selectively, but in every respect, and finally there was no-one left but yourself. For me you took on the enigmatic quality that all tyrants have whose rights are based on their person and not on their ideas.[23]

In a later passage Kafka writes:

> Hence the world was for me divided into three parts:
> one in which I, the slave, lived under the laws that had
> been invented only for me and which I could, I did not
> know why, never completely comply with: then a sec-
> ond world, which was infinitely remote from mine, in
> which you lived, concerned with government, with the
> issuing of orders and with annoyance about their not
> being obeyed: and finally a third world where everyone
> else lived happily and free from orders and from hav-
> ing to obey. I was continually in disgrace, either I
> obeyed your orders, and that was a disgrace, for they
> applied after all only to me, or I was defiant, and that
> too was a disgrace, for how could I presume to defy
> you, or I could not obey because for instance I had not
> your strength, your appetite or your skill, in spite of
> which you expected it of me as a matter of course; this
> was of course the greatest disgrace of all.[24]

A triple bind, therefore, in which the child, whatever he did,
was always in the wrong. It is not surprising that Kafka
writes to his father, "I had lost my self-confidence where you
were concerned, and in its place had acquired a boundless
sense of guilt."[25]

Kafka's complaint to his father that he, the slave, lived
under laws which existed for him alone, is expressed in the
parable "Before the Law," told by the priest to K. in the
penultimate chapter of *The Trial*. It will be recalled that a
countryman seeks access to the Law through a door which is
always open, but which is guarded by a doorkeeper who will
not allow the countryman in. After many years of importu-
nate waiting, the countryman is near his end. He complains:
" 'Everyone strives to reach the law . . . so how does it happen
that for all these many years no one but myself has ever
begged for admittance?' The doorkeeper . . . roars in his
ear: 'No one else could ever be admitted here, since this gate
was made only for you. Now I am going to shut it.' "[26]

Just as "The Law" is forever inaccessible, so "the Laws" can never be known. In one of his short fragments, "The Problem of Our Laws," Kafka writes, "Our Laws are not generally known; they are kept secret by the small group of nobles who rule us."[27] He goes on to speculate that it is possible that no body of Law really exists; that "the Law is whatever the nobles do."[28] The parallel with Kafka's view of his father as a tyrant whose domination was based upon his person and not on reason is inescapable.

The Trial also illustrates what Kafka called his "boundless sense of guilt." In the novel, K. is arrested without having done anything wrong. His guilt is taken for granted. As one of the warders who arrests him tells him, the high authorities who order his arrest are well informed about the reasons: "The authorities . . . never go hunting for crime in the populace, but, as the Law decrees, are drawn towards the guilty and must then send out us warders. That is the Law. How could there be a mistake in that?"[29]

K.'s crime is never specified, in spite of the fact that he is finally executed by stabbing. It does not need to be spelled out. In one passage, K. says: "It is a matter of countless subtleties in which the Court is lost sight of. And in the end, out of nothing at all, an enormous fabric of guilt will be conjured up."[30]

It is, I think, evident that K.'s sense of guilt is existential. No crime need be named, since he feels that it is a crime for him to be alive at all. It is a feeling which children who think of themselves as always in the wrong not infrequently develop. If guilt is boundless, if nothing the child does is ever right, and if he has no way of finding out what would be right, he cannot develop any confidence in himself as an authentic person with a separate identity. Earlier, I quoted R. D. Laing's example of a patient who had to withdraw from an argument because he felt that his very existence was threatened. If one has always felt oneself to be in the wrong, and then tries to assert one's separate existence by gently putting forward an opinion of one's own, anyone who rides roughshod over that opinion is a threat to that separate existence. It is not surprising that people whose childhood experience was like that of Kafka tend to withdraw into an ivory tower of isolation where interaction with others cannot threaten them.

That K.'s crime is his very existence is confirmed in the passage in which Kafka describes the impossibility of K. ever being able to complete a plea which could be presented to the Court in support of his case:

> One did not need to have a timid and fearful nature to be easily persuaded that the completion of this plea was a sheer impossibility. Not because of laziness or constructive malice, which could only affect the advocate, but because to meet an unknown accusation, not to mention other possible charges arising out of it, the whole of one's life would have to be passed in review, down to the smallest actions and accidents, clearly formulated and examined from every angle.[31]

This is one passage in which Kafka really does seem to anticipate the techniques of interrogation employed by both the Russian and Chinese interrogators when they wish to obtain confessions. When a person is arrested, a warrant may be produced and read, but the prisoner's supposed crimes are never specified. After a period of total isolation, the interrogation begins. The interrogator assumes that the prisoner is undoubtedly guilty and acts as though all his crimes are known to the authorities. The prisoner is told that there is no hope for him unless he makes a full confession. The whole of his past life is reviewed, and, in many instances, the prisoner is required to write a detailed autobiography which may have to be corrected over and over again. Most people have some feelings of guilt connected with past episodes in their lives, and religious people, especially, often have a deep sense of sin. It is not difficult for

Communist interrogators to make use of this, and to link real or imagined transgressions with so-called "crimes against the people" which the prisoner becomes ready to confess.

In Kafka's world, just as in a Communist state, there is no real possibility of acquittal. In *The Trial*, the painter Titorelli, whose aid K. seeks because he has access to the Judges whose portraits he paints, tells him the position. Even if K. is acquitted and allowed to walk out of the Court a free man, he is only

> ... ostensibly free, or more exactly, provisionally free.
> For the Judges of the lowest grade, to whom my
> acquaintances belong, haven't the power to grant a final
> acquittal, that power is reserved for the highest Court
> of all, which is quite inaccessible to you, to me, and to
> all of us. What the prospects are up there we do not
> know, and, I may say, do not even want to know.[32]

So the charge which may be temporarily lifted from K.'s shoulders may be laid upon him again at any time.

I suppose that, for most people, the sexual act is an important means of self-affirmation. Although it can be argued that sexual intercourse is impersonal, since it is designed by nature for the propagation of the species, the majority of people do not experience it in this way. Nor does the fact that many people feel a temporary loss of identity in merging with the beloved contradict their prior or simultaneous experience that, in sexual intercourse, they are expressing the essence of their physical and spiritual nature. But this way of affirming his identity as a man was barred to Kafka, at least initially. Kafka's first sexual experience was with a shopgirl, soon after his twentieth birthday. In a letter he wrote to Milena seventeen years later, he recalled that

> ... at the hotel the girl in all innocence made a tiny
> repulsive gesture (not worth mentioning), had uttered a

trifling obscenity (not worth mentioning), but the
memory remained—I knew at that moment that I
would never forget it and simultaneously I knew or
thought I knew that this repulsiveness and smut,
though outwardly not necessarily, was inwardly, however, very necessarily connected with the whole thing,
and that just this repulsiveness and obscenity (whose
little symptom had only been her tiny gesture, her
trifling word) had drawn me with such terrible power
into this hotel which otherwise I would have avoided
with all my remaining strength.[33]

Max Brod records that "in later years he steered clear of
dalliance, looked at the erotic side of life only from the most
serious angle, and never told a dirty story or even stood for
one being told in his presence. That is to say, he never
protested against one; it simply would not have occurred to
anyone to tell one in his presence."[34]

Although in the last year of his life Kafka was able to move
in with Dora Dymant and, one hopes, became able to enjoy
some of the rewards of physical closeness, he refers to the
step of actually living with her as "a reckless move which can
only be compared to some great historical event, like
Napoleon's Russian campaign."[35]

As everyone familiar with Kafka's life knows, Kafka did
from time to time have actual sexual involvements and,
according to Max Brod, fathered a son of whose existence
he remained ignorant. But, right up to, and including, his
relationship with Milena, he thought of sex and himself as
"dirty." Marthe Robert, in her recently translated book,
Franz Kafka's Loneliness, interprets Kafka's vacillation about
women in standard Oedipal terms.[36] She supposes that
Kafka was unable to venture on marriage because, for him,
all women were mothers, and sexual intercourse was therefore incestuous. This is a superficial interpretation which
shows no appreciation of the terrible dilemma which Kafka,
and others like him, actually face. Before his terminal relationship with Dora Dymant, Kafka's two most important

relationships with women were with Felice Bauer and with Milena Jesenská. Kafka contrived to keep these relationships almost entirely epistolary. During the five years of his relationship with Felice, the couple met no more than nine or ten times, often for no more than an hour or two. The same pattern was repeated, though for a shorter time, with Milena. Kafka perfectly exemplifies the schizoid dilemma: a desperate need for love nullified by an equally desperate fear of actual proximity.

In his letters to Felice, Kafka constantly abuses himself; says that he would be impossible to live with; that he is quite unable to manage life; that he is a hopeless person. This pattern of confessional self-abasement is repeated in the letters to Milena, to whom he also sent his diaries. There are people who feel themselves compelled to behave particularly badly with, and toward, those they love. They seem to be seeking something which they feel they never had: an unconditional love which accepts the very worst in themselves without rejection. Kafka, in these distressing letters, is seeking a total acceptance which demands nothing in return; the kind of love which a mother may be expected to offer her newborn baby who, although squalling, incontinent, and totally unaware of anyone else's needs, is nevertheless entitled to a loving acceptance of a kind which it will never again experience. This kind of total demand is made by psychiatric patients in analysis who have been deprived or neglected in early childhood, and especially by those who have had to learn, too early in life, that love is a reward for compliance rather than a gift which is freely given. Kafka is looking for a relationship in which he is not required to adapt to the other person, since, all his life, he has tended to lose his sense of identity by never asserting himself and by striving to comply with the demands of the other.

After Felice has accepted his proposal of marriage in June 1913, Kafka writes letters in which he demands to know everything about her life, down to the smallest detail: what she is wearing, how she spends her time, what her room is like, whom she sees, what she eats. These obsessive inquiries can be interpreted in more than one way. To know exactly what the beloved is doing, every moment of the day, is reassuring. Even if she is too far away for actual control to be exercised, as was true of Felice, she is, in imagination, pinned down, potentially accessible at any moment. One can guess that, had they ever lived together, Kafka would have infuriated her by demanding to know, as anxious, insecure spouses often do, when she was going out, when she would be back, and so on. And such inquiries would not have been pathological jealousy, though this may be a part of the picture, but rather the intense anxiety of the small child whose very existence depends upon his mother's actual presence.

Another way of looking at Kafka's anxious inquiries is to realize that, by knowing every detail about the life of the girl to whom he was writing, he would be able to give reality to a person who, because he saw her so seldom, remained largely a figure of his imagination. This is a technique employed by some novelists, who lend their characters verisimilitude by inventing for them all manner of details of dress, habits, and surroundings, so that they end by knowing exactly how a particular character would behave in any situation demanded by the plot of the novel. By not becoming actually, physically involved with the women he loved, Kafka was better able to make them into denizens of his inner, imaginative world, the only world in which he felt he could cope with them.

At the same time, Kafka's anxiety makes almost impossible demands. He used to carry Felice's letters around with him, saying that they gave him continuous support and made him feel better and more competent. If she fails to reply at once, he is absolutely desolate:

> Has there ever been, Felice, in the last three months, a single day on which you have not had news from me?

You see, there hasn't been such a day. But today, Tuesday, you leave me entirely without news; since four o'clock on Sunday I know nothing about you; until tomorrow's delivery that will be no less than sixty-six hours, filled in my mind with every alternating good and bad contingency.[37]

This absolute, total dependency, this aching, unassuageable need is combined with a fearful anxiety about what would happen if she were actually there:

You once said that you would like to sit beside me while I write. Listen, in that case I could not write (I can't do much anyway), but in that case, I could not write at all. For writing means revealing oneself in excess; that utmost of self-revelation and surrender, in which a human being, when involved with others, would feel he was losing himself, and from which, therefore, he will always shrink as long as he is in his right mind—for everyone wants to live as long as he is alive—even the degree of self-revelation and surrender is not enough for writing. Writing that springs from the surface of existence—when there is no other way and the deeper wells have dried up—is nothing and collapses the moment a truer emotion makes that surface shake. This is why one can never be alone enough when one writes, why there can never be enough silence around one when one is writing, why even night is not night enough.[38]

Kafka's anxiety is twofold. On the one hand, probably rightly, he feels that his need is so great that no one could possibly meet it; or, if any woman were to attempt to meet it, he fears that she would be drained and ultimately destroyed in the process. On the other hand, if she were to be with him, his independence, his identity, and therefore his capacity to write would be annihilated.

Kafka's anxiety in the presence of other people made him

diffident to the point of self-effacement. Once, when visiting Max Brod, he woke up the latter's father. "Instead of apologizing, he said, in an indescribably gentle way, raising a hand as if to calm him and walking softly on tiptoe through the room, 'Please look on me as a dream.' "39

It is characteristic of such a man that he should prefer Nature cures to conventional medicine, and, for long periods, be vegetarian. In an aquarium he was heard addressing the fish: "Now at last I can look at you in peace, I don't eat you any more."40 He drank no alcohol, tea, or coffee, and never smoked. It is also characteristic that he should plan an idealist "Guild of Workmen without Possessions" in which members were not to be allowed money or valuables, but only the minimum of clothing and books and materials necessary for work. Everything else in this Utopia was to belong to the poor.

Self-effacement and self-denial of this kind is the very opposite stance from the joyous affirmation of one's own identity to which I referred earlier. Kafka's anxiety not only made him reluctant to compete, but also made him almost too acutely aware of what the other person was feeling. Overadaptation to the other means loss of the self as a separate entity. Only in the silent watches of the night, when Kafka was entirely alone, could he get in touch with his innermost depths and be really and truly himself.

In his penultimate letter to Felice, written after he knew that he had tuberculosis, he demonstrates that his wish to please is not really based on concern for what others are feeling, but upon his own wish to be accepted and to gain love. It is a remarkable piece of insight:

> When I examine my ultimate aim, it shows that I do not actually strive to be good, to answer to a supreme tribunal. Very much the opposite. I strive to know the entire human and animal community, to recognize their fundamental preferences, desires, and moral ideas, to

reduce them to simple rules, and as quickly as possible
to adopt these rules so as to be pleasing to everyone.
Indeed (here comes the inconsistency), to become so
pleasing that in the end I might openly act out my
inherent baseness before the eyes of the world without
forfeiting its love—the only sinner not to be roasted. In
short, my only concern is the human tribunal, and I
would like to deceive even this, and what's more without actual deception.⁴¹

Everyone who tries to suppress all aggression and self-
assertion pays a price for doing so: "Naturam expellas furca,
tamen usque recurret." It is no surprise that Kafka, the
gentle ascetic, is haunted by horrific sado-masochistic fantasies: ". . . that I lie stretched out on the floor, sliced up like a
roast, and with my hand am slowly pushing a slice of the
meat towards a dog in the corner."⁴²

Torture, violence, flagellation are recurrent themes in
both Kafka's diaries and his fiction. But beyond and beneath
the suffering, there is also a glimmer of hope. On March 13,
1915, he writes in his diary, "Occasionally the feeling of an
unhappiness which almost dismembers me, and at the same
time the conviction of its necessity and of the existence of a
goal to which one makes one's way by undergoing every kind
of unhappiness."⁴³

In that most terrifying of all his stories, "In the Penal
Settlement," we can get an idea of what that goal really is.
When the officer in charge is explaining how the apparatus
of torture and execution really works, he points out that it is
so designed that the victim under the harrow does not die
until twelve hours have passed. However, after the needles
have been inscribing their message of judgment into the
victim's flesh for about six hours, a change comes over him:

> But how quiet the man grows at the sixth hour. Enlight-
> enment comes to the most dull-witted. It begins around
> the eyes. From there it radiates. A moment that might

tempt one to get under the harrow with him. Nothing
more happens after that, the man only begins to understand the inscription, he purses his mouth as if he were
listening. You have seen how difficult it is to decipher
the script with one's eyes; but our man deciphers it with
his wounds.[44]

The most striking sentence in this extract is surely that in
which the officer refers to his temptation to get under the
harrow with the victim. Perhaps, if a man suffers enough, as
he nears death, he will finally attain enlightenment: at last
understand what law it is that he has transgressed, and come
to terms with the guilt which is so deeply inscribed that it is
an inescapable part of his physical being. When, near the
end of the story, the officer does replace the condemned
man, the machine goes wrong. The officer is deprived of
enlightenment because he is killed prematurely and has not
therefore suffered for long enough.

How is it that long endurance of suffering can bring
enlightenment? Only, perhaps, when we do not try to
avoid it.

Wordsworth, in his ode "Intimations of Immortality from
Recollections of Early Childhood," regrets the passing of
the child's pristine vision of the world:

> Heaven lies about us in our infancy!
> Shades of the prison-house begin to close
> Upon the growing Boy.

But Wordsworth also recognizes that creativity has its origin
in early childhood and that it is vital to preserve what links
we can with what is past:

> But for those first affections,
> Those shadowy recollections,
> Which, be they what they may,
> Are yet the fountain-light of all our day,
> Are yet a master-light of all our seeing . . .[45]

From what Kafka wrote, in his diaries, in his letters, and in his fiction, we may surmise that it was Hell rather than Heaven which lay about him in his infancy, and the hounds of Hell continued to pursue him. But Kafka realized that, for him, as for Wordsworth, the link with his childhood must be preserved. Most of us paper over our miseries with a variety of defensive devices. We put on masks; we pretend that what is important does not matter; we betray ourselves and therefore we betray others; we twist and turn, pose and pretend, drink, fornicate, and try to forget. This why we so often end up stereotyped and sterile.

Kafka, until nearly the end of his life, was tempted by suicide. Like Georg Bendemann in "The Judgement," he was drawn to obey his father's injunction that he had no right to exist. But Kafka, the man with no identity, forever ironic, gentle, self-effacing, was, in his inner world, courageous, uncompromising, ruthlessly honest. If his fate was to live under the harrow, that was where he had to be, and he was not going to wriggle out from it. As a writer, he not only did not flinch, but discovered his real identity. In a letter to Felice written in August 1913, he complains of the inaccuracies of a graphologist to whom she has evidently shown his writing. The graphologist has attributed "artistic interests" to him. Kafka writes: "Even 'artistic interests' is not true; in fact, of all the erroneous statements, that is the most erroneous. I have no literary interest, but am made of literature, I am nothing else, and cannot be anything else."[46]

The self which he felt had been crushed in childhood, and which he feared would be crushed again by anyone who came too close to him, triumphantly asserts its uniqueness on the page; and we should not recognize and celebrate that uniqueness if Kafka had emancipated himself from suffering instead of laying hold upon it.

Kafka's fear of the external world, of involvement with others, and of the loss of his own identity, made him seek writing as a retreat. Writing was the only way which he could be entirely himself, and yet still preserve lines of communication. Schizophrenics protect themselves in similar fashion. They retreat into an inner world in which they achieve all manner of wonderful things in spite of the machinations of their enemies and their perpetual fear of being engulfed and overwhelmed. Those who feel powerless in the external world commonly develop a compensatory inner world in which they are omnipotent; in which the hard facts of reality are denied and replaced by psychotic fantasies in which the subject is all-important and possessed of magical powers. Jung quotes a striking example of a schizophrenic who told him that the world was his picture book: he had only to turn the pages to see a new vision.[47] Kafka was no stranger to omnipotence of thought. In his early story "Description of a Struggle," he writes of a traveler who flattens out a steep road, causes an enormously high mountain to rise, and forgets to let the moon come up.[48] Kafka also exhibited a paranoid side to his nature. In December 1917 he wrote to Max Brod about the mice who were invading his bedroom:

> My reaction towards the mice is one of sheer terror. To analyze its source would be the task of the psychoanalyst, which I am not. Certainly, this fear, like an insect phobia, is connected with the unexpected, uninvited, inescapable, more or less silent, persistent, secret aims of these creatures, with the sense that they have riddled the surrounding walls through and through with their tunnels and are lurking within, that the night is theirs, that because of their nocturnal existence and their tininess they are so remote from us and thus outside our power.[49]

Kafka was not psychotic; but I believe that it was his writing which prevented him from retreating into a world of psychotic fantasy. For writing is a means of communication, and therefore a means of retaining contact with others, albeit at a distance. Indeed, for people of Kafka's temperament, the gift of being able to write is an ideal way of expressing oneself, since it does not involve direct contact with others. Writing also serves another function for those plagued with horrors. Kafka told Janouch that writing "The Judgement" had exorcised a specter. So writing was not only a way of affirming his identity without direct involvement, but also a form of abreaction, of laying ghosts by confronting them and pinning them down in words. Kafka perfectly illustrates the fact that, for some people, writing, or some other form of imaginative activity, is a way of survival. I agree with Erich Heller, who writes of Kafka: "Of course, this is a disposition akin to madness, separated from it only by writing table, an imagination capable of holding together what appears to have an irresistible tendency to fall apart, and an intelligence of supreme integrity."[50]

Although writing may have saved Kafka from madness, writing is not, and can never be, a total substitute for living life in the world, and Kafka, with his customary insight, realized this. I think that "The Burrow" demonstrates this insight. Professor Thorlby, in his study of Kafka,[51] has given a very interesting interpretation of this story. If my emphasis is different, this is not only because I am a psychiatrist rather than a literary scholar, but because Kafka contains such multitudes that different interpretations of his work can often be complementary rather than contradictory.

"The Burrow" is the story of an animal's attempt to find security by constructing a hugely elaborate burrow in which it can find safety from potential enemies and a retreat from the external world. The burrow has taken a very long time to construct; the network of passages is elaborate. Not quite in its center, chosen to serve as a refuge in case of extreme danger, is a cell called the Castle Keep, in which the animal assembles its store of food. It is, as a rule, beautifully still within the burrow; the air is balmy, there is hardly any noise, and the animal feels that he can sleep "the sweet sleep of tranquillity, of satisfied desire, of achieved ambition."[52] But, in spite of all the complex defenses, certain anxieties cannot be altogether eliminated. There is, for example, the entrance. Although this is concealed by a covering of moss, and has so far not attracted the attention of enemies, it is impossible to be confident that this will be so forever. It is dangerous, but perhaps advisable, to look at the entrance from the ou⁺ ⸱de from time to time. Moreover, the burrow is rather confined, and the food outside is better. Sometimes the animal spends quite long periods outside, concealed from enemies, gloating over the burrow which lies waiting for him with its promise of infinite bliss. When he is in the burrow, it is difficult to leave it for the outside world. When he is in the outside world, it is equally difficult to descend into the burrow. One solution might be to enlist a confidant, who could keep watch over the burrow and warn of danger. But no, there is no one he can trust; and he could certainly never let anyone else into the burrow itself.

Kafka perfectly illustrates the dilemma in which he finds himself. He can neither be fully engaged in the external world, nor can he entirely withdraw into his inner world. In the story, the two worlds may even exchange their characteristics, so that what appeared tranquil becomes threatening, and vice versa.

At last, the animal settles for retreat. Exhausted by conflict and perpetual watchfulness, he makes his way to the safety of the Castle Keep. He sleeps for a prolonged period, but, after a while, is awakened by a disturbing whistling noise. At first he concludes that this noise is made by the small fry, the tiny animals which do not threaten him but are always around and constitute his food. But the noise grows louder and more insistent. It is, he decides, some new type of beast which he has never before encountered. Perhaps all his precautions against attack are insufficient. He tries to guess at its plans. One thing is certain; if they do encounter each other, there will be a bloody battle. He finally contents himself with the hope that the beast, although undoubtedly a threat, may never have heard of him. The story (of which the final pages are missing) ends on this note of unresolved unease.

Kafka is surely saying that security is not attainable, either in the external world or in the enclosed world of the imagination. The fate of those who are unable to risk loving and living, and who seek to be safely protected within the burrow of their own narcissism, is, inevitably, to be haunted by creatures of the imagination (like Kafka's own sado-masochistic fantasies) which will not leave them in peace.

The theme of this story seems to me to be similar to that of one of Henry James's most powerful tales, "The Beast in the Jungle." This is the story of John Marcher, who for years has led a futile existence because he is haunted by the con- viction that he is being reserved for an unusual, perhaps terrible experience, which he pictures as a beast tracking him through the jungle. He confides his story to a sympa- thetic woman who becomes his Platonic companion. Only when they become old and the woman is ill does he learn the truth. He has been haunted by the beast because he has avoided commitment and has lost the woman he might have loved. The beast is a product of his own blindness, self- centeredness, and lack of courage; and it springs when he realizes that his own life has been rendered sterile by his efforts to protect himself.

Kafka was originally driven to affirm his identity through writing because he found involvement with others threaten- ing; but it is clear that, through his writing, and through recognition of his talent by others, and their acceptance of the self which manifested itself in his stories, he became more confident. What would have happened to him if his life had not been prematurely brought to a close by tuber- culosis? My guess is that he would finally have been able to commit himself to Dora or to some other woman, and would have become more capable of living something approaching a normal life. What the effect upon his writing would have been is another matter. Kafka's writing is so bound up with the more pathological parts of his personality that, if he had become happier, his drive to write might have been greatly diminished.

NOTES

References are to Kafka's works unless otherwise noted.

1. Charles Rycroft, *A Critical Dictionary of Psychoanalysis* (London: Nelson, 1968), p. 68.
2. Erik Erikson, *Identity* (London: Faber and Faber, 1958), p. 19.
3. C. G. Jung, "The Development of Personality," in *Collected Works*, 20 vols., trans. R. F. C. Hull (London: Routledge and Kegan Paul, 1953–79), vol. 17, para. 289.
4. "Two Dialogues" (from a work later destroyed, "Description of a Struggle"), trans. Willa and Edwin Muir, in *Wedding Preparations in the Country and Other Stories* (Harmondsworth: Penguin, 1978), pp. 80–81.
5. Ibid., p. 80.
6. "Description of a Struggle," trans. Tania and James Stern, in *The Penguin Complete Short Stories of Franz Kafka*, ed. Nathan N. Glazer (London: Allen Lane, 1983), p. 33.
7. Ronald Hayman, *K: A Biography of Kafka* (London: Weidenfeld and Nicolson, 1981), p. 47.
8. *Letters to Felice*, trans. James Stern and Elizabeth Duckworth, ed. Erich Heller and Jürgen Born (London: Secker and Warburg, 1974), p. 271.
9. *The Letters of John Keats*, ed. M. B. Forman (Oxford: Oxford University Press, 1935), p. 228.
10. R. D. Laing, *The Divided Self* (London: Tavistock, 1960), p. 45.
11. *The Standard Edition of the Complete Psychological Works of Sigmund Freud*, 24 vols., ed. and trans. James Strachey (London: Hogarth Press, 1953–64), 19:26.
12. "Letter to His Father," trans. Ernst Kaiser and Eithne Wilkins, in *Wedding Preparations*, p. 32.
13. *The Diaries of Franz Kafka*, ed. Max Brod, vol. 1, *1910–1913*, trans. Joseph Kresh (Harmondsworth: Penguin, 1972), p. 50.
14. Ibid., p. 124.
15. "Wedding Preparations in the Country," trans. Ernst Kaiser and Eithne Wilkins, in *Wedding Preparations*, p. 10.
16. *Letters to Friends, Family and Editors*, trans. Richard and Clara Winston (London: Calder, 1978), p. 15.

17. *Diaries*, pp. 87–88.
18. Jonathan Swift, *Gulliver's Travels and Selected Writings in Prose and Verse*, ed. John Hayward (London: Nonesuch Press, 1968), p. 115.
19. "Letter to His Father," p. 34.
20. Ibid.
21. George Painter, *Marcel Proust*, 2 vols. (London: Chatto and Windus, 1959), 1:9.
22. *The Trial*, trans. Willa and Edwin Muir (Harmondsworth: Penguin, 1953), p. 145.
23. "Letter to His Father," p. 35.
24. Ibid., p. 38.
25. Ibid., p. 55.
26. "Before the Law," trans. Willa and Edwin Muir, in *Penguin Complete Short Stories*, p. 4.
27. "The Problem of Our Laws," trans. Willa and Edwin Muir, in ibid., p. 437.
28. Ibid., p. 438.
29. *The Trial*, p. 12.
30. Ibid., p. 165.
31. Ibid., pp. 142–43.
32. Ibid., p. 175.
33. *Letters to Milena*, ed. Willi Haas, trans. Tania and James Stern (London: Secker and Warburg, 1953), p. 164.
34. Max Brod, *Franz Kafka* (New York: Schocken Books, 1963), p. 116.
35. Quoted in Allan Blunden, "A Chronology of Kafka's Life," in *The World of Franz Kafka*, ed. J. P. Stern (London: Weidenfeld and Nicolson, 1980), p. 28.
36. Marthe Robert, *Franz Kafka's Loneliness*, trans. Ralph Manheim (London: Faber and Faber, 1982).
37. *Letters to Felice*, p. 23.
38. Ibid., pp. 155–56.
39. Brod, *Franz Kafka*, pp. 73–74.
40. Quoted in ibid., p. 74.
41. *Letters to Felice*, p. 545.
42. *Letters to Friends*, p. 95.
43. *Diaries*, p. 333.
44. "In the Penal Settlement," trans. Willa and Edwin Muir, in *Penguin Complete Short Stories*, p. 150.
45. William Wordsworth, *The Poems*, vol. 1, ed. John O. Hayden (Harmondsworth: Penguin, 1977), p. 525.

46. *Letters to Felice*, p. 174.

47. Jung, "The Relations Between the Ego and the Unconscious," in *Collected Works*, vol. 7, para. 228.

48. "Description of a Struggle," in *Penguin Complete Short Stories*, p. 22.

49. *Letters to Friends*, p. 174.

50. Erich Heller, *Franz Kafka* (New York: Viking, 1975), p. 15.

51. Anthony Thorlby, *Kafka: A Study* (London: Heinemann, 1972).

52. "The Burrow," trans. Willa and Edwin Muir, in *Penguin Complete Short Stories*, p. 327.

3

Isaac Newton

ISAAC NEWTON IS generally acknowledged to have been one of the greatest creative men of genius who ever existed. It also happens that he showed many striking abnormalities of personality, and at one time was considered mad by his contemporaries. His early history, moreover, is such that, to my mind, it is not surprising that he grew up to be eccentric. I want to examine two questions that may or may not be related. Firstly, how far were his adult peculiarities the consequence of his childhood circumstances, and, secondly, were his scientific achievements in any way connected with his personality?

There are those, even among psychiatrists, who deny that the experiences of early childhood play any important part in the formation of adult character, believing this to be the consequence of inheritance, hardly modified by circumstance. I do not find myself among their number, although I recognize that heredity must not only influence a child's response to adverse circumstance but may also determine which experiences he perceives as harmful. Newton's early childhood, however, was, as we shall see, so classically traumatic that I find it impossible to believe that it did not play a major part in shaping his personality.

The relation between his personality and his achievement is more dubious. Some like to believe that scientific discovery is entirely the result of intelligence combined with application. When I ventured to suggest that the structure of Newton's character and his discoveries might be related, Sir Karl Popper, who was at the meeting at which I spoke, said:

> I do not believe in the currently fashionable psycho-pathological interpretation of Newton. I think that Newton's theory is a clear answer to a definite problem situation. The problem situation was set by the work of Galileo and Kepler, and subsequent to their work various people attempted to solve the problem that Newton eventually solved. Newton was certainly one of the greatest geniuses of all time, and he exhibited talents of a very special order; but to explain his work as the result of, say, an obsession with unity seems to me empty talk, and to represent a very dangerous kind of psychologistic approach.[1]

I should, I suppose, have been abashed by being put in my place by one who has been described as the greatest living philosopher of science. Despite Karl Popper's strictures, however, I find it difficult to believe that intellectual achievement can take place in isolation from other features of personality. Although the mind of a scientist may seem, at times, to act like an impersonal calculator, there are, it seems to me, traits of character and circumstances that render this possible that are not shared by all of us. Even the most detached intellectual operations are motivated, I believe, by forces that are emotional in origin rather than purely rational, a conclusion supported by the philosopher Hume, who wrote, "Reason is, and ought only to be, the slave of the passions, and can never pretend to any other office than to serve and obey them."[2] This is not to say that I subscribe to the kind of interpretations that the more fundamentalist psychoanalysts are only too ready to advance. I do not believe that the wish to make sense out of the universe is a sublimation of sexual or aggressive drives in any direct or simple sense, but I do consider it likely that those who, like Newton and Einstein, prove capable of creating new models of the universe are unusual in ways besides the obvious one of being unusually intelligent.

Isaac Newton was born prematurely on Christmas Day, 1642. He was so tiny that his mother often remarked that at birth he was small enough to fit into a quart pot. His father, a yeoman without education, unable even to sign his name, had died three months before Newton was born. For his first three years Newton enjoyed the undivided attention of his mother without suffering competition from any rival. Indeed, as premature children often require special care, he may have had even more of her attention than was customary. Then on January 27, 1646, when Newton was just past his third birthday, his mother remarried. She not only presented Newton with an unwanted stepfather but added insult to injury by abandoning him, leaving him to be reared by his maternal grandmother under the legal guardianship of a maternal uncle. Although his mother, with her new husband, moved to a house that was only a short distance away, we know that Newton passionately resented what he felt to be a betrayal. When Newton was about eleven his stepfather died and his mother returned, bringing with her two little girls and a boy, the offspring of her second marriage. According to contemporary accounts, Newton's mother was a remarkable woman of strong personality. Although his feelings toward her were ambivalent, Newton remained attached to her and looked after her during her last illness in 1679, when he was thirty-six; but Westfall records that he paid her few visits during his time at Cambridge despite living quite close to home.

As a child Newton is reported as spending more time

making ingenious mechanical models than playing with his fellows. A contemporary observed that "he was always a sober, silent thinking lad, and was never known scarce to play with the boys abroad, at their silly amusements."[3] If this was really his attitude toward boyish games, it is not surprising that his schoolfellows are reported as being "not very affectionate toward him. He was commonly too cunning for them in everything. They were sensible he had more ingenuity than they, and 'tis an old observation, that in all Societys, even of men, he who has most understanding, is least regarded."[4] There is a story, which Newton himself repeated, that on one occasion when he did deign to compete, he beat the other boys at jumping by first noting the direction and then taking advantage of the gusts of a strong wind that was blowing that day. Westfall, who has examined what is known of his aggressiveness and disobedience in boyhood, writes that he must have been insufferable.

Evidence suggests that as a boy Newton was often so abstracted as not to be aware of either his schoolbooks or what was going on about him. His ability was recognized by his schoolmasters, but examination of the curriculum offered at Grantham Grammar School, to which Newton went when he was twelve, shows how little mathematics was taught. Yet Newton invented the calculus four years after leaving school. His mother's servants are said to have been glad to part with him, declaring that he was "fit for nothing but the 'Versity.' "[5]

In June 1661, when he was eighteen, Newton was sent to Trinity College, Cambridge. In February 1664 he was elected scholar and took his B.A. in 1665. In 1667 he became a minor fellow, in 1668 an M.A. and major fellow. In 1669, when still only twenty-seven, he became Lucasian professor of mathematics. Charles II provided, by letter patent, a special dispensation which allowed Newton to take this chair without at the same time taking holy orders, a step that was normally demanded of all fellows.

What was Newton like as a young man? According to a contemporary account, he was a recluse, the archetype of the absentminded, solitary scholar:

> I never knew him to take any recreation or pastime either in riding out to take the air, walking, bowling, or any other exercise whatever, thinking all hours lost that was not spent in his studies, to which he kept so close that he seldom left his chamber unless at term time, when he read in the schools as being Lucasianus Professor, where so few went to hear him, and fewer understood him, that ofttimes he did in a manner, for want of hearers, read to the walls. . . . So intent, so serious upon his studies that he ate very sparingly, nay, ofttimes he has forgot to eat at all, so that, going into his chamber, I have found his mess untouched, of which, when I have reminded him, he would reply—"Have I!" and then making to the table, would eat a bite or two standing, for I cannot say I ever saw him sit at table by himself. . . . He very rarely went to bed till two or three of the clock, sometimes not until five or six.[6]

Newton in youth was predominantly solitary, seldom receiving visitors or calling upon others. In old age he told a relative that he had never "violated Chastity," and it seems probable that he died a virgin. There are hints that he had some obsessional traits: "He was very curious in his garden, which was never out of order, in which he would at some seldom times take a short walk or two, not enduring to see a weed in it."[7]

Newton must have been physically robust, as he not only survived the hazards of prematurity but lived until he was nearly eighty-five. Despite this he was notably hypochondriacal, dosing himself with homemade remedies and recommending medicine to others, and he was often preoccupied with death.

* * *

Newton's religious beliefs were unorthodox. He was an Arian, a secret Unitarian, which is not only peculiar in a fellow of a college named after the Trinity but at that time was regarded as dangerously heretical. He believed that worshipping Christ as God was idolatry, and that Athanasius, who routed Arius in the fourth century in that famous controversy between Homoousians and Homoiousians that so amused Gibbon, had corruptly distorted the early texts of the Christian Fathers. Despite this Newton remained a member of the Church of England, professed orthodoxy when he needed to, and was a determined adversary of Roman Catholicism. When James II ordered that a Benedictine monk be admitted to the degree of M.A. without taking an oath of loyalty to the established church, Newton was one member of the university who bitterly opposed what he saw as an attempt to infiltrate Cambridge with papists. Indeed, he put himself at risk by appearing as one of the university's delegates before the high commission, chaired by the notorious Judge Jeffreys who had presided over the so-called Bloody Assizes, which had been appointed to inquire as to why the university had not instantly obeyed the King's command.

Newton's religious beliefs were puritanical. Notebooks exist showing that at the time of his entry to Trinity he was obsessed with sin. In 1662 he wrote a confession in which he catalogued no less than fifty-eight sins of which he found himself to have been guilty. Most of these were concerned with his failures in religious observance or in his love for and obedience to God. Thus he records that as a child he had been guilty of "eating an apple at Thy house"; "making a mousetrap on Thy day"; "twisting a cord on Sunday morning"; and "squirting water on Thy day." He also records trivial instances of stealing food, gluttony, and "having uncleane thoughts words and actions and dreamese."[8] He also recorded his aggressive thoughts towards his mother and stepfather: "Threatning my father and mother Smith to burne them and the house over them."[9] There are many

depressive ideas about his own lack of worth, dread of punishment, and fear of future disaster. As one biographer
notes:

> The word love never appears, and expressions of glad-
> ness and desire are rare. A liking for roast meat is the
> only strong sensuous passion. Almost all the statements
> are negations, admonitions, prohibitions. The climate
> of life is hostile and punitive. Competitiveness, orderli-
> ness, self control, gravity,—these are Puritan values
> that became part of his being.[10]

At this date, therefore, the picture is that of a predominantly depressive character, self-punitive, anxious, and insecure, with poor interpersonal relationships and little
capacity for enjoyment. Whiston, his successor in the Lucasian chair, described Newton as possessing a "prodigiously
fearful, cautious, and suspicious Temper."[11]

A lasting distrust of others, which I think it reasonable to
derive from his sudden maternal deprivation, led to fear
that critics would harm him and that his discoveries would
be stolen. Brodetsky, one of his biographers, writes:

> He was always somewhat unwilling to face publicity
> and criticism, and had on more than one occasion
> declined to have his name associated with published
> accounts of some of his work. He did not value public
> esteem as desirable in itself, and feared that publicity
> would lead to his being harassed by personal relation-
> ships—whereas he wished to be free of such entangle-
> ments. . . . Apparently Newton hardly ever published a
> discovery without being urged to by others: even when
> he had arrived at the solution of the greatest problem
> that astronomy has ever had to face he said nothing
> about it to anybody.[12]

One of Newton's most famous and lengthy quarrels originated from his reluctance to publish. This was with
the philosopher and mathematician Leibniz. Both men

independently invented the calculus, but Newton did not publish his discovery until 1687, although it is clear from his papers that he invented the method in the years 1664–66, when most of his major discoveries were made. Leibniz invented his variety of calculus in 1675–76 and published it in 1684. It was natural that he should claim priority. The dispute was vituperative on both sides, but Newton's violence and vengefulness seem to have been out of all proportion. In one set of memoirs Newton is recorded as saying "pleasantly" that "he had broke Leibniz's heart with his reply to him."[13]

Newton was notably reluctant to acknowledge his indebtedness to others, and this seems to have been the occasion of another quarrel, with Flamsteed, the astronomer royal. For Flamsteed had provided Newton with astronomical observations and felt that his contribution to the Newtonian synthesis had not been sufficiently recognized.

Another running battle was with Robert Hooke, a secretary of the Royal Society and a distinguished scientist. But Hooke not only had the temerity to criticize Newton's theory of light, which led to Newton's threatening to resign from the Royal Society, but also claimed priority in discovering the inverse square law. In one sense this was probably true, but, as Newton claimed, Hooke had been unable to prove the law, while he, Newton, had demonstrated it mathematically.

These are far from being the only disputes in which Newton was involved, but enough has been said to show that along with the depressive traits in his character was a strongly paranoid streak. Newton was no more able to cope with the hostility of others than he was with his own, and was apt to see slights when none were intended and to exaggerate any that were. Even his friend, the philosopher Locke, said of him, "A nice man to deal with [meaning touchy and hypersensitive] and a little too apt to raise in himself suspicions where there is no ground."[14]

In line with Newton's isolation and suspiciousness was his lack of trust in the senses, a characteristic familiar to psychiatrists who treat schizoid persons, for they are commonly "out of touch" with physical experience. In one passage Newton wrote, "The nature of things is more securely and naturally deduced from their operations one upon another than upon our senses."[15] In this connection it is worth noting that Newton's style of writing, even when he is not dealing with mathematics or physical phenomena, is devoid of metaphor and nearly bare of adjectives. He was suspicious of the poetic and the imaginative, and his arid style reflects this.

In his Freud memorial lecture, "The Nature of Genius,"[16] Ernest Jones points out that one feature of Freud's psychology was a peculiar skepticism, a refusal to acquiesce in the generally accepted conclusions of others. He goes on to say that in certain areas, Freud also displayed an unexpected credulity, which at times bordered on superstition. Jones goes on to suppose that this combination of opposites in one person is characteristic of genius and quotes Newton as one of several examples. In his scientific work Newton took nothing on trust and was rigorous in demanding that his hypotheses be supported by mathematical proof. But there was another side to his character. Until he left Cambridge for London in 1696, he was deeply preoccupied with alchemy. This preoccupation was not merely scientific interest in what was partly the precursor of chemistry but a reflection of his belief that the secrets of nature had been revealed to the ancients and that the alchemists possessed esoteric knowledge concealed in hieroglyphs that required decipherment. As Sherwood Taylor writes in his book on alchemy: "Alchemy . . . was essentially religious. Its philosophy aimed at the unification of all nature in a single scheme, the author of which was avowed to be God."[17] This was also Newton's aim, and he left a vast pile of manuscripts concerned with alchemy, which has always disconcerted scientists who like to imagine him as possessing a rational intellect unclouded by superstition.

Newton was credulous also in that he was euhemeristic, a term derived from the name of Euhemerus of Messina (300 B.C.), who believed the classical gods to have been actual people deified. Newton believed that myths represented real events in human history, albeit requiring interpretation in many instances. He spent much time and effort in constructing a system of chronology on the supposition that if the position of the sun relative to the fixed stars could be determined, past events could be dated with certainty. But the key date on which he based his revision of the traditional system was that of the expedition of the Argonauts led by Jason to recover the golden fleece. Newton found it to have taken place in 936 B.C., which cut about four hundred years off the accepted record of Greek history. French historians attacked Newton's chronology with vigor, much to his chagrin.

Newton was passionately anti-pagan as well as anti-Catholic, and it seems that many of his historical studies were designed to prove that the Israelites, rather than the heathens, had introduced humanity into the ancient world. He seems to have believed that originally all mankind worshipped one God and acknowledged one universal law. Both his major works, the *Principia* and the *Opticks,* have religious endings.

I am not asserting that a scientist cannot be both devoutly religious and rigorously objective in experiment, but Newton's religious beliefs seem to have been peculiar, even for his age, and certainly misled him in his historical studies. Lord Keynes suggests that he thought that God had left clues that could be deciphered, and that he regarded the riddle of the universe in theological terms: "He looked on the whole universe and all that is in it *as a riddle,* as a secret which could be read by applying pure thought to certain evidence, certain mystic clues which God had laid about the world to allow a sort of philosopher's treasure hunt to the esoteric brotherhood."[18]

Keynes gained possession of most of a collection of secret papers that Newton assembled on leaving Cambridge for London in 1696. These papers consisted of nearly a million words on church history, alchemy, prophecy, and other biblical writings, besides disclosing the Unitarianism that he had sought to conceal. These writings led Keynes to remark:

> In the eighteenth century and since, Newton came to be thought of as the first and greatest of the modern age of scientists, a rationalist, one who taught us to think on the lines of cold and untinctured reason. I do not see him in this light. I do not think that anyone who has pored over the contents of that box which he packed up when he finally left Cambridge in 1696 and which, though partially dispersed, have come down to us, can see him like that. Newton was not the first of the age of reason. He was the last of the magicians, the last of the Babylonians and Sumerians, the last great mind which looked out on the visible and intellectual world with the same eyes as those who began to build our intellectual inheritance rather less than 10,000 years ago.[19]

Newton's religious and historical studies were so extensive that J. W. N. Sullivan calculates that he cannot have given to physics and mathematics more than about a third of his time. Sullivan ends his biography by saying that Newton "was a genius of the first order at something he did not consider to be of the first importance."[20]

Newton became mentally ill in 1693, when he was just over fifty. "He broke with his friends, crawled into a corner, accused his intimates of plotting against him, and reported conversations that never took place."[21] In September of that year he wrote to the diarist Pepys, abruptly terminating their relationship. It is significant that in this letter Newton admits that his psychotic episode, like so many others, was preceded by anorexia and insomnia. He also retains some insight: "I am extremely troubled at the embroilment I am in, and have neither ate nor slept well this twelve month, nor have my former consistency of mind."[22] It has been suggested that Newton, who performed chemical experiments in his rooms, was suffering from poisoning by mercury; but, although insomnia, loss of memory, and delusions do occur in this condition, there is no mention of the characteristic features of tremor and loss of teeth, and the symptoms subsided too quickly for the diagnosis to be likely.

Newton alleged that a fellow of Magdalene called Millington had importuned him with messages from Pepys and made him promise that he would visit Pepys in London, but this allegation is thought to have been delusional. Newton continues: "I never designed to get anything by your interest, not by King James's favour. . . . I am now sensible that I must withdraw from your acquaintance, and see neither you nor the rest of my friends any more, if I may leave them quietly."[23]

A letter to the philosopher Locke, evidently written when his disturbance was beginning to subside, runs:

> Being of opinion that you endeavoured to embroil me with women and by other means I was so much affected with it as that when one told me you were sickly & would not live I answered twere better if you were dead. I desire you to forgive me this uncharitableness. For I am now satisfied that what you have done is just & I beg your pardon for my having hard thoughts of you for it & for representing that you struck at the root of morality in a principle you laid down in your book of Ideas & designed to pursue in another book & that I took you for a Hobbist. I beg your pardon also for saying or thinking that there was a designe to sell me an office or embroile me.[24]

Both Pepys and Locke realized that Newton was ill and were solicitous in offering help. The period at which Newton was

accusing his friends was succeeded by depression, as may
be deduced from the letter from which I have just quoted;
and it seems probable that the paranoid ideas that Newton exhibited were in fact secondary to depression, just
as in youth his diaries show more of self-accusation than of
accusation of others. But Newton possessed a mixture
of traits that were manifested in exaggerated form during
his illness.

The faults of which he accused others were clearly his
own. His preoccupation with place-seeking, soon to be
rewarded, may be traced to his ambition: his fear of being
embroiled with women, to his almost total suppression of
sexuality. His calling Locke a Hobbist, which meant atheist,
may have been related to his own doubts about the nature of
God. Three years earlier Newton had written a vehemently
anti-Trinitarian tract but had withdrawn it from publication. Professor Manuel lays great emphasis on Newton's
affection for a much younger man, a Swiss scientist named
Fatio de Duillier, and supposes that his breakdown may have
been precipitated by his recognition that this affection contained homosexual elements.[25] Newton certainly wrote to
the young man in terms more intimate than those he usually
employed. "Yours most affectionately to serve you," he ends
one letter. In another he offers him money to pay doctors
when he is ill. Freud would certainly have agreed with Professor Manuel in supposing that Newton's breakdown was
the result of homosexual impulses that he found intolerable
breaking the chains of repression, but firm evidence seems
to me to be lacking. I find it at least as convincing to suppose
that Newton's illness was primarily a mid-life depression in
which he had to come to terms with the fact that his great
days of inventiveness were over. As Manuel points out, he
had published the *Principia—Philosophiae Naturalis Principia
Mathematica,* to give it its full title—only in 1687, and he may
well have felt that this marked the zenith of his creativity.
After his illness he did little fresh work, though Dr. White-
side, who is editing Newton's mathematical papers, informs

* only however ex post facto

me that he was still capable of original work. His creativeness declined, but his appetite for power found ample fulfillment.

Although Newton's illness was short-lived, rumors that he was mad spread far and wide, fueled no doubt by envy and the delight that lesser mortals often experience when great men run into trouble. Newton made a good recovery in most respects, however, and became an able administrator. In 1696 he became warden of the Mint, then master of the Mint, and in 1703 president of the Royal Society. He was also knighted. As master of the Mint one of his duties was to prosecute forgers and coiners. He did this with efficiency and relish, and seems personally to have conducted the interrogation of such criminals in the Tower. In Chapter 1, "Churchill: The Man," I drew attention to the fact that those who carry within themselves aggressive impulses that they have difficulty discharging find relief in acquiring a legitimate enemy. For Newton the coiners served the same function as did Hitler for Churchill.

Newton died in March 1727, in his eighty-fifth year. No other scientist, until the appearance of Einstein, has won such universal acclaim. As we have seen, his personality was unusual. I think it legitimate to attribute many of his pathological traits to the circumstances of his early life, his prematurity, his lack of a father, and his abandonment by his mother. I turn now to the much more difficult and controversial question of whether his personality and his discoveries can in any way be related to one another.

Newton's main discoveries were made in 1664–66, between the ages of twenty-one and twenty-three. It is characteristic of physicists and mathematicians to make their major contributions early in life, which is unlike creative people working in the arts, who may not come to maturity until much later. During those two years Newton formulated his basic laws of mechanics, his optical observations on the nature of light, the calculus, and the law of universal grav-

itation. This latter discovery is generally supposed to have
been made in his mother's garden in Lincolnshire, for Newton twice left Cambridge (from June 1665 to March 1666,
and from June 1666 to April 1667) to avoid the great
plague, which closed the university. He himself recalled: "All
this was in the two plague years of 1665 and 1666 for in
those days I was in the prime of my age for invention, and
minded Mathematicks and Philosophy more than at any
time since."[26]

The Newtonian synthesis was based on the discoveries of
Kepler, who had been able to describe the motions of the
planets round the sun, combined with those of Galileo, who
had described the laws of motion of objects upon the earth.
Until Newton these two sets of laws seemed to be quite
separate. But when Newton made the leap of imagination
that led him to suppose that gravity was a universal that
acted at enormous distances, he combined the discoveries of
Kepler and Galileo in such a way that the motions of bodies
in the heavens and bodies on earth could be seen to obey the
same universal laws. The law of gravitation, which states that
"every body attracts every other with a force inversely pro-
portional to the square of the distance between them," has
been described as the greatest generalization achieved by
the human mind. To prove his law Newton had to show that
the path of the moon round the earth could be accounted
for by the interaction of the gravitational force on it, which
he supposed the earth to be exerting, together with the
centrifugal force of the moon, the formula for which had
already been discovered by Huygens. His mathematical gift
enabled him to accomplish this. He then computed the sun's
attraction on the planets and showed that their orbits, which
Kepler had described but for which he could not account,
complied with the same laws. Newton left a diagram that
anticipates the possibility of artificial satellites by showing
that increasing the velocity of a projectile will eventually
result in its circling the earth at the same velocity forever.

But action at a distance worried Newton just as much as it has worried later scientists. In a letter to Richard Bentley, the master of Trinity, he wrote:

> It is inconceivable that inanimate brute matter should, without the mediation of something else, which is not material, operate upon, and affect other matter without mutual contact: as it must do, if gravitation, in the sense of Epicurus, be essential and inherent in it. And this is one reason, why I desired you would not attribute innate gravity to me. That gravity should be innate, inherent, and essential to matter, so that one body may act upon another at a distance through a vacuum, without the mediation of anything else, by and through which their action and force may be conveyed from one to another, is to me so great an absurdity, that I believe no man who has in philosophical matters a competent faculty of thinking can ever fall into it. Gravity must be caused by an agent acting constantly according to certain laws; but whether this agent be material or immaterial, I have left to the consideration of my readers.[27]

The material agent to which Newton refers was the hypothetical interstellar "ether," in which Newton himself probably no longer believed. The immaterial agent is God, and Sullivan thinks that Newton came to regard gravitational phenomena as due to the direct intervention of the deity. It is, therefore, interesting to note that Newton's religious beliefs may have prevented him from traveling further along the path towards relativity. I do not pretend to understand relativity in its entirety but can comprehend that in considering the motions of bodies it is impossible to define absolute rest or absolute uniform motion. The only physically detectable states of uniform motion are the relative motions of one observer with respect to another. According to Jeremy Bernstein in his book on Einstein, "Newton himself was aware of the difficulty of specifying states of

absolute motion." But "Newton resolved the problem theo-
logically. For him, a devout Christian mystic, it was enough
that rest and motion were distinguishable in the consciousness of God. God, in other words, provides the absolute
frame of reference in Newtonian mechanics."[28]

As we have seen, Newton's adult character presented both
depressive and schizoid traits; and these, in part, may justifiably be related to the sudden severance, at an age before it
could have been reasonably understood by him, of an
unusually close tie with his mother. Being suddenly left by
one's only parent can, I believe, make self-esteem difficult to
achieve. For self-esteem seems primarily dependent on the
sense of value derived from being loved, and the withdrawal
of love is likely to result in a child doubting his own worth.
Newton, in youth, wondered whether he would be fit for
anything, as he himself recorded. I think that the part of his
achievement that can be attributed to ambition (and what
great achievement does not owe something to this source?)
took origin from his need to obtain self-esteem in ways other
than by gaining the affection of his fellows. We cannot
assume that even a man as intelligent as Newton necessarily
achieved as much as he did without some compulsive force
fueling that intelligence.

Although Newton guarded his work jealously, and might
have gained public recognition earlier than he did if he had
not been reluctant to publish, it seems certain that his self-
esteem was almost entirely bound up with his work, and that
this is why he was so touchy about questions of priority and
anxious always to be in the right in any dispute. Like other
people of similar temperament, Newton may have felt that,
though he himself might be of little worth, the amount and
quality of his work would bring him fame, as indeed it did.
Fame often serves as a partially effective substitute for love
in those who are uncertain of obtaining love; and work is

often substituted for the self as a focus of self-esteem in those in whom a tendency toward depressive self-denigration is manifest. In later life, when his creative days were past, Newton found an alternative in seeking and obtaining power, much as in Wagner's opera *Das Rheingold,* when the dwarf Alberich, spurned in his pursuit of love by the Rhine-maidens, foreswears love in exchange for the power conferred by Rhinegold, which he steals from his mockers.

There are other aspects of his achievement that may, not unreasonably, be related to his early experience. To an infant the world must seem arbitrary and unpredictable, as the fulfillment of his needs, indeed, his very existence, depends on the whim of those on whom he is dependent. If his needs are met he develops what Erik Erikson has aptly called a sense of basic trust. If, on the contrary, his needs are not met or he is suddenly deprived by his mother's death or disappearance, he is likely to develop a sense of basic distrust with regard to people and an exaggerated anxiety about the arbitrary and unpredictable nature of the world. The writer Kafka, better than anyone else I know, described in his novels and short stories what it is like to feel oneself helplessly at the mercy of people who are not only powerful but also remote, inaccessible, and entirely arbitrary in their actions.

It seems likely that an exaggerated sense of helplessness in the face of the unpredictable in infancy may lead some gifted people to strive especially hard to master and control as many facets of existence as possible. Could Newton's basic mistrust have been one motive force that spurred him to solve some of the most difficult problems with which science has been confronted? Manuel has no doubt of it, and I am inclined to agree with him. As he puts it, "To force everything in the heavens and on earth into one rigid, tight frame from which the most minuscule detail would not be allowed to escape free and random was an underlying need of this anxiety-ridden man."[29]

An absence of intimacy with other persons often goes hand in hand with being cut off from one's own emotions; out of touch with bodily experience, which, more than thought, seems to be the common basis of our closest relationships with others, as the phrase "out of touch" indicates. In some instances failure to achieve later intimacy seems to follow as a consequence of an interruption of the physical relation of the child with its mother, leading to distrust of the senses. Such distrust may, in gifted people, enhance certain capacities even if it deprives them of the chance of closeness with others.

One human capacity that is enormously important in certain kinds of creative achievement is that of abstraction, the ability to divorce thinking from feeling and to be more concerned with the relation between concepts than with the objects from which the concepts originated. Both Newton and Einstein distrusted the senses. The latter believed that understanding the world depended on concepts of objects becoming to a high degree independent of the sense impressions that originally gave rise to them. Einstein said himself that his supreme aim was to perceive the world by thought alone, leaving out everything subjective.

Most human beings are, to some extent, capable of abstraction in the sense in which I am using the word. Indeed, in my book *The Dynamics of Creation,* I attribute man's inventiveness, and hence his supremacy, in part to this capacity. But most of us do not find it easy to escape from the subjective for long periods, from the demands of the body or our need for interpersonal relationships. Those men of genius who are responsible for the greatest achievements of abstract thought seem particularly often to have formed no close personal ties and to have been largely indifferent to, or else repelled by, bodily needs and functions. Newton shared his absence of close personal ties with Descartes, Locke, Hobbes, Hume, Pascal, Spinoza, Kant, Leibniz, Schopenhauer, Nietzsche, Kierkegaard, Wittgenstein—in short, with many of the world's greatest thinkers. This is also true of two of the greatest historians: Gibbon and Macaulay. Some of these men of genius were celibate or homosexual; others had transient affairs with women. Descartes fathered a daughter on a servant girl; Schopenhauer, in spite of his notorious misogyny, had a number of short-lived involvements with women. Nietzsche fell in love with Lou Andreas Salomé, who later became a psychoanalyst and intimate friend of Freud. He had himself and another admirer of Lou, Paul Rée, photographed with Lou brandishing a whip, apparently driving a cart to which both men were roped. Within a few months the relationship broke up and Nietzsche coined his famous phrase, "You go to women? Don't forget the whip." Whatever passing relationships these men had, none of them married, and most of them lived alone for the greater part of their lives. The point I want to make is amply shown. Although, especially in youth, sexual preoccupations and the need for personal relations may distract a man from his work, emotional isolation, with or without celibacy, goes hand in hand with supreme abstract mental achievement.

There is, of course, a simpler, more obvious relation between solitude and thinking. Lord Keynes, in the essay on Newton from which I have already quoted, wrote:

> I believe that the clue to his mind is to be found in his unusual powers of continuous concentrated introspection. . . . His peculiar gift was the power of holding continuously in his mind a purely mental problem until he had seen straight through it. . . . I believe that Newton could hold a problem in his mind for hours and days and weeks until it surrendered to him its secret. Then being a supreme mathematical technician he could dress it up, how you will, for purposes of exposition, but it was his intuition which was pre-eminently extraordinary.[30]

This kind of prolonged concentration requires solitude. Without going into any elaborate speculations about the sublimation of the sexual drive, let me make the simple point that if intense periods of concentration over long periods are required to attain fundamental insights, the family man is at a disadvantage. In answer to a question as to how he came to make his discoveries, Newton himself said, "I keep the subject constantly before me, and wait till the first dawnings open slowly by little and little into the full and clear light."[31] If Newton had been subject to the demands of a wife for companionship or interrupted by the patter of tiny feet, it would certainly have been less easy for him to concentrate so intensely over long periods of time.

The field of pathography has been so muddied by Freudian overstatement that it is small wonder that Popper and other critics entirely dismiss psychopathological interpretations of historical figures. Here I have tried to limit myself to discussing psychological matters that, though they may provoke disagreement, are accessible to common sense. In a subject in which so much is controversial, it behooves both the psychiatrist and the historian to be modest in their claims to psychological understanding.

NOTES

1. In Hans A. Krebs and Julian H. Shelley, eds., *The Creative Process in Science and Medicine* (Amsterdam: Excerpta Medica, 1975), p. 115.

2. David Hume, *A Treatise of Human Nature*, 2d ed., ed. L. A. Selby-Bigge (Oxford: Oxford University Press, 1978), p. 415.

3. William Stukeley, *Memoirs of Sir Isaac Newton's Life*, ed. A. Hastings White (London: Taylor and Francis, 1936), pp. 45–46.

4. Ibid., pp. 46–47.

5. Ibid., p. 51.

6. Humphrey Newton, letter to Conduitt, quoted in Frank Manuel, *A Portrait of Isaac Newton* (Cambridge: Harvard University Press, 1968), p. 105.

7. Ibid.

8. Quoted in Manuel, *Portrait of Newton*, pp. 62–63.

9. Quoted in Richard S. Westfall, *Never at Rest: A Biography of Isaac Newton* (Cambridge: Cambridge University Press, 1980), p. 53.

10. Manuel, *Portrait of Newton*, p. 59.

11. William Whiston, *Authentick Records*, 2:107, quoted in Westfall, *Never at Rest*, p. 650.

12. S. Brodetsky, *Sir Isaac Newton* (London: Methuen, 1972), pp. 69, 89.

13. William Whiston, *Historical Memoirs of the Life of Dr. Samuel Clarke* (London: F. Gyles, 1730), p. 132.

14. Quoted in Peter King, *The Life of John Locke*, 2 vols., 2d ed. (London: H. Colburn and R. Bentley, 1830), 2:38.

15. Quoted in Manuel, *Portrait of Newton*, p. 75.

16. Ernest Jones, "The Nature of Genius," in his *Sigmund Freud: Four Centenary Addresses* (New York: Basic Books, 1956), p. 22.

17. Sherwood Taylor, *The Alchemists* (London: Heinemann, 1951), p. 235.

18. John Maynard Keynes, "Newton the Man," in *Essays in Biography*, ed. Geoffrey Keynes (London: Hart-Davis, 1951), p. 313.

19. Ibid., pp. 310–11.

20. J. W. N. Sullivan, *Isaac Newton: 1642–1727* (London: Macmillan, 1938), p. 275.

21. Manuel, *Portrait of Newton*, p. 214.

22. Quoted in ibid., p. 215.

23. Quoted in ibid.

24. Quoted in ibid., p. 216; and in Maurice Cranston, *John Locke* (Oxford: Oxford University Press, 1985), p. 372.

25. Manuel, *Portrait of Newton*, p. 197.

26. Quoted in Sullivan, *Isaac Newton*, p. 13.

27. Quoted in ibid., pp. 169–70.

28. Jeremy Bernstein, *Einstein* (New York: Viking, 1973), p. 40.

29. Manuel, *Portrait of Newton*, p. 380.

30. Keynes, "Newton the Man," p. 312.

31. Quoted in E. F. King, *A Biographical Sketch of Isaac Newton*, 2d ed. (Grantham: S. Ridge, 1858), p. 66.

4

C. P. Snow

I FIRST MET C. P. SNOW in October 1939, when I arrived at Christ's College, Cambridge, as an undergraduate. Although he did not actually teach me, he was my tutor in the sense that he was responsible for looking after my progress, my behavior, and my welfare. At that time, Snow looked much older than his thirty-four years. Heavily built and already balding, he continued to look much the same until his death. I don't remember seeing very much of him during my first year as an undergraduate. He was often in London; for this was the first year of the war, and Snow already had a toehold in the corridors of power as member of a group set up by the Royal Society to advise upon the best way of using scientists to promote the war effort. In my second year, however, I aroused his particular interest; we became fast friends, and remained so until his death. The reason was the death of my father in 1940. I had to go to Snow to seek permission to attend my father's funeral. I made some remark indicating that I regarded such ceremonies as otiose but that I felt I had to go for form's sake. This remark, I suppose, made him think that I might be less conventional than some public schoolboys. He invited me to dine with him at High Table; and from then on, I was a frequent visitor to his rooms. It also happened that my father died leaving no money, not even enough to pay the modest fees demanded by Cambridge at that date. Friends of my father's clubbed together to raise enough to see me through my medical training, but Snow also persuaded the College to contribute a modest sum. He thought the College mean not to do more for me, but I was delighted. In fact, this gesture gave an enormous boost to my self-esteem. I was a diffident and insecure young man; I showed no particular promise as a medical student; and the fact that Snow thought well enough of me to persuade the College that I was worth supporting meant a great deal to me.

Of course, I became an ardent admirer of C. P. Snow and bought each of his novels as soon as it was published. In those days, he had only published three: *Death Under Sail, New Lives for Old,* and *The Search,* which made his name as a novelist. While I was still an undergraduate, *Strangers and Brothers,* the first of the series of novels which bears that name, was published; and I remember Snow's pleasure when Desmond MacCarthy gave it a long and favorable review. I later met Bert Howard, the schoolmaster who was the original of George Passant in the novel, and who, so Snow told me, looked over his shoulder while he was writing certain passages to make sure that the portrait Snow was painting of him was accurate.

Snow's rooms at Christ's were a meeting place for his friends. I recall particularly C. H. Waddington, the biologist, and J. B. Trend, the Spanish scholar and friend of Falla. It was my first introduction to a society in which very clever men discussed everything under the sun without talking down to the younger and less experienced. It was a marvelously exhilarating and different atmosphere from the Victorian, clerical household in which I had been reared. In Snow's world there was little room for disapproval, and he put a liberal interpretation upon the duties of a moral tutor. When, while an undergraduate, I embarked upon my first "affair," it seemed natural to ask Snow to dinner to meet the young woman.

Like his schoolmaster and friend Bert Howard, Snow was a liberator. But what I chiefly remember was the intellectual stimulus of his conversation, his openness to new ideas, and his unflagging interest in every oddity of human nature. Snow was interested in psychology and psychiatry, and, when I suggested that I might become a psychiatrist, said, "I think you'd make a very good one," a remark which clinched my resolve. At that time, Snow was much taken with Jung's extravert/introvert dichotomy, and also with the work of W. H. Sheldon, the American who originated the technique of "somatotyping," in which temperamental traits were linked with physical characteristics. While I, in those days, was reading Freud and Jung with enthusiasm, fascinated by the possibility of altering personality by psychoanalysis, Snow remained firmly convinced that temperament, as well as physique, was genetically determined, and that, while individuals could be helped to come to terms with their innate characteristics, not much could be done to alter them. It was some years before I came round to agreeing with him.

As I have already indicated, Snow's own physique was massive. He was also physically inept to a degree I have never seen equaled. He was incapable of doing up, or even undoing, a parcel. It was no surprise to learn that in one set of examinations—I think in chemistry—he had obtained the highest marks in theory and the lowest marks in the practical which had ever been recorded. I cannot think that he could ever have been a successful experimental scientist. His hands and arms resembled flippers, rather than human appendages. In addition, he often suffered from lumbago, which made his gait shambling and at times totally disabled him. I am sure that his physical awkwardness was, in early life, something which made him self-conscious and uncertain of himself, especially with the opposite sex. He was intensely sensitive about his personal appearance. I remember lunching with him during the war at a little restaurant near St. James's Park Underground station. The question of his physical appearance cropped up, and one of us, I think Harry Hoff, suggested "senatorial" as an appropriate adjective, which Snow accepted. Then I put my foot in it by saying that I couldn't imagine him in a toga, and laughing. I realized instantly that I'd hurt his feelings, and suffered agonies of embarrassment myself. I think it was his own experience of feeling ill at ease which made Snow so tolerant of, and sympathetic to, that uneasy mixture of arrogance and diffidence which is so characteristic of clever undergraduates.

Snow dealt with his physical maladroitness by getting others to do for him anything which might require the minimum of physical skill. He became expert at finding helpers; and when, during the war, he left Cambridge for London, he always ensured that someone, secretary or girl-friend, would minister to his needs and do up his parcels. I don't know if his physical ineptitude was in any way connected with his fear of air raids. Right through the war, it was a torment to Snow to endure the bombing, far more of a torment than it was for most of us. I have always considered myself to be a physical coward, and was so when playing games at school. But when the air raids started, I found them exhilarating rather than frightening. Snow was just the opposite; and we used sometimes to discuss the oddity and irrationality of human fear. Both of us realized that praise or blame didn't come into the matter. That sort of fear, or lack of it, has nothing to do with moral excellence; and I admired Snow for stoically enduring something which I was lucky enough not particularly to mind.

A good many of the people whom Snow portrays in his novels were known to me. Not all his characters were taken direct from life, but, when they were, they were painted with wonderful accuracy. Many years after I first read *The Search*, I took part in a weekend conference at which J. D. Bernal was one of the speakers. I had never met him before, but, after listening to him for a while, I recognized him. "You," I said to myself, "are Constantine in *The Search*." Indeed, he was; and I'm told wasn't best pleased with the portrait. I wonder how many people have recognized a person in real life from first encountering them in a novel?

Snow was, perhaps, too much tied to the actual ever to scale the heights of art. Art is both life and something more; something which transcends the mundane and may transmute the mundane into the eternal. Snow, I believe, distrusted fantasy; and without fantasy it is difficult to capture the imagination of the reader in the way that the greatest novelists are able to do. Snow's prose style has sometimes been described as pedestrian. In fact, it was a serviceable instrument which aptly fulfilled his sober purposes. It may be relevant that Snow had little ear for music. I recall that a friend once persuaded him to listen to a recording of Beethoven's Ninth Symphony. Snow said he was able to recognize that this work possessed a certain majesty; but music meant virtually nothing to him, and I doubt if he ever considered how any sentence he wrote would actually *sound*.

Snow's portraits of actual people are, I think, the best work he did. Although Snow was an unusually compassionate man, there were others besides J. D. Bernal who were hurt by Snow's descriptions of them; but he himself always maintained that most of those he knew would rather appear in one of his novels than be disregarded, even if this meant including "warts and all." One example where possible hurt was avoided was *The Conscience of the Rich,* that masterly portrayal of possessive paternal love in an upper-class Jewish family. The original of Charles March told Snow that his portrait of his father would desperately upset the old man, and asked him not to publish it until his father had died. With great reluctance Snow agreed, although it threw out his whole plan for the *Strangers and Brothers* sequence. *The Conscience of the Rich* should have come second. In fact, it did not appear until six of the series were already in print. I think that a remarkable instance of Snow's generosity.

Although most of Snow's portraits of actual people occur in his novels, he also wrote *Variety of Men,* a collection of essays on some of the eminent people he had encountered, including H. G. Wells, Einstein, and Lloyd George. I don't think anyone who has read it could ever forget his picture of the mathematician G. H. Hardy, whose book *A Mathematician's Apology* has become a classic. Hardy was one of Snow's heroes. He was also notably eccentric; and Snow's account combines humor, insight, and intense sympathy with this lonely man who, not long before his death from natural causes, became so depressed that he tried to kill himself.

Variety of Men is an apt title; for no one can have known, and known intimately, a wider variety. Snow came from the lower middle-class and ended up in the House of Lords. Although he gave up science himself, he kept in close touch with science and scientists. He was fascinated by politics, and, although his sympathies remained with the left, he made friends on both sides of the House. For instance, I can remember one of his parties including both Harold Wilson and Lord Hailsham; and Snow became intimate with Harold Macmillan, who not only shared his enthusiasm for Trollope, but also made a masterly speech at the party which launched Snow's book on the novelist. In spite of moving in high society, Snow was not a social snob. Unlike many of those who rise in the world, Snow never disowned his origins. He was proud of having achieved so much without the advantages of birth or inherited wealth. I cannot imagine that this generous and tolerant man would ever have disowned a friend. Snow was sometimes imposed upon, cheated, or stabbed in the back by former acquaintances who were envious of him; but he continued to be magnanimous even toward those who treated him badly. Indeed, he had a peculiar sympathy with tricky characters of doubtful honesty.

He could, of course, show resentment; and did so, quite properly, when subjected to a venomous attack by F. R.

Leavis, although he did not himself reply to it until years afterward. At the time, it was left to his friends to object, which they did in, among other places, the *Spectator* of March 16, 1962. I was glad to be among them. There was one other attack which deeply disturbed him. At one time, he had to go into Moorfields Hospital to have an operation on his eye. His sight was threatened; and *Private Eye* chose to make a cruel joke about the country of the blind in which the one-eyed man is king. That he found hard to forgive.

Snow liked to think of himself as a realist; and when he wrote a book about novelists whom he admired, he gave it the title *The Realists*. Some might think that it was stretching the category to include within it Dickens and Dostoyevsky. However, Snow prided himself on possessing an earthy, somber view of the human condition. Human beings were fallible, limited, incapable of much foresight or much self-sacrifice. Western lack of concern for the Third World was ample evidence of that. Moreover, human beings often possessed what he called a "sadic" streak (he meant "sadistic") which inclined them toward cruelty and which decent men had to fight against in themselves. The motives of men were invariably mixed, and there was a dark side to what appeared to be the most disinterested actions. It was part of human nature to pursue one's own interest, and men deceived themselves if they believed they could do otherwise. The quest for "goodness" was real enough; but others were likely to be harmed in its pursuit. Snow was very tolerant of, and compassionate toward, the compulsions of the flesh. His own early experience of love had been desperately unhappy, and he was in his forty-fifth year when he finally found contentment in marriage.

I think that he was much more of a romantic than he acknowledged. The pursuit of success remained for him a romantic quest. He enjoyed the honors which came his way. I remember the first he was awarded, during the war. He put on a show of modesty. "My friends tell me I should accept it," he said, but neither of us was deceived by this disclaimer. He enjoyed being a successful novelist, a member of the House of Lords, and a resident of Eaton Terrace, and I don't think these trappings ever lost their charm for him. I believe that his early uncertainty about himself meant that he never took these manifestations of success for granted. He remained delighted and surprised that he had got so far, and, because of this, never became disenchanted. He also greatly enjoyed any success which his friends attained. His geese habitually turned into swans, and, at a party, he once clasped both my hands and called me "The most successful of my pupils," a title which I certainly did not deserve. It was, I believe, this romantic streak which made his presence life-enhancing. Snow might take a pessimistic view of human beings in general, but about his friends he was warmly, irrationally optimistic. As J. H. Plumb wrote of him in an obituary which appeared in the Christ's College magazine, "He possessed that great quality of making all whom he met feel larger than life, better scientists, better writers, better historians; indeed, better men."

Science also retained for him the glamor of a romantic quest. His posthumous book, *The Physicists,* not only demonstrates his remarkable memory, but also illustrates the fact that understanding the structure of matter, adding to the scientific edifice, remained for him as exciting an endeavor as when he portrayed it so well in his early novel *The Search.* "Insight" was one of Snow's favorite words; and he applied it equally to those who exhibited it in science and to those who understood human nature. He himself bridged the "two cultures" which he described better than anyone else I have known.

Of all those who have influenced me, Snow stands out as the man to whom I owe most. His warmth, his generosity, and his belief in me at a time when I had little belief in myself are unforgettable, and I am glad to have this opportunity to pay tribute to his memory.

5

Othello and the Psychology of Sexual Jealousy

JEALOUSY IS a complex feeling which, because it is compounded of more than one emotion, is not easily defined. The *Oxford Dictionary* illustrates the difficulty when it first states that jealousy is "zeal or vehemence of feeling against some person or thing," and goes on to say that it is also "zeal or vehemence of feeling in favour of a person or thing." One can be jealous of someone one hates, and jealous to preserve someone one loves. The *Oxford Dictionary* continues its definitions with "solicitude or anxiety for the preservation of well-being of something," and "vigilance in guarding a possession from loss or damage." Only after these definitions does the *OED* proceed to how we more usually think of jealousy: "the state of mind arising from the suspicion, apprehension or knowledge of rivalry," and "fear of being supplanted in the affections."

The word "jealousy" is often used as if it were synonymous with envy; but I think the distinction worth preserving. Jealousy is predominantly concerned with the fear of loss of something one possesses, envy with the wish to own something another possesses. Othello suffers from the fear that he has lost Desdemona's love. Iago suffers from envy of the position held by Cassio, to which he feels entitled.

Ambrose Bierce's *The Devil's Dictionary* is often tiresomely facetious, but also contains wit and some wisdom. Bierce calls jealousy "the seamy side of love," and defines the adjective "jealous" as "unduly concerned about the preservation of that which can be lost only if not worth keeping."[1] Jealousy is complex because, like hate, it is so closely related to love. It is only those we love who are capable of arousing our most intense resentment. It is not surprising that murder is overwhelmingly a domestic crime in which murderer and victim are linked emotionally.

Jealousy, like being "in love," is an emotion which contains a markedly irrational, subjective component. When we are in love, the person who is the object of our infatuation may be objectively admirable and lovable; but this is not what makes him or her the center of our universe. Freud wrote that being in love is "the normal prototype of the psychoses."[2] But jealousy, however objectively justified, is as crazy as being in love, and a more dangerous state of mind. Both the state of being in love and the state of being in hate or being jealous can be so subjective as to be quite unrelated to anything which the object of such emotions does or feels. It is when a person's beliefs and feelings appear to have no foundation in fact, no relation to reality, that we call them delusional and label the person insane. But, as we shall see, there is really no hard and fast line between sanity and madness where these powerful emotions are concerned.

The extreme irrationality of both jealousy and being in love is probably related to the way that human beings develop from infancy onward. The human infant, if he or she is to grow up happy, confident, and able to make fruitful relationships with others, seems to require the kind of totally irrational adoration with which healthy mothers usually greet their newborn infants. Certainly, evidence is accumulating that children who have not been adored and welcomed in this way suffer emotional difficulties. For example, mothers who are themselves depressed are less able to involve themselves in the lives of their children, and are less capable of communicating with them or showing them affection. The children of depressed mothers are more likely than those of normal mothers to show later emotional problems.

The human infant requires more than being fed, kept warm, and protected from danger. It seems to need a mother who, at any rate for a time, considers it the most important person in the world, the temporary center of her universe. When adults fall mutually in love, this experience of irrational adoration is repeated. It so powerfully ministers to self-esteem that the threat of a partner turning elsewhere is dangerously alarming; and this is still true even when the element of sexual infatuation has long since declined. In reality, few human beings are so important or so unusual that they are not easily replaceable. But that is not how most people feel either about their partners or about themselves. From infancy onward, most of us need intimate ties which minister to our narcissism; which make us feel "special," even though we may in fact be very ordinary.

Freud, in a paper first published in 1922, wrote:

> Jealousy is one of those affective states, like grief, that may be described as normal. If anyone appears to be without it, the inference is justified that it has undergone severe repression and consequently plays all the greater part in his unconscious mental life. The instances of abnormally intense jealousy met with in analytic work reveal themselves as constructed of three layers. The three layers or grades of jealousy may be described as (1) *competitive* or normal, (2) *projected*, and (3) *delusional* jealousy.[3]

Freud thinks that "normal" jealousy is compounded of grief at the thought of losing the loved object combined with pain from the injury to self-esteem: the "narcissistic wound," as he calls it. The emotion is further complicated by self-criticism (What am I or what have I done to lose him or her?), and by feelings of enmity toward the rival. In Freud's view, even "normal" jealousy is not wholly rational, "for it is rooted deep in the unconscious, it is a continuation of the earliest stirrings of the child's affective life, and it originates in the Oedipus or brother-and-sister complex of the first sexual period."4

For Freud, loss of the loved object is primarily loss of sexual fulfillment. Later theorists, like John Bowlby, have widened this by referring to loss of an "attachment figure," a concept to which I shall return.

Freud's second grade of jealousy is based upon the well-known psychological mechanism of projection. Freud writes, "It is a matter of everyday experience that fidelity, especially that degree of it required in marriage, is only maintained in the face of continual temptations."5 Those who are unwilling to admit this fundamental truth about themselves repress their own impulses toward infidelity, and are apt to attribute such impulses to their partner: "It isn't I who wish to be unfaithful, but my spouse." This mechanism provides relief to the person who employs it, and also a kind of reassurance, in that the spouse is perceived as having the same kind of impulses toward infidelity which the subject finds it so hard to acknowledge. Freud makes the point that social convention makes some allowance for the partial expression of sexual feelings toward persons other than the partner by permitting mild degrees of flirtation, followed by satisfaction in return to faithfulness. He goes on to say, "A jealous person, however, does not recognize this convention of tolerance; he does not believe in any such thing as a halt or turning-back once the path has been trodden, nor that a flirtation may be a safeguard against actual infidelity."6 In other words, the person who is particularly prone to jealousy is by nature rigid; a creature of absolutes, who allows no latitude to the expression of impulses which he can neither admit in himself nor tolerate in his partner.

When Freud was twelve years old, in 1868, the first of thirty-two sixpenny numbers of an English novel appeared, *He Knew He Was Right,* by Anthony Trollope. This novel perfectly illustrates the type of character Freud describes in his paper of 1922. We know that Freud read some of the novels of Dickens, Fielding, Thackeray, Disraeli, George Eliot, Arnold Bennett, Galsworthy, Kipling, Victoria Sackville-West, and even those of James Hilton and Dorothy Sayers. Whether or not he ever ventured upon Trollope I have been unable to discover. Freud would certainly have recognized Trollope's portrait of Louis Trevelyan, and paid tribute to its accuracy.

Not everyone who enjoys Trollope is familiar with this novel, which is less well known than it deserves. There are, it is true, a number of subsidiary characters and subplots which do not entirely hold the reader's interest; but the portrait of Louis Trevelyan, the jealous man who persuades himself that his wife is playing him false, is convincing, subtle, and true to life. James Pope Hennessy, in his book on Trollope, writes: "As in the novels of Balzac, jealousy in all its varied forms plays a great part in Trollope's works. There seems to have been nothing about jealousy that Trollope did not know, or could not imagine."[7] Trollope was well aware that intense jealousy is closely allied to mental illness. The borderland of madness is a subject which lends wings to Trollope's sometimes pedestrian pen. Mr. Crawley, in *The Last Chronicle of Barset,* another rigid, tormented man, is one of the great characters of fiction.

Trollope's delineation of jealousy has something to teach us about that disturbing emotion which is relevant and which closely matches what Freud wrote over fifty years later. Louis Trevelyan, recently married, objects to the attentions paid to his wife by Colonel Osborne, a man of over fifty, who has been an intimate friend of his wife's father, who had known her in early childhood, and who might therefore be thought to be above suspicion. Nevertheless, Colonel Osborne is in fact something of a philanderer: a bachelor who enjoys the company of young, attractive married women. With delicate skill, Trollope makes it plain that, although Emily Trevelyan is undoubtedly faithful to her husband, there is an undercurrent of sexuality between herself and Colonel Osborne; the sort of licensed, mild flirtation to which Freud refers as a safety valve for extra-marital desires which we all have, but which are in no way threatening to those to whom we are committed. Trevelyan's perception that there is something between the two is, therefore, correct.

But Trevelyan is rigid, threatened, and intolerant. He forbids his wife to see Colonel Osborne again. She feels insulted, and their relationship goes from bad to worse. Trevelyan gradually becomes more and more disturbed in mind. His friends desert him because they feel that he is treating his wife unfairly. His feeling that he is being disregarded and despised becomes a self-fulfilling prophecy, as often happens with such people. Throughout his gradual decline into near-madness, physical illness, and final death, Trollope makes it clear that he does not really believe that his wife has been unfaithful, but that he cannot tolerate her refusal to obey him, to submit herself utterly to his unreasonable demands. Trollope writes, "He was jealous of authority, fearful of slights, self-conscious, afraid of the world, and utterly ignorant of the nature of a woman's mind."[8] The weakness of the petty tyrant who cannot afford to yield or to admit error has seldom been better portrayed.

Trollope accurately pinpoints the relation between weakness, rigidity, and jealousy. Trevelyan is unable to recognize his own fallibility, his own hostility, or, presumably, his own impulses toward infidelity. Like many weak people, he is hypersensitive to anything which might be construed as an attack upon him or a threat to his absolute authority. When such attacks or such threats appear, he takes them as alone constituting reality and disregards the love and the esteem which, much more importantly, surround him. People of this kind live in a black-and-white world in which others are either totally hostile or totally on their side.

Freud's third grade of jealousy is "delusional." Freud states that this type of jealousy also

> has its origin in repressed impulses towards unfaithfulness; but the object in these cases is of the same sex as the subject. Delusional jealousy is what is left of a homosexuality that has run its course, and it rightly takes its position among the classical forms of paranoia. As an attempt at defence against an unduly strong homosexual impulse it may, in a man, be described in the formula: "*I* do not love him, *she* loves him!" In a delusional case one will be prepared to find jealousy belonging to all three layers, never to the third alone.9

Whether or not one accepts Freud's psychopathological formulation, the fact is that delusions of infidelity occur in a variety of mental illnesses. When men accuse their wives of infidelity, it is often because they themselves are wholly or partially impotent. Diabetes sometimes causes impotence; and so do various diseases of the spinal cord. Partial impotence is sometimes found together with brain damage. This occurs in chronic alcoholism and also in punch-drunk boxers. Delusions of infidelity also occur in cases of the psychosis known as paranoia, in which there is no brain damage and no physical illness. A few cases of severe depression also exhibit paranoid delusions. There is no doubt that latent homosexuality plays a part, as Freud supposed. Enoch and Trethowan report two cases of women who accused their husbands of taking more interest in erotic magazines than they did in marital relations. It turned out that both women had lesbian inclinations and themselves wanted to make sexual contact with the pinups who were depicted.[10]

It is interesting that Freud's supposition that paranoid delusions arise from the denial and projection of homosexual desires is better supported by research than are many of his theories. Fisher and Greenberg, in their book *The Scientific Credibility of Freud's Theories and Therapy,* write, "It is a fact that the majority of the experimental studies have demonstrated that the paranoid has a unique pattern of reaction to anything that has the potential for conjuring up homosexual images."[11]

Delusions of a partner's infidelity not infrequently lead to murder. In Britain, one third of those who commit murder are found, on examination, to be insane. In addition, one third of all suspects in cases finally recorded as murder commit suicide. If one assumes that those who commit suicide are mentally abnormal, it follows that about 70 percent of all murderers in England and Wales are mentally abnormal.

Jealousy is a common motive for murder, both in murderers who are rated sane and in those who are found to be mentally ill. Norwood East, examining the records of two hundred sane murderers, found jealousy to be the main motive in forty-six.[12] Abrahamsen said of murder because of jealousy: "The psychological mechanism behind such an act is that the person's self-esteem and prestige is injured. The individual believes he not only possesses the partner, but also that he has the right to possess and this makes him jealous. By killing the partner his self-esteem is restored."[13]

Mowat made a careful study of murderers whose crimes had been directly related to delusions of infidelity. Of male insane murderers admitted to Broadmoor over a period of twenty years, 12 percent committed their crime because of morbid jealousy. Female insane murderers exhibited delusions of infidelity in only 3.3 percent of cases. This difference does not mean that women are less prone to jealousy than men, but that the buildup of aggression to the pitch required to commit murder happens less frequently. In fact, this percentage is a serious underestimate of how often morbid jealousy is a motive in murder. It is obviously impossible to examine the motives of the third of murderers who commit suicide immediately after their crime. But one can be sure that jealousy played an important part in a number of such cases. Attempts at suicide had been made by nearly 10 percent of the murderers in which jealousy was the main motive.[14]

As I pointed out earlier, murder is predominantly a domestic crime in which men kill their wives or mistresses and women kill their children. In 80 percent of murders, the murderer and the victim are either related or previously acquainted. As Norval Morris writes: "You are safer on the streets than at home; safer with a stranger than with a friend or relative."[15] In murders provoked by jealousy, it is very rare for the rival to be the victim. It is the supposedly unfaithful person who inflicts the greater injury to self-esteem.

How does one distinguish between delusional jealousy and normal jealousy? By the presence or absence of other evidence of insanity than that provided by ideas of infidelity alone. Delusions rarely exist singly. The person with delusions of infidelity in the partner commonly shows evidence of disordered judgment in other areas. For example, ideas that the spouse is damaging potency by administering poison are not uncommon. The pathologically suspicious person usually feels that his spouse has become cold toward him. He seizes on details which seem to him to confirm his suspicions. The fact that a piece of furniture has been moved indicates that another man has been in the house. So does a cigarette end in the fireplace, a stain on underwear, the fact that she has changed her clothes. Advertisements put through the letter box are a way of communicating through a code. A light left on by accident is a signal to the lover.

Such delusions usually arise on the basis of a change in the subject himself which is then attributed falsely to the spouse. As I suggested above, the morbidly jealous man is not infrequently impotent himself, or sexually abnormal. Whether or not delusions of infidelity have any actual justification plays little part in making the diagnosis. The types of mental illness in which delusions of infidelity flourish usually take some time to develop; and it would not be surprising if, during the course of a gradual deterioration in the marital relationship, a wife occasionally looked elsewhere for comfort. As William Burroughs says, "A paranoid is a man who knows a little of what is going on."[16] The point I want to make is that, even if there is some actual basis for suspicion, the difference between the sane and insane person is usually obvious because of other considerations.

Let us turn to examine *Othello* in the light of what is known about jealous murders. In Cinthio's original story, from which Shakespeare took his plot, it is jealousy, rather than envy, which inspires Iago's campaign of poisonous suggestion. For Iago is depicted as himself being in love with Desdemona, rather than merely being envious of Cassio's promotion. Which is the more powerful motive for Iago's evil behavior? Boito, Verdi's librettist, clearly thought that envy was not a sufficient motive. In his skillfully compressed libretto, he actually feels it necessary to add something to underline Iago's wickedness: the famous "Credo," in which Iago states his belief in a cruel God who has created him in his image. Iago claims that whatever evil he thinks or does was decreed for him by fate, and that fate is essentially unjust. Life is a mockery which ends in death; Heaven is an illusion; and Death is therefore nothingness.

I can understand why Boito felt it necessary to add Iago's "Credo," but I must confess that I have found it an unconvincing excuse. Human beings who perform evil acts do so for a variety of reasons, of which envy and jealousy are two. They do not commit crimes because God or fate has made them essentially evil. In Rossini's opera *Otello*, which Byron

saw in Venice in February 1818, Iago is depicted as both
being envious of the Moor's success as a military leader, and
also as having at one time wished to marry Desdemona.
Byron wrote to John Murray before he saw the opera that it
was reputed to be one of Rossini's best. After seeing it, he
wrote to Samuel Rogers that the music was "good but lugu-
brious," and complained, "But as for the words! All the real
scenes with Iago cut out—and the greatest nonsense
instead."[17] Rossini's librettist was Francesco Berio, Marchese
di Salsa. His plot is no nearer to Cinthio's, and much further
removed from Shakespeare's, than Boito's version. Did
Byron know that Berio, enthused by reading *Childe Harold*,
had written an ode to him?

Stendhal, who saw the opera in Naples, wrote: "Nothing
colder. It must have taken a lot of *savoir-faire* on the part of
the writer of the libretto to render insipid to this degree the
most impassioned of all dramas."[18] However, if one puts
Shakespeare out of mind altogether, it is possible to enjoy
Rossini's *Otello* for the sake of the music, some of which is
beautiful.

Returning to Shakespeare, I must first affirm that discussing the motives of invented characters as if they were
real people is a dubious exercise. We cannot know what Iago
or Othello "really" felt, because neither "really" existed.
Ernest Jones, in his essay on Hamlet and Oedipus, says that
he proposes to pretend that Hamlet was a living person. In
the latter part of the essay, he goes on to consider Shakespeare's own presumed psychopathology in some detail.
Jones writes, "It is noteworthy that Shakespeare's famous
victims of jealousy, Othello, Leontes, Posthumus, all display
extraordinary credulousness, which at times makes the
audience impatient with them, and have perfectly innocent
wives."[19]

Was Othello's credulousness really so extraordinary? As
Shakespeare depicts him, Othello certainly does not belong
to that group of murderers who are obviously insane. There
is no evidence of madness other than his mistaken belief

that Desdemona was unfaithful. And had he not a variety of reasons for believing what Iago told him? In the first act (dropped by both Berio and Boito), Othello is warned by Desdemona's father, Brabantio. Brabantio at first believes that Desdemona must have been seduced by witchcraft:

> O thou foul thief, where hast thou stow'd my daughter?
> Damn'd as thou art, thou hast enchanted her,
> For I'll refer me to all things of sense,
> (If she in chains of magic were not bound)
> Whether a maid, so tender, fair, and happy,
> So opposite to marriage that she shunn'd
> The wealthy curled darlings of our nation,
> Would ever have (to incur a general mock)
> Run from her guardage to the sooty bosom
> Of such a thing as thou?[20]

When Brabantio has been convinced, in front of the Duke, that magic has not been used, he has to accept the validity of the clandestine marriage he so much deplores. But in spite of the Duke's assurance—"Your son-in-law is far more fair than black"—Brabantio's parting shot to Othello is "Look to her, Moor, have a quick eye to see: She has deceiv'd her father, may do thee."[21]

Iago reverts to this when, in Act III, Scene 3, he says to Othello: "She did deceive her father, marrying you."[22] Immediately prior to this remark, Iago has said:

> I know our country disposition well;
> In Venice they do let God see the pranks
> They dare not show their husbands: their best conscience
> Is not to leave undone, but keep unknown.[23]

Although Othello is a general, who must, one presumes, have resided in Venice for some considerable period to attain such eminence, Iago is playing on the fact that he is a foreigner who is not so familiar with the ways of Venetian women as he is with those of women in his own country.

Venice enjoyed a reputation for sexual license over several centuries. At the end of the sixteenth century, there are said to have been 2,889 patrician ladies in Venice, 2,508 nuns, and 1,936 burgher women; but there were 11,654 courtesans![24] In the Fitzwilliam Museum, you can see Guardi's portrait *A Woman of Venice*. Bejeweled, elaborately coiffed, painted, and elegantly dressed, she is clearly designed both for ostentation and for enjoyment. It is said that a Venetian husband pointed out to a friend a stone figure carved on a wall above a bridge. "There is the only honest woman in Venice," he remarked. The bridge is known as the Bridge of the Honest Woman to this day.[25]

In fact, being in a foreign country does tend to increase any tendency toward suspiciousness which an individual may possess. I well recall seeing a patient who was a Government employee concerned with energy policy. He was quite high in the hierarchy, and his position demanded that he travel abroad from time to time. On two occasions when he did so, he suffered a breakdown in which paranoid suspicions were the main feature. As long as he stayed at home, he remained stable; but when he was in a country in which the language was unfamiliar to him, he began to feel uneasy because he felt that people were making disparaging remarks about him which he could not understand.

Although Othello's case is different, in that we may assume that he spoke Italian sufficiently well to command an army, it is reasonable to assume that his foreignness might make him more gullible.

Iago goes on to suggest that Desdemona is less to be trusted because she has chosen a black husband:

> Not to affect proposed matches,
> Of her own clime, complexion, and degree,
> Whereto we see in all things nature tends;
> Fie, we may smell in such a will most rank,
> Foul disproportion; thoughts unnatural.[26]

Othello takes this insult lying down, as if, like so many subjects of color prejudice, he himself acquiesces to some extent in the notion that black is inferior or even evil. Anthony Burgess, in his coffee-table book on Shakespeare, writes, "The status of Othello shows, incidentally, that there was no colour-prejudice in those days, however much anti-semitism was rife."[27] This seems to me nonsense. We have to remember that blacks were supposed to be descended from Noah's son Ham. Because Ham had seen his father's naked-ness when Noah was drunk, his descendants were con-demned to serve the other brothers, Shem and Japheth, and the black color assigned to them was a mark of divine dis-favor.

Then, as now, prejudice was apt to see sexual union between black and white as repellent, although other emo-tions may have entered in as well. During World War II, I happened to be a patient in a hospital ward full of soldiers. The conversation turned to the relations between black men and white women: "Once a woman has had a black man, she's never going to be satisfied with a white again. You see, they're bigger made than we are." Whether this super-stitious mixture of envy and jealousy was current in Shake-speare's day, I do not know. If it was, it may well have increased the repugnance to the union between Othello and Desdemona which both Iago and Brabantio display. Iago, telling Desdemona's father of her marriage, refers to "the gross clasps of a lascivious Moor."[28] I have already quoted Brabantio's own remark about Othello's "sooty bosom." Iago suggests to Roderigo that Desdemona is bound to tire of Othello because of his appearance:

> Her eye must be fed, and what delight shall she have to look on the devil? When the blood is made dull with the act of sport, there should be again to inflame it, and give satiety a fresh appetite, loveliness in favour, sympa-thy in years, manners and beauties; all which the Moor is defective in: now, for want of these requir'd conve-

niences, her delicate tenderness will find itself abus'd,
begin to heave the gorge, disrelish and abhor the Moor,
very nature will instruct her to it, and compel her to
some second choice."[29]

Othello, however well endowed physically he may have
been, is inevitably more prone to suspect his wife's fidelity
than if he had been white. Although he had "done the state
some service," and taken the Christian side against the
Turks, it was nevertheless a state in which his black color
labeled him as an inferior and a probable infidel.

Another reason prompting Othello's willingness to
believe Iago is his trust in the latter's honesty. Bradley says:
" 'Honest' is the word that springs to the lips of everyone who
speaks of him. It is applied to him some fifteen times in the
play, not to mention some half-dozen where he employs it, in
derision, of himself."[30] Whom is Othello more likely to
trust? A newlywed Venetian bride or a tried comrade-in-
arms whom everyone calls "honest"? The state of being in
love is one in which it is accepted that illusions flourish; but
battle tests what a man is really made of.

I conclude that Othello does not exhibit the "extraordinary credulousness" which Ernest Jones attributes to him.
There are good reasons why he should trust Iago more than
Desdemona, and good reasons why he should be uncertain
of his place in her affections. There is nothing approaching
delusional jealousy in Othello's attitude. Although Iago
threatens, "Othello shall go mad,"[31] Othello shows no sign
of doing so. His momentary loss of consciousness is evidence
of stress, but not of insanity. There are none of the other
signs or symptoms which are generally found together with
delusions of jealousy in people suffering from mental illness. And, although Othello commits murder, and although
a high proportion of murderers are suffering from mental
illness, his crime is surely to be rated as a *crime passionel*,
which, it is generally believed, is the type of murder most
likely to be committed by normal people. We must remem-

ber that notions of male honor, in Shakespeare's day, more closely resembled those which, in quite recent times, provoked murderous family vendettas in Italy and other Mediterranean countries.

It remains for me to consider why sexual jealousy releases such powerful emotions of anger and hatred. Most people take this for granted, and assume that everyone feels the same; but this is not actually the case. My experience leads me to believe that people vary a good deal in the extent to which they experience jealousy. I do not believe that, in most instances, jealousy is merely based upon fear of losing a person who provides sexual release and satisfaction. There is one form of jealousy in which this may be true, but it is rare. I refer to those cases in which the person, usually a woman, who has had previous lovers, is submitted to relentless questioning about the actual details of her sexual encounters. Such questioning may go on for hours; and whatever the victim admits she has done with her lovers never satisfies the questioner. In his distorted mind, there are always closer intimacies or perversions which she has practiced with other men and has not practiced with him. This obsessional type of questioning is really a sign of profound sexual insecurity. The person suffering from it has carried into adult life some of the uneasiness typical of early adolescence, when a shy boy may easily feel that grown-ups or "real men" possess sexual secrets to which he has no access. This kind of retrospective jealousy is seldom, if ever, found together with delusions of infidelity in the present.

In more normal forms of jealousy, such an emphasis upon the sexual relationship to the exclusion of everything else does not occur. Sexual intimacy, though an important part of an intimate attachment, is only a part. And sexual infatuation, though temporarily threatening, is often transient, whereas intimate attachments tend to persist. When dangers like illness or poverty or war threaten a relationship,

sexual desire is often diminished while the need for attachment and mutual support becomes enhanced.

In recent years, the human need for attachment has been
emphasized by John Bowlby, whose studies of the ties
between small children and the mother have proved so fruitful. In the third volume of his book *Attachment and Loss*,
Bowlby writes:

> Intimate attachments to other human beings are the
> hub around which a person's life revolves, not only
> when he is an infant or a toddler or a schoolchild but
> through his adolescence and his years of maturity as
> well, and on into old age. From these intimate attach-
> ments a person draws his strength and enjoyment of
> life and, through what he contributes, he gives strength
> and enjoyment to others. These are matters about
> which current science and traditional wisdom are at
> one.[32]

Freud's instinct theory was primarily concerned with the
individual's search for pleasure in the form of sexual gratification, and human relationships assessed chiefly in terms
of their potential for providing such satisfaction. Bowlby
conceives that the need for intimate attachments extends far
beyond sexuality. As the sociologist Peter Marris puts it:

> The relationships that matter most to us are charac-
> teristically to particular people that we love—husband
> or wife, parents, children, dearest friend—and some-
> times to particular places—a home or personal terri-
> tory—that we invest with the same loving qualities.
> These specific relationships, which we experience as
> unique and irreplaceable, seem to embody most cru-
> cially the meaning of our lives.[33]

It seems to me that this view of intimate attachments can
help us to understand why jealousy is such a powerful feeling. A person who has achieved a modicum of sexual satis-

faction with one partner can reasonably expect to find another. Most people have had more than one sexual partner during the course of their lives and have not necessarily found that losing one and taking on another is desperately traumatic. But losing the meaning of one's life is another matter. This is why bereaved persons so often feel that, for a time, life has become meaningless. As Marris puts it, "Losing someone you love is less like losing a very valuable and irreplaceable possession than finding the law of gravity to be invalid."[34] Jealousy occurs when loss of the loved person is threatened by their forming a new attachment. Transient sexual infatuations do not necessarily threaten long-term attachments; and it seems to me doubtful whether adultery, in the absence of other reasons, should be a ground for divorce. The threats that really count are not so much to sexual pride as to the central meaning of a person's life.

This seems to be the case with Othello. Why, otherwise, should he believe that Desdemona's supposed infidelity should threaten the end of his career as a soldier? One can surely lose a wife without losing one's job as well. Yet, in his famous speech in Act III, Othello bids farewell not only to the tranquil mind and to content, but to "the pride, pomp, and circumstance of glorious war! . . . Farewell, Othello's occupation's gone!"[35] This surely implies that, because he can no longer trust Desdemona, the whole meaning of his life has been put in jeopardy.

But, you may argue, although intimate attachments may constitute the meaning of life for the majority of people, they do not do so for all. What about monks and nuns? What about isolates like Isaac Newton or most of the great philosophers of the Western world, whose wish or capacity to form intimate relationships is conspicuous by its absence?

I am sure that Peter Marris is right in thinking that intimate relationships constitute the meaning of life for most people. However, human beings are wonderfully various. For some, meaning appears to be constituted by something far more abstract than relationships with other human beings. For example, Newton showed passionate jealousy about his discoveries. He was reluctant to publish them for fear that they should be stolen, and had numerous quarrels, throughout the creative part of his life, with other scientists, such as Leibniz and Hooke, over questions of priority. It is clear that, for this isolated, suspicious man, the meaning of his life was to be found in scientific discovery, in his alchemical, religious, and historical research, and not in relations with others.

Newton was, for definable psychological reasons, pathologically incapable of close relationships. When, in mid-life, he suffered a depressive breakdown, he exhibited paranoid delusions, broke with his friends, and accused them of plotting against him. He exemplifies the fact that jealousy need not necessarily be based upon love, if love is not the prime source of self-esteem. Along a scale from the extreme represented by Newton to the so-called normal may be found all kinds of human beings, from those to whom relationships with others mean very little, to those for whom relationships are all-important. It is, I think, this kind of difference between people which may be one reason why the capacity to feel sexual jealousy seems also so widely to vary.

NOTES

1. Ambrose Bierce, *The Enlarged Devil's Dictionary*, ed. E. J. Hopkins (Harmondsworth: Penguin, 1971), p. 195.
2. *The Standard Edition of the Complete Psychological Works of Sigmund Freud*, 24 vols., ed. and trans. James Strachey (London: Hogarth Press, 1953–64), 13:89.
3. Freud, *Standard Edition*, 23:223.
4. Ibid.
5. Ibid., 23:224.
6. Ibid.
7. James Pope Hennessy, *Anthony Trollope* (London: Cape, 1971), p. 292.
8. Anthony Trollope, *He Knew He Was Right* (Oxford: Oxford University Press, 1948), pp. 257–58.
9. Freud, *Standard Edition*, 23:225.

10. David Enoch and William H. Trethowan, "The Othello Syndrome," in *Uncommon Psychiatric Syndromes* (Bristol: Bristol Classical Press, 1979).

11. Seymour Fisher and Roger P. Greenberg, *The Scientific Credibility of Freud's Theories and Therapy* (New York: Basic Books, 1977), p. 268.

12. Norwood East, *Society and the Criminal* (London: His Majesty's Stationery Office, 1949).

13. D. Abrahamsen, *Crime and the Human Mind* (Montclair, N.J.: Patterson Smith, 1944), pp. 161–63.

14. Ronald R. Mowat, *Morbid Jealousy and Murder: A Psychiatric Study of Morbidly Jealous Murderers at Broadmoor* (London: Tavistock, 1966).

15. Norval Morris and Gordon Hawkins, *The Honest Politician's Guide to Crime Control* (Chicago: University of Chicago Press, 1970), p. 57.

16. Quoted in Jonathon Green, ed., *The Cynic's Lexicon* (London: Routledge and Kegan Paul, 1984), p. 36.

17. Quoted in Herbert Weinstock, *Rossini* (Oxford: Oxford University Press, 1968), p. 66.

18. Quoted in ibid., p. 67.

19. Ernest Jones, *Hamlet and Oedipus* (London: Gollancz, 1949), pp. 116–17.

20. Act I, scene 2, lines 62–71.

21. Act I, scene 3, lines 292–93.

22. Act III, scene 3, line 210.

23. Ibid., lines 205–8.

24. James Morris, *Venice* (London: Faber and Faber, 1964), p. 69.

25. Ibid., p. 70.

26. Act III, scene 3, lines 233–37.

27. Anthony Burgess, *Shakespeare* (New York: Knopf, 1970), p. 146.

28. Act I, scene 1, line 126.

29. Act II, scene 1, lines 224–34.

30. A. C. Bradley, *Shakespearean Tragedy* (London: Macmillan, 1924), p. 214.

31. Act IV, scene 1, line 100.

32. John Bowlby, *Loss, Sadness and Depression*, vol. 3 of *Attachment and Loss* (London: Hogarth Press/Institute of Psycho-Analysis, 1980), p. 442.

33. Peter Marris, "Attachment and Society," in *The Place of Attachment in Human Behavior*, ed. C. Murray Parkes and J. Stevenson-Hinde (London: Tavistock, 1982), p. 185.

34. Ibid., p. 195.

35. Act III, scene 3, lines 360, 363.

6

Aspects of Adult Development

WHEN I WAS a young doctor, starting to specialize in psychiatry, the notion of adult development scarcely impinged. Those of us who were psychoanalytically inclined were particularly interested in early childhood development and its supposed effect upon future mental health and character structure. We accepted the Freudian postulate, shared by the Jesuits, that the experiences of the first five years of life and the emotional influences affecting the child during that early period were all-important in shaping adult personality. Some of my contemporaries, strongly influenced by the ideas of Melanie Klein, went still further. They supposed that accurate reconstructions could be made of the infant's experience from birth onward, and alleged that the first few months of extrauterine existence shaped the child's fate for good or ill.

This concentration upon the individual's early childhood, accompanied by the assumption that recall and reconstruction of the events of that period were essential to the restoration of psychic health, had the consequence that psychoanalysts showed little interest in later periods of life. The

early psychoanalysts, although oversanguine about their
ability to disinter the infant vicissitudes of their patients,
were not at all confident about ameliorating the problems of
older people, and could seldom be persuaded to take them
on as patients. Freud himself wrote in an early paper:

> The age of patients has this much importance in deter-
> mining their fitness for psycho-analytic treatment,
> that, on the one hand, near or above the age of fifty the
> elasticity of the mental processes, on which the treat-
> ment depends, is as a rule lacking—old people are no
> longer educable—and, on the other hand, the mass of
> material to be dealt with would prolong the duration of
> the treatment indefinitely.[1]

One implication of this statement was clear. If the powerful
tool of psychoanalysis was unable to affect those approaching middle age, they must indeed be fixed in their ways.

This impression was, in the 1940s and 1950s, reinforced
by clinical and educational psychologists who told us that
optimum performance in intelligence tests occurred at
about the age of sixteen. Following this peak, all we had to
look forward to was a daily loss of some thousands of brain
cells, accompanied by a progressive decline in intellectual
ability. When, at the age of twenty-seven, I was in training at
the Maudsley Hospital, I recall my gloom at realizing that I
was already eleven years past my best.

Nor had the zoologists any comfort to offer. Students of
animal behavior were interested in the development of animals from birth to sexual maturity, but showed little interest
in any period, when such existed, beyond that at which the
animal had fulfilled its reproductive potential. Once an animal had produced a family, or several families, and given
them enough support and protection to ensure their own
capability of reproduction, there seemed little left to live for.

When I was still an undergraduate at Cambridge, my
tutor, C. P. Snow, introduced me to *A Mathematician's Apology*,

by his friend G. H. Hardy. In this classic account of the pleasures and rewards of being a mathematician, Hardy affirms that mathematics, more than any other art or science, is a young man's game.[2]

Hardy reinforces this statement by pointing out that Newton's greatest ideas came to him at about the age of twenty-four, and alleges that, although he continued to make discoveries until he was nearly forty, he did little but polish his earlier ideas after this, and gave up mathematics altogether when he was fifty (but see Chapter 3). Hardy states that "Galois died at twenty-one, Abel at twenty-seven, Ramanujan at thirty-three, Riemann at forty. . . . I do not know an instance of a major mathematical advance initiated by a man past fifty."[3]

Hardy's book appeared in 1940. Had it been delayed for sixteen years, he would certainly have included Einstein in his list. Einstein's greatest work belonged to his early years. He was born in 1879, published the special theory of relativity in 1905, and followed it with the general theory of relativity in 1916, when he would have been thirty-seven. The last half of his life was spent in searching for a unified field theory which would cover all the forces of nature at once. But he took a wrong turning. C. P. Snow records, "Einstein's tremendous instinct for physics had sadly gone astray, and led him up a blind alley for the last forty years of his life."[4]

When people so diverse in temperament and interests as psychoanalysts, zoologists, experimental psychologists, and mathematicians all concur in giving the impression that life, if not actually over at forty, is so ossified that not much change can be expected, a climate of opinion is created in which the concept of anything called "adult development" can scarcely be entertained. The study of adult decline, although it may be of interest to a few specialists working on dementia, is not an alluring topic.

However, this predominantly gloomy picture was gradually modified. A few bold spirits had the temerity to suggest that it was untrue to suppose that, from forty onward, life ground slowly to a halt. Some claimed that interesting changes took place around the mid-life period. Others proposed that even psychological developments proceeding into old age were well worth studying.

Various attempts were made to subdivide the life cycle into a series of stages traversed by the individual in the course of normal development. Erik Erikson, whose first book, *Childhood and Society*,[5] was published in 1950 and became a best seller, postulated "Eight Ages of Man," the last three of which pertained to adulthood. All these stages are characterized by antinomies representing different psychosocial tasks or problems, each of which Erikson believes to be characteristic of a particular age period. The first stage, for example, is "basic trust versus mistrust," a concept which is relevant to the understanding of the people whom psychiatrists label schizoid, and which fits quite well with Melanie Klein's notion of the "paranoid-schizoid position" in infantile development. Erikson proposes three adult stages. In early adulthood, he suggests, the main issue to be resolved is that of "intimacy versus isolation." He compares this stage of development with Freud's end point of "genitality," that is, the capacity to make a mature heterosexual relationship which is likely to progress toward creating a new generation.

Erikson's next stage, which pertains to middle adulthood, centers on what he calls "generativity versus stagnation." He defines generativity primarily as concern with establishing and guiding the next generation, but extends the concept to include productivity and creativity. Whether or not such a stage can be objectively demonstrated, the notion is still well within the bounds of a biological, evolutionary schema. Man's infancy and childhood, relative to his total life-span, is considerably prolonged as compared with other primates. This extension of dependency is adaptive because it provides time for learning. The development of speech has made possible adaptation by means of the transmission of culture. For this to be effective, postponement of the age of attaining sexual maturity is desirable, since the child is thereby kept dependent and teachable. If the human child's rate of development kept up the pace of the first five years, sexual maturity could be expected around the age of eight or nine; but the intervention of the so-called latency period postpones puberty for some years after this. If human adaptation requires the prolongation of childhood in order to provide time for learning, it is obviously desirable that adulthood should also be prolonged in order to ensure a supply of teachers: more especially, of teachers who have finished the task of reproducing themselves and who are therefore able to spread their attention beyond their own immediate families.

In this connection, it is pertinent to recall one observation of a zoologist working with baboons, which indicates that there is some interest in studying the behavior of animals which have passed their reproductive period. John Crook reports a personal communication from Robin Dunbar, who had been looking at the social organization of gelada baboons. When a younger male takes over the harem of an old male, the latter is not banished or killed, as happens in some other species. Instead, "the old male remains loosely attached to the harem and spends a great deal of time caring for his infants. No longer active sexually, he now invests his time and energy in caring for his last offspring."[6]

Erikson's postulated third and final stage of adult development takes us beyond the biological in the sense that its utility in Darwinian terms cannot easily be defined. Erikson formulates it as "ego integrity versus despair." He writes:

> Only in him who in some way has taken care of things and people and has adapted himself to the triumphs and disappointment adherent to being, the originator

> of others or the generator of products and ideas—only in him may gradually ripen the fruit of these seven stages. I know no better word for it than ego integrity.7

Erikson's concept of ego integrity includes the notion that the individual has come to terms with the inevitability of death by an acceptance of his own life cycle as something that had to be, that could not really have been different. He contrasts this attitude of constructive resignation with despair, which he conceives as arising from the feeling that it is now too late to reach ego integrity by any other path. Despair, in this sense, is linked with the fear of death. Although many criticisms can be made both of Erikson's stages of life and of the clumsy, turgid prose in which he struggles to express himself, clinical observation confirms that those who are most afraid of death are those who have been most afraid of some aspects of life, and who therefore continue to feel that, if they had shown more courage, life would have been more fulfilling.

In recent years, various other workers have been attracted to the idea that the developmental stages of adulthood are worthy of study. At Yale, Daniel Levinson and his associates have studied the life cycle in males.8 Like Erik Erikson, they conclude that there are "developmental tasks" characterizing different stages of life which every individual is compelled to tackle. Levinson's original procedure was to study in depth the life cycles of a small number of American males: ten factory workers, ten biologists, ten business executives, and ten novelists. He claims to have detected a pattern of change in each individual which, both in nature and timing, is closely similar. By taking individuals from such different backgrounds and with such different interests, Levinson has at least avoided the common error of assuming that the life cycles of other people necessarily coincide with one's own.

According to Levinson, the life cycle alternates between stable periods of consolidation and less stable periods of transition. The first of the periods of transition occurs between adolescence and full entry into the adult world. In our culture, this stage usually occupies the years between eighteen and twenty-two. After settling into an occupation and perhaps embarking upon marriage, there is usually another transition period between the ages of twenty-eight and thirty-two. This is a time when the young man is apt to question his original choices of occupation and of marital partner, and may well change both. Between thirty-two and about forty-one is another period of consolidation. This is succeeded by the mid-life transition, between thirty-nine and forty-two.

Like other writers, Levinson emphasizes the storminess of the mid-life transition, often referred to as the mid-life crisis. It is sometimes a period of agonizing reappraisal, when many men have to come to terms with the fact that they cannot hope to fulfill all their youthful dreams. It is also a period at which neglected parts of the self clamor for expression. Levinson, like Jung, believes that the achievement of conventional goals in Western society involves making choices which necessarily exclude or minimize certain aspects of the person as a whole. This one-sidedness is apt to cause trouble in the mid-life period. Clinically, when faced with cases of mid-life depression, I have found it useful to encourage the patient to recall the daydreams and interests of his adolescence. This brings to light aspects of the self which have been neglected and which, if pursued, have a compensatory therapeutic effect.

Levinson's explorations of later adulthood are incomplete and will not be pursued further here. The sequences of crises and resolutions which he describes seem too closely tied to narrow time spans and are also rather tediously similar. The period of transition at adolescence, or the mid-life transition, may occur at very different times in different individuals. Human beings mature at different rates, both mentally and physically.

However, there may be a valid underlying principle in

Levinson's scheme, although he himself does not spell it out. In our Western culture, though not in all cultures, man seems so constituted that he can never rest upon his laurels. The moment he has achieved something, be it a position in the world, marriage and a family, a successful piece of research, a new book, painting, or musical composition, he is driven to question its value and look for something more. If problems are not there, he will invent them. Man seems to be a problem-seeking as well as a problem-solving animal. We are programmed to change, develop, and meet new challenges until we die. We are compelled to be perpetual travelers. If we travel hopefully, that is as much as we ought to expect. If we do not, we become depressed. The idea that we can ever arrive at a stable state in which life's problems are settled is an illusion. The only "final solution" is death.

Another study worth looking at is by George Vaillant, a Harvard psychiatrist.[9] His subjects were Harvard students. Vaillant's emphasis is quite different from Levinson's. He is not so concerned with stages of the life cycle but more with "patterns of defense" in the Freudian sense; that is, with how the individual comes to terms with instinctual drives. As examples of pathological defenses, he cites the following: the paranoid one of always blaming others for one's own shortcomings; retreating into a world of fantasy; or "acting out" with overtly disturbed behavior. Healthy mechanisms of defense include suppression as opposed to repression, altruism, and sublimation. Vaillant's study, in contrast with what might be expected from early Freudian theory, indicates that childhood trauma is a poor guide to predicting adult neurosis or health. However, children who have not developed "basic trust," or who have not been encouraged to be autonomous, are likely to show delay in maturation. As in Terman's famous studies of gifted children,[10] physical health and mental health generally march hand in hand, although there are some exceptions.

But what emerges most strikingly from these biographical

studies is the fact that more development toward maturity takes place during adult years than most psychiatrists had imagined. Even highly disturbed adults who have habitually employed one of the pathological defenses already mentioned, and who may have been labeled "psychopathic," can lose their symptoms, abandon their disturbed patterns of behavior, and adopt maturer mechanisms of defense. Vaillant discovered that a surprisingly large number of adults only feel free to "do their own thing" by the time they are fifty or older. This finding is relevant to the changes which occur in some notably creative people, which are discussed below. It looks as if the length of the period during which the human child is educable may carry with it the disadvantage of embedding his early training so firmly within him that emancipation from its influence is difficult when this is needed.

I referred before to the reluctance of the early psychoanalysts to treat middle-aged patients. However, C. G. Jung, after he parted company with Freud in 1913, developed a psychotherapeutic practice which consisted largely of older patients. Jung's ideas about the development of personality are explored in Chapter 9 of this book. In this context, it should be emphasized that he was a pioneer in the study of adult development. In Chapter 9, Jung's own experience of going through a mid-life crisis is related to the growth of his interest in the problems of the middle-aged. In 1931, Jung wrote:

> The clinical material at my disposal is of a peculiar composition: new cases are decidedly in the minority. Most of them already have some form of psychotherapeutic treatment behind them, with partial or negative results. About a third of my cases are not suffering from any clinically definable neurosis, but from the senselessness and aimlessness of their lives. I should not object if this were called the general neurosis of our age. Fully two thirds of my patients are in the second half of life.[11]

Jung's own subjective upheaval was partly responsible for directing his attention to such patients, but there were other reasons as well. Jung did not share Freud's assumption that the events of early childhood were the prime cause of neurosis, and did not therefore believe that getting the patient to recall his first five years was always essential.

Jung also accumulated older patients who had had previous treatment because he became famous enough to be regarded as a last resort who might succeed where other analysts had failed. Some of those who were suffering from the "senselessness and aimlessness of their lives" were undoubtedly Americans like the Mellons and Fowler McCormick who possessed enormous wealth and did not know what to do with themselves. At Mary Mellon's first appointment with Jung, her opening words were "Dr. Jung, we have too much money. What can we do with it?"[12]

I earlier referred to my own practice of asking patients to recall their adolescent fantasies and interests. This psychotherapeutic technique is taken from Jung, who wrote:

> The nearer we approach to the middle of life, and the better we have succeeded in entrenching ourselves in our personal attitudes and social positions, the more it appears as if we had discovered the right course and the right ideals and principles of behaviour. For this reason we suppose them to be eternally valid, and make a virtue of unchangeably clinging to them. We overlook the essential fact that the social goal is attained only at the cost of a diminution of personality. Many—far too many—aspects of life which should also have been experienced lie in the lumber-room among dusty memories; but sometimes, too, they are glowing coals under grey ashes.[13]

Jung then comments upon statistics which show an increased incidence of depression around the age of forty in men, rather earlier in women. He believes that these disturbances are often evidence of an important change taking place in the psyche which has its origin in the unconscious. Occasionally, these changes can be almost catastrophic. Jung quotes the case of an excessively pious and intolerant church-warden who became more and more morose and moody. Finally, at the age of fifty-five, he sat up in bed one night and said to his wife, "Now at last I've got it! I'm just a plain rascal." Jung reports that he spent his declining years in riotous living![14] This is a crude and comical example of Jung's notion of self-regulatory compensation, described in Chapter 9.

Why should this process of compensation be particularly noticeable at the mid-life period or later? Jung considered that the first half of life was primarily concerned with the young person establishing himself or herself as a separate entity, with breaking the emotional ties with parents and home, with achieving a position in the world, and with beginning a new family. When all this had been accomplished, it might well happen that the person concerned became depressed; feeling perhaps that there was nothing to aim for, no definite direction to go in. Jung's way of treating such problems is outlined in Chapter 9.

Whereas Jung interpreted the mid-life crisis in terms of the reemergence of aspects of the self which had been neglected and were seeking recognition, other observers took a different view. One of these is Elliott Jaques, whose paper "Death and the Mid-Life Crisis"[15] has become a classic. Elliott Jaques qualified in medicine at Johns Hopkins, obtained a Ph.D. in social relations at Harvard, and also trained as a Kleinian analyst. He was, for some years, head of the School of Social Sciences at Brunel University in West London. Jaques is one of the very small number of psycho-analysts who have taken an interest in industrial relations. His work on management in industry has become deservedly famous.

Jaques became interested in the mid-life period when he became aware of

a marked tendency towards crisis in the creative work
of great men in their middle and late thirties. . . . This
crisis may express itself in three different ways: the
creative career may simply come to an end, either in a
drying-up of creative work, or in actual death; the
creative capacity may begin to show and express itself
for the first time; or a decisive change in the quality and
content of creativeness may take place.

Jaques studied a random sample of 310 creative men of
genius and found a sudden jump in the death rate between
the ages of thirty-five and thirty-nine. This group included
Mozart, Raphael, Chopin, Rimbaud, Purcell, Baudelaire,
and Watteau.

As an example of "drying-up," Jaques cites Racine, who
had thirteen years of success, culminating with *Phèdre* at
the age of thirty-eight. For the next twelve years he produced nothing. Another example is that of Ben Jonson,
who had produced all his best plays by the time he was
forty-three, although he continued to write masques and
some other plays which are generally considered of less
interest.

Gauguin, who gave up his job in a bank at the age of
thirty-three, is an obvious example of an artist who did not
really get going until the mid-life period. George Eliot did
not turn to fiction until she was nearly forty. *Studies in Hysteria,* the first psychoanalytic book, was not published until
Freud was thirty-nine.

Donatello and Goethe are quoted as examples of men of
genius whose styles, in their late thirties, showed considerable change. Jaques might also have referred to Ibsen. It was
not until Ibsen was thirty-eight that he achieved considerable success with the publication of *Brand.* At the same time,
his manner, appearance, and even his handwriting under-
went considerable changes.

Jaques's explanation of the significance of the mid-life
period is that this is the period when individuals become

truly aware that they must die; a possibility which, in youth, seems infinitely remote.

Jaques alleges that, in earlier years, creative production tends to be intense, spontaneous, lyrical, and rapid. After the mid-life crisis, works become more "sculpted," that is, more carefully considered, worked over, and externalized. He associates the first kind of creativity with the idealism and optimism of youth, quoting Shelley as an example of someone who, according to his wife's account, thought that all the evil in the world would disappear if only men would will it to be so.

In Kleinian terms, such an idealistic attitude is based on unconscious denial of reality and the employment of manic defenses. The change which takes place at the mid-life period is consequent upon an acceptance of the existence of hate and destructive impulses within the self, as well as upon recognizing and accepting the reality of death. Jaques uses the phrase "constructive resignation," which aptly expresses this change of attitude. Mature insight leads to serenity, and this manifests itself in an artist's work.

Jaques illustrates his thesis, rather convincingly, by quoting the opening of *The Divine Comedy,* which was begun by Dante after his banishment from Florence at the age of thirty-seven.

> Midway upon the journey of our life
> I found that I was in a dusky wood;
> For the right path, whence I had strayed, was lost.
> Ah me! How hard a thing it is to tell
> The wildness of that rough and savage place,
> The very thought of which brings back my fear!
> So bitter was it, death is little more so.[16]

Jaques argues that the poem is an account of the poet's first conscious, full encounter with death. He has to be led by Virgil through both hell and purgatory before he eventually finds his own way into Paradise.

One might argue that the mid-life crises of creative people are hardly typical of the general run of mankind. However, I am inclined to agree with Jaques that what can be more easily discerned in men and women of genius because it is recorded in their works also occurs in some form or other in more ordinary mortals. Indeed, the changes taking place in adult life can perhaps best be studied by considering the records left by creative artists. Longitudinal studies of change in ordinary people from adulthood to death are still hard to come by, although I earlier referred to some attempts in this direction. But there is certainly a consensus among observers writing from very different theoretical standpoints that, somewhere around the late thirties or early forties, changes in attitude take place in many human beings which are often accompanied by emotional upheavals. How far such changes are a product of our particular culture is an open question.

Jung and Jaques are content to delineate two main periods of adult life, separated by the mid-life crisis. In the case of creative people, however, critics have often defined three periods rather than two. The so-called "third period" is of particular interest. As I have written about it at some length elsewhere,[17] I shall refer to it only briefly. The first period in an artist's life is one in which he is learning his craft and in which, in varying degree, he still exhibits indebtedness to his teachers. The second period is the time at which the artist has achieved mastery of his art, and has also found his own, individual way of expressing himself. Some artists reach this second period without difficulty. Others, like Giacometti, may go through agonies before they feel that they have succeeded in reaching the essence of an individual vision. Many of the greatest geniuses have not passed beyond this second stage because they have died prematurely, like Mozart, Schubert, Mendelssohn, Purcell, and the others referred to earlier.

The mid-life crisis may occur at any time between the ages of thirty-five and forty-five. When an artist lives long enough to be said to have entered a third period of creative production, he will usually be in his fifties or sixties.

Third-period works are those of an artist who is looking inward rather than outward. He is concerned with an internal process rather than with appealing to his public. Very often, third-period works are unconventional in form. They seem to be exploring remote, suprapersonal areas of experience and may, for this reason, appear incomprehensible. The last quartets of Beethoven, which exhibit all the qualities to which I have just referred, were initially considered impossibly "difficult." From Beethoven's death in 1827 until the beginning of this century, performances of the last five quartets were rare. Today, they are among our most treasured musical possessions; but everyone who knows anything about music agrees that this last set of quartets is in an entirely different category from the six of Opus 18, or the five quartets which are usually grouped together as belonging to the middle period.

The same kind of late change can be seen in the works of Liszt, Brahms, Richard Strauss, and J. S. Bach. It can also be detected in the novels of Henry James, whose three periods are sometimes facetiously referred to as those of James I, James II, and James the Old Pretender.

Michelangelo is an interesting example of an artist who is claimed by Jaques as having had a long fallow period in mid-life, between forty and fifty-five. What Jaques does not mention is that Michelangelo turned to poetry. The majority of his sonnets were written during the last thirty years of his long life. A very late change of style can be detected in the last sculpture of Michelangelo, the *Rondanini Pietà,* on which he was still working six days before his death at the age of eighty-nine. Michael Ayrton has described this piece in his introduction to Michelangelo's sonnets:

> The *Rondanini Pietà* is a statue so stripped, so bare, so passive and so patient that all the spent strength of the titan is drained away and only the spirit remains within

a slim and fragile shell of stone. . . . The Dead Christ,
slim and worn as a sea-washed bone, is as remote from
the all-conquering athlete of *The Last Judgement* as sleep
is from earthquake. The thrust is gone, the weight is
gone, the articulation no longer describes energy. In
the *Rondanini Pietà* is the still centre.[18]

Enough has been said to illustrate the point that, even
toward the end of life, psychological changes are still taking
place. There is often a lessening of interest in interpersonal
relationships. Both Jung and Freud survived into their
eighties; and both almost abandoned interest in psychotherapy in favor of abstract ideas. Instead of being concerned with conventional achievement or with impressing
others, there is a wish to be rid of superfluities, a greater
concern with essentials. So far as we know, man is the only
creature who can see his own death coming. The realization
concentrates the mind wonderfully. He prepares for death
by freeing himself from mundane goals and attachments,
and turns toward the cultivation of his own interior garden.
This is surely the common factor which links Jaques's "constructive resignation" with Erikson's "ego integrity" and
Jung's "individuation."

We are living in a culture in which the proportion of the
elderly and old is constantly increasing. At the same time,
unemployment is a major problem, and one which brings
increasing pressure on those in work to seek early retirement. It is important that psychologists and psychiatrists
should devote more attention to adult development, and to
increasing our understanding of psychological changes taking place in older people. It is still too often the case that
retirement is seen as having to give up work because of
incapacity, and hence often accompanied by depression. It is
known that a good many people die shortly after losing a
spouse. I am impressed with the number who die shortly
after retirement, though I cannot give statistics. My friend
Kingsley Martin, the famous editor of the *New Statesman,*

dreaded retirement because, he said, all the editors he had known had died within two years of doing so. Within three years of his own retirement, he had a stroke. Although he did not die, he was never really well again.

Suppose that properly controlled studies demonstrate that the processes we see taking place in creative people are examples of a more general pattern, a part of normal human development. Our attitude to retirement might change, and the prospects of keeping our aging population well and happy might improve. If retirement could be looked upon as an opportunity for self-development and fulfillment rather than as a kind of defeat, it would greatly increase the happiness of a large number who now regard the prospect with dread, and also encourage them to get out of the way of the young. Perhaps we should all retire at fifty. There seems no realistic prospect of decreasing the number of the unemployed in most Western countries in the foreseeable future.

NOTES

1. *The Standard Edition of the Complete Psychological Works of Sigmund Freud*, 24 vols., ed. and trans. James Strachey (London: Hogarth Press, 1953–64), 7:264.
2. G. H. Hardy, *A Mathematician's Apology* (Cambridge: Cambridge University Press, 1940), p. 10.
3. Ibid., pp. 11, 12.
4. C. P. Snow, *The Physicists* (London: Macmillan, 1981), pp. 132–33.
5. Erik Erikson, *Childhood and Society* (Harmondsworth: Penguin, 1965).
6. John H. Crook, *The Evolution of Human Consciousness* (Oxford: Oxford University Press, 1980), p. 83.
7. Erikson, *Childhood and Society*, p. 259.
8. Daniel J. Levinson, with Charlotte N. Darrow, *The Seasons of a Man's Life* (New York: Knopf, 1978).
9. George E. Vaillant, *Adaptation to Life* (Boston: Little, Brown, 1977).
10. L. M. Terman and Melita H. Oden, *The Gifted Child Grows Up* (New York: Oxford University Press, 1947).

11. C. G. Jung, "The Aims of Psychotherapy," in *Collected Works*, 20 vols., trans. R. F. C. Hull (London: Routledge and Kegan Paul, 1953–79), vol. 16, para. 83.

12. Quoted in William McGuire, *Bollingen* (Princeton: Princeton University Press, 1982), p. 20.

13. Jung, "The Stages of Life," in *Collected Works*, vol. 8, para. 772.

14. Ibid., para. 775.

15. Elliott Jaques, "Death and the Mid-Life Crisis," *International Journal of Psycho-Analysis* 46, part 4 (1965). Reprinted in *Work, Creativity and Social Justice* (London: Heinemann, 1970), pp. 38–63.

16. Dante Alighieri, *The Divine Comedy*, trans. Lawrence Grant White (New York: Pantheon, 1948), p. 1.

17. Anthony Storr, *Solitude: A Return to the Self* (New York: Free Press, 1988).

18. Michael Ayrton, introduction to *The Sonnets of Michelangelo*, trans. Elizabeth Jennings (London: Folio Society, 1961), pp. 14–15.

7

Psychoanalysis and Creativity

ALTHOUGH FREUD'S WRITINGS on art and artists constitute a comparatively small fraction of his total output, the editors of the English *Standard Edition* list twenty-two references to writings "dealing mainly or largely with Art, Literature or the theory of Aesthetics."[1] Freud's papers "Leonardo da Vinci," "The Moses of Michelangelo," and "Dostoevsky and Parricide" will be known to every student of his work.

There is no doubt that Freud had a deep appreciation, and love, of poetry and other forms of literature. His schooling had made him familiar with the Latin and Greek classics, and, throughout his life, he read widely, not only in German, but also in English, French, Italian, and Spanish. After Freud abandoned neuropathology for the study and treatment of neuroses, his writings contain far more references to novelists and playwrights, more especially to Shakespeare and to Goethe, than to the writings of other psychiatrists.

Freud's own talent as a writer was recognized early in his life. When he was only seventeen, he wrote to his friend Emil Fluss:

At the same time my professor told me—and he is the first person who ventured to tell me this—that I had what Herder so neatly calls an "idiotic" style, i.e. a style at once correct and characteristic. I was duly surprised at this amazing fact and hasten to spread the news of this happy event abroad as far and wide as possible—the first of its kind. To you, for instance, who, I am sure, have until now not been aware that you are exchanging letters with a German stylist. So now I would counsel you, as a friend, not as one with a vested interest—preserve them—bind them together—guard them well—you never know.[2]

In 1930, Freud became the fourth recipient of the Goethe Prize for Literature awarded by the city of Frankfurt. He could hardly have written so well himself if he had been unable to appreciate style in literature, but his aesthetic appreciation of the other arts was far more limited. Music, for example, was actually distasteful to him. When Freud was a boy, his sister Anna began to have music lessons. But the sound of her practicing disturbed the studies of the *wunderkind* and Freud's parents had the offending piano removed from the apartment. Freud's own children were not allowed to pursue music in the home, and his nephew Harry wrote of him: "He despised music and considered it solely as an intrusion. . . . He never went to a concert and hardly to the theater."[3] Had Freud been musical, he would have been forced to pay more attention to aesthetic form, since the content of music cannot be verbally defined with any precision, while its effect, at any rate in classical music, is highly dependent upon the forms chosen by the composer. However, as Freud modestly acknowledged in his paper "The Moses of Michelangelo," aesthetic form remained a puzzle to him:

I may say at once that I am no connoisseur in art, but simply a layman. I have often observed that the subject-matter of works of art has a stronger attraction for me than their formal and technical qualities, though to the artist their value lies first and foremost in these latter. I am unable rightly to appreciate many of the methods used and the effects obtained in art. I state this so as to secure the reader's indulgence for the attempt I propose to make here.

Nevertheless, works of art do exercise a powerful effect on me, especially those of literature and sculpture, less often of painting. This has occasioned me, when I have been contemplating such things, to spend a long time before them trying to apprehend them in my own way, i.e. to explain to myself what their effect is due to. Wherever I cannot do this, as for instance with music, I am almost incapable of obtaining any pleasure. Some rationalistic, or perhaps analytic, turn of mind in me rebels against being moved by a thing without knowing why I am thus affected and what it is that affects me.

This has brought me to recognize the apparently paradoxical fact that precisely some of the grandest and most overwhelming creations of art are still unresolved riddles to our understanding. We admire them, we feel overawed by them, but we arc unable to say what they represent to us. I am not sufficiently well-informed to know whether this fact has already been remarked upon; possibly, indeed, some writer on aesthetics has discovered that this state of intellectual bewilderment is a necessary condition when a work of art is to achieve its greatest effects. It would only be with the greatest reluctance that I could bring myself to believe in any such necessity.[4]

Freud's disclaimer was not false modesty. His lack of aesthetic appreciation of the visual arts is attested from another source. Freud was a passionate collector of antiquities, especially of Roman, Etruscan, Assyrian, and Egyptian statuettes. In May 1938, a few days before Freud's journey to

England from Nazi-occupied Vienna on June 4, the photographer Edmund Engelman recorded for posterity the appearance of that famous apartment at Berggasse 19.[5] Freud's consulting room and study are overflowing with an unbelievable number of antique statuettes, crowded together so closely that the outline of any individual piece is hardly discernible. These are not the rooms of an aesthete, but those of a compulsive collector. Freud once told Jung that, were he to suffer from a neurosis, it would be of obsessional type. His accumulation of objects and the manner in which he arranged them bears this out.

Freud's principal interest, therefore, was in the subject matter of works of art, not in the skill, style, or manner in which they were presented. In *An Autobiographical Study*, Freud wrote that analysis "can do nothing toward elucidating the nature of the artistic gift, nor can it explain the means by which the artist works—artistic technique."[6] And in his paper on Dostoyevsky, he wrote, "Before the problem of the creative artist analysis must, alas, lay down its arms."[7]

Since content, rather than style, was the problem to which Freud addressed himself, it was reasonable that he should apply the same method of interpretation to works of art as he did to dreams, fantasies, and neurotic symptoms. The subjects which an artist selects, and the ways in which he chooses to present those subjects are, of course, partly dictated by the conventions of his time. But his choices are also determined partly by his personality and by his personal history, even though, in some instances, he may himself be unconscious of the connection.

As an example of Freud's procedure, one cannot do better than turn to his essay on Leonardo. In recent years, this monograph of 1910 has been somewhat discredited, since Freud's interpretation of a fantasy memory of Leonardo's, in which a bird is supposed to have struck his lips with its tail, has been shown to be based upon a mistranslation. The bird was a kite and not a vulture; and whereas vultures can be shown to have mythological connections with the mother, kites cannot. However, this error of Freud's does not invalidate the other interpretations which he advances.

Freud is careful to point out that he does not regard Leonardo as a neurotic, although he suggests that he may have had some obsessional traits of character. On the basis of slender information, Freud nevertheless builds up a convincing explanation of Leonardo's homosexual orientation. Leonardo was an illegitimate child, and for his first few years lived only with his mother. Freud supposes, with reason, that the absence of a father combined with the excessive caresses of a lonely mother might well have made heterosexuality difficult of achievement. When Freud comes to discuss Leonardo's paintings, what interests him is the presumed relation of their content to the circumstances of Leonardo's childhood. The famous, ambiguous smile which appears on the faces of some of Leonardo's subjects is traced back to a presumedly similar smile on the face of the artist's mother; and the androgynous appearance of some of his portraits is attributed to Leonardo's homosexuality. Freud comments at some length upon the picture of the Virgin and Child with St. Anne.[8] As many critics have observed, St. Anne seems hardly older than her daughter, the Virgin Mary. Freud first notes that the subject of mother, grandmother, and child may have suggested itself to Leonardo because, once he had been removed from the sole care of his mother, he was brought up in a household which included his paternal grandmother as well as his stepmother. Freud goes on to suggest that the similarity in age between the Virgin and St. Anne may be a reflection of the fact that Leonardo did, in effect, have two mothers: his real mother and then his stepmother, who was also supposed to have been devoted to him. As it appears that this subject is one rarely chosen by artists, Freud's interpretations carry conviction. However, this method of interpretation can only be applied to representational art. What, one wonders, would

Freud have said if he had been confronted by a canvas of Mark Rothko's? It can also be said, with justice, that Freudian interpretation always leads back to the artist's personality: that is, it may reveal something about the artist, but does not tell us much about the work of art itself.

It has sometimes been alleged that, because Freud used the same methods of interpretation for works of art as he did for neurotic symptoms, he did not distinguish between the two. But it must be remembered, as Richard Wollheim has pointed out in a lecture on Freud and the interpretation of art, that Freud was aiming at a general theory of how the mind works, and that his interpretation of art appears, at any rate at first sight, to be consistent with such a theory. We all express, in our speech and in our actions, desires and wishes of which we are only partially conscious, to which psychoanalytic interpretation can be applied. There is no reason to exclude works of art from this kind of scrutiny. In the Freudian scheme, works of art are regarded as being largely the result of sublimation; that is, of a mechanism by which instinctual impulses are diverted from direct expression and transformed into something more acceptable to society. Although sublimation is technically classified as a mechanism of defense, it is described by Anna Freud as pertaining "more to the study of the normal than to that of neurosis."9 However, although sublimation is a mechanism of defense employed by normal people, Freud was evidently of the opinion that artists needed to, or were driven to, employ sublimation more than most of us, and were therefore closer to neurosis than the average. As late as 1917, in the twenty-third *Introductory Lecture on Psycho-Analysis,* Freud wrote:

> An artist is once more in rudiments an introvert, not far removed from neurosis. He is oppressed by excessively powerful instinctual needs. He desires to win honour, power, wealth, fame and the love of women; but he lacks

the means for achieving these satisfactions. Conse-
quently, like any other unsatisfied man, he turns away
from reality and transfers all his interest, and his libido
too, to the wishful constructions of his life of phantasy,
whence the path might lead to neurosis.[10]

Freud considered that fantasy was derived from play, and
regarded both activities in a negative light since they were,
in his view, a denial of, or turning away from, reality:

> The growing child, when he stops playing, gives up
> nothing but the link with real objects; instead of *play-
> ing*, he now *phantasies*. He builds castles in the air and
> creates what are called *day-dreams*.[11]

> The creative writer does the same as the child at play.
> He creates a world of phantasy which he takes very
> seriously—that is which he invests with large amounts
> of emotion—while separating it sharply from reality.[12]

Freud proceeds to consider the nature of fantasy:

> We may lay it down that a happy person never phan-
> tasies, only an unsatisfied one. The motive forces of
> phantasies are unsatisfied wishes, and every single
> phantasy is the fulfilment of a wish, a correction of an
> unsatisfying reality.[13]

Although not everyone who engages in fantasy becomes
neurotic, and, as we shall see, creative people are a special
case because their creative abilities make it possible for them
to link their fantasies with reality, fantasy is a dangerous
activity. For "neurotics turn away from reality because they
find it unbearable—either the whole or parts of it."[14]

Freud conceived that, at the beginning of life, the infant
was dominated by the pleasure principle and that the pleasures sought were entirely sensual in nature. From time to
time, the Nirvana-like bliss of the satisfied infant would be

disturbed by "the peremptory demands of internal needs"[15] for food, for warmth, and so on. Freud goes on:

> When this happened, whatever was thought of (wished for) was simply presented in a hallucinatory manner, just as still happens today with our dream-thoughts every night. It was only the non-occurrence of the expected satisfaction, the disappointment experienced, that led to the abandonment of this attempt at satisfaction by means of hallucination. Instead of it, the psychical apparatus had to decide to form a conception of the real circumstances in the external world and to endeavour to make a real alteration in them. A new principle of mental functioning was introduced; what was presented to the mind was no longer what was agreeable but what was real, even if it happened to be disagreeable. This setting-up of the *reality principle* proved to be a momentous step.[16]

So, fantasy is equated with hallucination, with dreaming, with turning away from reality, with the persistence of an infantile mode of mental functioning which Freud called "primary process." Proper adaptation to the external world is by means of deliberate thought and planning; by postponement of immediate satisfaction; by the abandonment of wish-fulfilling fantasy. Freud wrote:

> Art brings about a reconciliation between the two principles in a peculiar way. An artist is originally a man who turns away from reality because he cannot come to terms with the renunciation of instinctual satisfaction which it at first demands, and who allows his erotic and ambitious wishes full play in the life of phantasy. He finds a way back to reality, however, from this world of phantasy by making use of special gifts to mould his phantasies into truths of a new kind, which are valued by men as precious reflections of reality. Thus in a certain fashion, he actually becomes the hero, the king,

the creator, or the favourite he desired to be, without following the long roundabout path of making alterations in the external world. But he can only achieve this because other men feel the same dissatisfaction as he does with the renunciation demanded by reality, and because that dissatisfaction, which results from the replacement of the pleasure principle by the reality principle, is itself a part of reality.[17]

This is surely a strange conception of both art and artist. It implies that, though the artist wins out in the end, and may even escape neurosis, his art is still an indirect way of obtaining satisfactions which, if he was fully adapted to reality, would be unnecessary. Even those who admire and enjoy what the artist has produced are still turning away from reality in the direction of fantasy. The implication must be that art is primarily escapist and that, in an ideal world in which everyone had matured sufficiently to replace the pleasure principle by the reality principle, there would be no place for art.

Yet, in an earlier paper Freud had written:

But creative writers are valuable allies and their evidence is to be prized highly, for they are apt to know a whole host of things between heaven and earth of which our philosophy has not yet let us dream. In their knowledge of the mind they are far in advance of us everyday people, for they draw upon sources which we have not yet opened up for science.[18]

This is, perhaps, not quite such a positive view of the artist as it appears, since Freud is hinting that, once the sources upon which the artist draws have been opened up by science, so much will be known about the mind that the creative writer's art will not be needed. This is borne out by what Freud says about science in that same paper on the two principles of mental functioning from which I have already quoted. After noting that religions, also, advocate the post-ponement of immediate satisfaction, Freud writes:

> *Religions* have been able to effect absolute renunciation of pleasures in this life by means of the promise of compensation in a future existence; but they have not by this means achieved a conquest of the pleasure principle. It is *science* which comes nearest to succeeding in that conquest; science too, however, offers intellectual pleasures during its work and promises practical gain in the end.[19]

So science is to be equated with the abandonment of fantasy; with postponement of immediate satisfaction; with "secondary process" mental functioning; with thinking that is adapted to reality. Freud states that thinking acts as a restraint upon discharge:

> Thinking was endowed with characteristics which made it possible for the mental apparatus to tolerate an increased tension of stimulus whilst the process of discharge was postponed. It is essentially an experimental kind of acting, accompanied by displacement of relatively small quantities of cathexis together with less expenditure (discharge) of them.[20]

Freud also wrote, "It is one of the principal functions of our thinking to master the material of the external world psychically."[21]

Freud was certainly right in assuming that intellectual functioning is related to the ability to postpone responses to immediate stimuli. David Stenhouse, in his book *The Evolution of Intelligence,* defines intelligent behavior as "behaviour that is adaptively variable within the lifetime of the individual."[22] The lower we descend down the evolutionary scale, the more likely we are to find that behavior is not variable, but rather consists of preprogrammed, rigid, invariable responses to incoming stimuli. Stenhouse suggests that, if the evolution of intelligent behavior is to occur,

> the most important factor is that which gives the individual animal the power not to respond in the usual way to the stimulus-situation which previously initiated an instinctive sequence culminating in a consummatory act. This power not to respond may be absolute, or may be merely the ability to delay the response—withhold it provisionally as it were—but its absence would negate the very possibility of adaptive variability in behaviour.[23]

But is scientific thinking really so removed from the sphere of fantasy as Freud assumes? It is clear that, if scientific hypotheses are to gain acceptance, they must be related to the real world, and be proven to increase our understanding of how the real world functions. Although science progresses by the refutation of hypotheses, and each scientific theory is ultimately supplanted by another which includes still more phenomena within its grasp, yet each theory has to be proven by experiment and shown to correspond with external reality. But proving a scientific hypothesis is secondary. Scientific thinking takes its origin from fantasy in exactly the same way as telling stories or any other creative activity. Einstein attributed his creative success not to his abilities as a mathematician and physicist, but to his imagination. Einstein's own attempt to define "thinking" is worth quoting:

> What, precisely, is thinking? When at the reception of sense-impressions, memory pictures emerge, this is not yet "thinking." When, however, a certain picture turns up in many such series, then—precisely through such return—it becomes an ordering element for such series in that it connects series which in themselves are unconnected. Such an element becomes an instrument, a concept. I think that the transition from free associa-

tion or "dreaming" to thinking is characterized by the more or less dominating role which the "concept" plays in it. It is by no means necessary that a concept must be connected with a sensorily cognizable and reproducible sign (word); but when this is the case thinking becomes by means of that fact communicable.[24]

Einstein goes on to say that thinking is "a free play with concepts," and that the justification for this kind of thinking, far removed as it may still be from any consensus of what constitutes "truth," is that in this way the thinker can emancipate himself from the experience of the senses. In his *Notes for an Obituary*, Einstein wrote, "Perception of this world by thought, leaving out everything subjective, became, partly consciously, partly unconsciously, my supreme aim."[25] Einstein was sure that most thinking went on without the use of words and that it was, to a considerable degree, unconscious. Freud would have agreed with this part of Einstein's statement. Indeed, he wrote, "It is probable that thinking was originally unconscious, in so far as it went beyond mere ideational presentations and was directed to the relations between impressions of objects, and that it did not acquire further qualities, perceptible to consciousness, until it became connected with verbal residues."[26] But Freud goes on to say:

> With the introduction of the reality principle one species of thought-activity was split off; it was kept free from reality-testing and remained subordinated to the pleasure-principle alone. This activity is *phantasying*, which begins already in children's play, and later, continued as *day-dreaming*, abandons dependence on real objects.[27]

But are not the greatest achievements of the human mind only possible because human beings are capable of abandoning dependence on real objects, in other words, capable of fantasy? Is not Einstein's definition of thinking as "a free play with concepts" a form of what Freud pejoratively dismissed as fantasy? Freud treated fantasy as though it was always escapist, but this is not necessarily the case; nor is it true of dreams.

Freud, I believe, was never at ease when thinking strayed too far from the body and physical sensation, which seemed to him to constitute reality. Freudian interpretation always strives to reduce abstractions, such as the notion of beauty, to something physical. For example, Freud writes, "There is to my mind no doubt that the concept of 'beautiful' had its roots in sexual excitation and that its original meaning was 'sexually stimulating.' "[28]

For Einstein, creative thinking had to be as far removed from sense impressions as possible, since he regarded the latter as unreliable. Einstein wrote, "I believe that the first step in the setting up of a 'real external world' is the formation of the concept of bodily objects of various kinds." So far, Freud would have agreed with him. But Einstein goes on:

> The second step is to be found in the fact that, in our thinking (which determines our expectation), we attribute to this concept of the bodily object a significance, which is to a high degree independent of the sense impression which originally gives rise to it. This is what we mean when we attribute to the bodily object "a real existence." The justification of such a setting rests exclusively on the fact that, by means of such concepts and mental relations between them, we are able to orient ourselves in the labyrinth of sense impressions. These notions and relations, although free statements of our thoughts, appear to us as stronger and more alterable than the individual sense experience itself, the character of which as anything other than the result of an illusion or hallucination is never completely guaranteed.[29]

Einstein's new model of the universe depended upon his being able to emancipate himself from "real objects."

Indeed, in order to conceive the special theory of relativity, he had to free himself from the subjective prejudice implicit in being a dweller upon earth, and imagine how the universe would appear to an observer traveling at near the speed of light. Is not this fantasy, albeit fantasy which was later shown by experiment to explain phenomena which did not fit in with Newton's model?

It might be affirmed that my disagreement with Freud is no more than a semantic issue. Perhaps he is using the word fantasy in one sense, while I am using it in another. It is certainly true that there are such things as escapist fantasies and idle daydreams. These play their part in rather lowly forms of creative activity like "romantic" fiction or the James Bond novels of Ian Fleming. But not all fantasies are of this kind. Freud was convinced that all mental activity which was not dependent on "real objects" was mere wish fulfillment. Yet, just as play can be preparatory for, and hence directed toward, adult activities like fighting, hunting, and sexual intercourse, so daydreaming can also be a form of anticipatory practice. I have often daydreamed about the formidable task of delivering a lecture, and my fantasies about my auditors' shafts of criticism and expert scrutiny have made me more scrupulous in my presentation than I might otherwise have been.

Freud's theory of dreams is equally open to question. Freud was particularly enthusiastic about his dream theory. In his preface to the third English edition of *The Interpretation of Dreams*, he wrote, "Insight such as this falls to one's lot but once in a lifetime."[30] He even allowed himself the fantasy that, one day, a marble tablet would be placed on the house in which he first studied dreams seriously. This would read, "Here the secret of dreams was revealed to Dr. Sigm. Freud on July 24, 1895."[31] It is ironic that the discovery of which Freud was proudest does not withstand critical scrutiny. Freud's mature theory of dreams claims that every dream, even a nightmare or an anxiety dream, is an attempt to fulfill a wish; and that every dream represents a wish fulfillment dating from early childhood as well as a wish fulfillment from current mental life. Because these wishes are for the most part unacceptable, they appear in dreams in disguised form. Hence, what the dreamer actually recalls is only the "manifest content" of the dream. The true meaning of the dream, its so-called "latent content," can only be revealed when the dreamer's associations to the images in the dream have been subjected to psychoanalytical scrutiny and interpretation.

The function of the dream, Freud believed, was to preserve sleep by giving disguised expression to wishes of an aggressive or sexual kind which, if they had been allowed to occur to the dreamer in undisguised form, would have been likely to have wakened him.

Although dreams are not couched in the language of everyday speech, there is really no evidence that all dreams are concealing something unacceptable. Nor is there sufficient reason to believe that all dreams represent unfulfilled wishes, although this is certainly true of some. Freud himself recognized that an exception had to be made when considering the dreams of people who have been subjected to some "traumatic" incident, like an accident or an explosion. Such people often have dreams in which the incident itself recurs in undisguised form. Freud guessed that, in such cases, the dream might be an attempt at coming to terms with, or mastering, a disturbing stimulus; a way of looking at dreams which is actually more fruitful than Freud's original theory.

Jung, who cooperated with Freud for some years in the early 1900s, but who then parted company with him to found his own school, took a very different view of dreams. He did not consider that dreams were concealments, but rather that they were expressed in a symbolic language, which, though it might be difficult to understand, was, in essence, a natural form of human expression. Poetry is another kind of human utterance in which symbol and metaphor play a predominant role, but we do not think of most poetry as willfully obscure on this account.

Dreams seem frequently to be concerned with unsolved problems. A man I knew once dreamed that he was looking into the window of a shop. Inside was a statuette of a beautiful woman standing upon a square base. Since both the statuette and its base were made of some translucent material, the dreamer could see that there were letters carved upon the underside of the base. He knew that what was written there was "The Secret of Life." But because from his viewpoint the letters were both upside down and the wrong way round, he could not read them. A dream with an extraordinarily similar theme is reported by Dr. Rycroft in his book *The Innocence of Dreams.*[32] A man dreamed that he noticed in the window of an antique shop an old book which he knew contained "The Truth." On inquiring inside, he was told that the book was the only copy of an otherwise unknown work of Immanuel Kant. But it was written in a language which no one could understand.

These dreams do not provide solutions to the problems which they raise. Although most creative inspiration comes to people when they are in a state of reverie rather than actually asleep, there are a number of authentic instances of problem-solving during sleep, or of new ideas coming out of a dream. In one experiment, students were presented with a variety of difficult problems which they were required to study for fifteen minutes before going to sleep. Many had dreams related to the problems, and a few reported finding solutions. People have reported dreams in which a game of chess was played, an algebraic problem solved, and a bookkeeping error detected. Robert Louis Stevenson said that the plot of *Dr. Jekyll and Mr. Hyde* came to him in a dream; and the composer Tartini named a composition "The Devil's Trill Sonata" because he had a dream in which the Devil took up a violin and played it to him.

Stanley Palombo, in his book *Dreaming and Memory,*[33] suggests that dreaming is a way of processing information. During the day, every one of us is exposed to a vast number of incoming stimuli and presented with a mass of "information." Only a small proportion of this information will be remembered, even for a short time, and still less will be transferred from the short-term memory system to the long-term memory store. However, our adaptation to the environment is largely dependent upon our being able to compare our current experience with our past experience, which is stored in the memory. It is the unfamiliar which engages our attention, while we take the familiar for granted; but we only recognize the unfamiliar as being so because we have a memory of what has gone before. Palombo thinks that dreams are one way in which the experience of the day is matched with the residues of previous experience before being assigned to the long-term memory.

This theory of dreams goes some way to explaining why it is that dreams so often seem to be such a curious mixture of events of the previous day with memories from the remote past. There is a kind of scanning process going on, perhaps selecting things which go together because they share a similar emotional tone rather than because they happened together in time.

If we try to put together these varying notions of dreams—that they are concerned with mastering disturbing experiences; that they are sometimes attempts at solving problems; and that they may be a way of processing information—we might hazard the proposition that dreams are in some way an attempt of the mind to order its own experience. This is borne out by the fact that so many dreams are cast in the form of a story which links together the various episodes of the dream, however absurd or incongruous these separate episodes may appear.

Many forms of play are also concerned with order. In his book *Homo Ludens*, Johan Huizinga, the Dutch historian, convincingly supposes that play is the primeval soil in which all cultural manifestations are rooted. Without play, we should have neither craft nor art, neither poetry nor music. Huizinga points out that

> in some languages the manipulation of musical instruments is called "playing," to wit, in the Arabic language on the one hand and the Germanic and Slavonic on the other. Since this semantic understanding between East and West can hardly be ascribed to borrowing or coincidence, we have to assume some deep-rooted psychological reason for so remarkable a symbol of the affinity between music and play.[34]

Games, also, are a way of ordering experience. Games allow for the controlled expression and mastery of competitive and aggressive impulses within a structure of rules and defined area or framework like a playing field.

So it appears that the three activities, play, fantasy, and dreaming, which Freud linked together as escapist or hallucinatory, can equally well be regarded as adaptive; as attempts to come to terms with reality, rather than to escape from it; as ways of selecting from, and making new combinations out of, our experience of both the external world and the inner world of the psyche. None of these activities is as far removed from "thinking" as they appeared to him; and, as we have seen, Freud considered that a principal function of thinking was to master the material of the external world psychically.

If Freud had been able to accept that play, fantasy, and dreaming were attempts to come to terms with, and master, reality rather than to escape from it, he would not have had to lay down his arms before the problem of the creative artist nor have felt that the grandest creations of art were unsolved riddles to his understanding. Art and science, though very different activities, have certain aims in common. Both are concerned with seeking order in complexity, and unity in diversity. As the Gestalt psychologists were the first to affirm, the human tendency toward pattern-making is inborn and inescapable. We cannot see three dots but that we make them into a triangle. Human beings have to order their experience, both spatially and temporally, as part of their biological adaptation to reality, and the forces which impel them to do so are just as "instinctive" as sex. Although Freud did not call it that, I am sure that he appreciated the aesthetic aspect of scientific discovery; the intense satisfaction which accompanies solving a problem or inventing a new explanatory principle. The "eureka" experience is a pleasure closely allied to aesthetic appreciation; for part of what we admire about a painting or a piece of music is the order which the artist has imposed upon what would otherwise have appeared disconnected or chaotic. The nearest Freud comes to acknowledging this kind of pleasure is in his book on jokes. Having recognized that all jokes are tendentious, that is, ways of expressing sexual or aggressive feelings, he reluctantly admits that the techniques of jokes are themselves sources of pleasure. When things which appear incongruous are linked together, Freud supposes that we are economizing our expenditure of psychic energy. This brings pleasure, but of a rather minor variety. Freud calls it a "fore-pleasure"; that is, a slight pleasure which leads on to and makes possible a much greater pleasure. Freud supposes that the form in which writers dress up their fantasies is a kind of fore-pleasure or "incentive bonus" designed to bribe the reader into enjoying something much deeper; the work's imaginative content, which the writer had to clothe in enticing form in order to make it acceptable.

Because Freud thought of the id as a chaotic cauldron of seething instincts entirely governed by the pleasure principle, in which form was notably lacking, he regarded the need to select, to order, and to impose form upon experience as predominantly a conscious, rational phenomenon. Modern psychoanalysts, particularly Marion Milner and Anton Ehrenzweig, have realized that the drive toward order arises unconsciously. Indeed, Ehrenzweig called his last, posthumously published book *The Hidden Order of Art*.[35]

Sir Ernst Gombrich, in his book *The Sense of Order*,[36] links man's need for pattern-making with his exploratory tendencies. In discovering more about our environment we create internal patterns or schemata. By doing so, we reduce the need to pay equal attention to every impinging stimulus, and only need to take notice of those stimuli which are novel; that is, those which do not fit in with our preformed schemata. A simple instance of this is descending a straight staircase. We only need to pay detailed attention to where it begins and ends, because we assume that each stair will be the same height and width as its fellows. Information theory, originally derived from practical work with telephone cables and other carriers of information, has thrown light on how we economize our intake by taking parts for wholes, and only pay attention to the unexpected. If we had no prior conception of regularity, we could not begin to make corrections to it; and if there were no regularities at all, our environment would be entirely unpredictable; a nightmare, as Gombrich calls it. One modern theory of schizophrenia suggests that sufferers lack some aspect of selective discrimination. Overwhelmed by stimuli which they can neither order nor disregard, they are compelled to withdraw as far as possible from the impact of the world.

As we have seen, Freud's idea was that the motivation of the artist and the motivation of the scientist could be sharply distinguished. The driving force behind the artist's need to create was unsatisfied instinct, expressing itself originally in escapist fantasy. The driving force behind the scientist's activity (about which Freud says little) is to master the material of the external world psychically. I hope I have convinced you that these two creative activities have more in common than Freud supposed. Both artists and scientists are concerned with creating order, a basic drive or need which, because we share it, makes us able to appreciate, and perhaps envy, what the great creators achieve.

This way of looking at creative endeavor raises an obvious problem. If scientific and artistic creativity have so much in common, in what ways are they different? It is clear that a scientific hypothesis is not a work of art, nor is a work of art a scientific hypothesis.

Leonard Meyer, discussing this question in his paper "Concerning the Sciences, the Arts—AND the Humanities,"[37] points out that scientists are discovering something which is already there, like the double helix, whereas artists create something which has never previously existed, like the C-sharp minor quartet of Beethoven. We assume, with good reason, that the structure of the DNA molecule was, and always has been, the same. Watson and Crick did not create its structure but discovered it. But nothing like the C-sharp minor quartet existed before Beethoven composed it. He did not discover it; he created it.

Meyer goes on to point out that there is a temporal progress in science which makes even the greatest generalizations, like Newton's law of universal gravitation, out of date. It follows that scientists have no need to study in detail the original papers of Newton or any other innovator, since their discoveries will have become part of the general scientific edifice.

The same is not true of works of art. Although styles change in the course of time, Beethoven is not an advance on Mozart, nor Picasso on Cézanne: they are simply different. Students of music and painting need to study all four. Meyer discusses a number of other differences which I need not pursue. What I am concerned with here is the similarity between the actual process of creative discovery as it takes place in the mind of an artist and that in the mind of a scientist. A new scientific hypothesis and a new work of art have in common that both are the product of mental activity in which abstraction, fantasy, and playing with various com-

binations of concepts all take part. Often, both are concerned with combining and transcending opposites. In my
paper "Individuation and the Creative Process,"[38] I have
taken as a scientific example Newton's synthesis between the
discoveries of Kepler and those of Galileo, which resulted in
a theory which transcended both: the law of universal gravitation. This is a classic example of how two sets of laws
which were previously thought to be entirely separate could
be both reconciled and superseded by a new hypothesis.

My example from the arts was Beethoven's "Grosse Fuge,"
the movement originally designed as the final movement of
the Quartet in B-flat, opus 130. Martin Cooper wrote of
this:

> What grips the listener is the dramatic experience of
> forcing—for there is frequently a sense of violence in
> this mastery—two themes which have, by nature, noth-
> ing in common, to breed and produce a race of giants,
> episodes or variations that have no parallel in musical
> history.[39]

Newton's synthesis is concerned with the facts of the external world; Beethoven's with what he found in his internal
world. It seems to me probable that the mental processes
employed by each man of genius in seeking his solution
were not dissimilar.

Whereas the scientist is pointed toward discovering order
in the external world, the artist is directed toward creating
order within: toward making sense out of his subjective
experience. What points the scientist in one direction, the
artist in the other, is still obscure—although Liam Hudson
has thrown some light upon the subject in his studies of the
temperamental differences between young people who
choose the arts and those who choose the sciences as subjects
of study. Both types of creativity are, I believe, motivated by
a "divine discontent" which is part of man's biological
endowment. Mystery and disorder spur man to discovery, to

the creation of new hypotheses which bring order and pattern to the maze of phenomena. But mystery and disorder pertain to our own natures as well as to the external world. I venture to suggest that, just as it is inconceivable that all the laws of Nature will ever be discovered, so it is equally impossible to believe that the complexities of human nature can ever be grasped in their entirety.

> Ah, but a man's reach should exceed his grasp,
> Or what's a heaven for?[40]

NOTES

1. *The Standard Edition of the Complete Psychological Works of Sigmund Freud,* 24 vols., ed. and trans. James Strachey (London: Hogarth Press, 1953–64), 21:213–14.
2. Sigmund Freud, "Some Early Unpublished Letters," *International Journal of Psycho-Analysis* 50 (1969):425.
3. Harry Freud, "My Uncle Sigmund," in *Freud As We Knew Him,* ed. Hendrik M. Ruitenbeek (Detroit: Wayne State University Press, 1973), p. 313.
4. Freud, *Standard Edition,* 13:211–12.
5. Edmund Engelman, *Bergasse 19: Sigmund Freud's Home and Offices, Vienna 1938* (New York: Basic Books, 1976).
6. Freud, *Standard Edition,* 20:65.
7. Ibid., 21:177.
8. Ibid., 11:59–137.
9. Anna Freud, *The Ego and the Mechanisms of Defence* (London: Hogarth Press, 1968), p. 44.
10. Freud, *Standard Edition,* 16:376.
11. Ibid., 9:145.
12. Ibid., 9:144.
13. Ibid., 9:146.
14. Ibid., 12:218.
15. Ibid., 12:219.
16. Ibid.
17. Ibid., 12:224.
18. Ibid., 9:8.
19. Ibid., 12:223–4.

20. Ibid., 12:221.

21. Ibid., 21:212.

22. David Stenhouse, *The Evolution of Intelligence; A General Theory and Some of Its Implications* (London: Allen and Unwin, 1974), p. 31.

23. Ibid., p. 67.

24. Quoted in Paul Arthur Schilpp, ed., *Albert Einstein: Philosopher-Scientist* (Evanston, Ill.: Library of Living Philosophers, 1949), pp. 7–8.

25. Quoted in Antonina Vallentin, *Einstein: A Biography* (London: Weidenfeld and Nicolson, 1954), p. 9.

26. Freud, *Standard Edition,* 12:221.

27. Ibid., 12:222.

28. Ibid., 7:156.

29. Albert Einstein, *Out of My Later Years* (London: Greenwood Press, 1956), pp. 60–61.

30. Freud, *Standard Edition,* 4:xxxii.

31. Ernest Jones, *The Young Freud 1856–1900,* vol. 1 of *Life and Work of Sigmund Freud* (London: Hogarth Press, 1953), p. 388.

32. Charles Rycroft, *The Innocence of Dreams* (London: Hogarth Press, 1979), p. 124.

33. Stanley Palombo, *Dreaming and Memory: A New Information-Processing Model* (New York: Basic Books, 1978).

34. Johan Huizinga, *Homo Ludens: A Study of the Play Element in Culture* (London: Maurice Temple Smith, 1970), p. 182.

35. Anton Ehrenzweig, *The Hidden Order of Art: A Study in the Psychology of Artistic Imagination* (London: Weidenfeld and Nicolson, 1967).

36. Ernst Gombrich, *The Sense of Order: A Study in the Psychology of Decorative Art* (Oxford: Phaidon, 1979).

37. Leonard Meyer, "Concerning the Sciences, the Arts—AND the Humanities," *Critical Inquiry* 1 (September 1974):163–217.

38. Anthony Storr, "Individuation and the Creative Process," *Journal of Analytical Psychology* 28 (1983):329–43.

39. Martin Cooper, *Beethoven: The Last Decade* (Oxford: Oxford University Press, 1970), pp. 388–89.

40. Robert Browning, *Andrea del Sarto,* lines 97–98.

8

Intimations of Mystery

IN HIS LECTURE "Belief and Creativity" William Golding writes, "I have always felt that a writer's books should be as different from each other as possible."[1] He doesn't tell us why, and professes to envy those authors who write the same book over and over again. I suspect that he is a man who feels compelled to challenge himself; always to set himself new tasks, to solve new problems. I have just reread all his published novels, and they are indeed so different from one another that it is hard to delineate connecting threads. The studied pastiche of *Rites of Passage* is remote from the visionary passion of *The Spire*. The ostensibly autobiographical *Free Fall* has next to nothing in common with *The Inheritors*. Yet, because this series of very different books is the work of one man, however many-sided, it must be possible to find some linking factors, some vision of man's nature which runs through all his work.

Bertrand Russell wrote of Joseph Conrad, "He thought of civilized and morally tolerable human life as a dangerous walk on a thin crust of barely cooled lava which at any moment might break and let the unwary sink into fiery depths."[2] I think these words apply equally to William Golding. Although Golding calls himself an optimist, there is little evidence in his novels to support that claim. The madness of violence, of lust, and of fanaticism seem always just below the surface. Like Koestler, Golding sees man as a species which is irredeemably flawed, and which is only too likely to bring about its own destruction. This is, of course, particularly obvious in what is still his most popular book, *Lord of the Flies*. Has Golding ever read accounts of those American experiments in which boys were taken to a holiday camp, divided into two groups, and set against each other? The experiments had to be brought to an end lest murder be committed. Golding doesn't need to read such mundane stuff. He knows it all already, both from his experience as a schoolmaster and from searching his own heart. "Kill the pig. Cut her throat. Spill her blood."[3] A savage chant and the putting on of war paint are enough to make Jack and his hunters lose their inhibitions against violence. The signal fire forgotten, it isn't long before the sand is stained with human blood as well as with that of pigs.

Sex, also, is more a matter of violent compulsion than of loving tenderness. Golding hates Freud, as well as Marx and Darwin. He calls them "the three most crashing bores of the Western world."[4] Yet, in *The Inheritors*, when Lok and Fa observe two of "the new people" having sexual intercourse, it looks to them like a fight:

> The two people beneath the tree were making noises fiercely as though they were quarrelling. In particular the woman had begun to hoot like an owl and Lok could hear Tuami gasping like a man who fights with an animal and does not think he will win. He looked down at them and saw that Tuami was not only lying with the fat woman but eating her as well for there was black blood running from the lobe of her ear.[5]

Golding may dislike Freud, but this is precisely Freud's picture of the child's interpretation of the "primal scene": "If children at this early age witness sexual intercourse between adults . . . they inevitably regard the sexual act as a sort of ill-treatment or act of subjugation: they view it, that is, in a sadistic sense."[6]

Sadism crops up in other places in Golding's work. Evie, the tarty girl in *The Pyramid*, cries, "Hurt me, Olly! *Hurt* me—"[7] But, at eighteen, he doesn't know how to hurt her, nor how to adapt to the sexual rhythm she requires. Evie allows Captain Wilmot to beat her, and shocks the adolescent Oliver when her weals are displayed. In *Pincher Martin*, Mary so maddens Chris by her poised inaccessibility that he fantasizes:

> Those nights of imagined copulation, when one thought not of love nor sensation nor comfort nor triumph, but of torture rather, the very rhythm of the body reinforced by hissed ejaculations—take that and that! That for your pursed mouth and that for your pink patches, your closed knees, your impregnable balance on the high, female shoes—and that if it kills you for your magic and your isled virtue![8]

She agrees to go out with him, refuses to comply. Driving dangerously enough to scare her, he brings the car to a screaming stop and attempts to rape her on the verge of the road. In *Free Fall*, Sammy is frustrated by the utter passivity of Beatrice, the girl he adores but whom he cannot get to respond to him:

> What had been love on my part, passionate and reverent, what was to be a triumphant sharing, a fusion, the penetration of a secret, raising of my life to the enigmatic and holy level of hers became a desperately shoddy and cruel attempt to force a response from her somehow. Step by step we descended the path of sexual exploitation until the projected sharing had become an infliction.[9]

The relationship doesn't last. Sammy finds himself another girl, and the passive Beatrice ends up in a mental hospital, with Sammy wondering whether he is responsible for her total retreat into chronic mental illness. In *The Paper Men*,

Wilfred Barclay behaves with the utmost cruelty to Rick, the American academic who is pursuing him; the sadism of power rather than of sex, but sadism nonetheless.

Golding dislikes homosexuality, but he is expert at describing its compulsions. The inhibited, paranoid Father Watts-Watt in *Free Fall;* the drunken, effeminate Mr. de Tracy in *The Pyramid;* the egregious, pedophilic Mr. Pedigree in *Darkness Visible;* the appalling Mr. Colley in *Rites of Passage*—all are memorable figures whose sexual preferences are even more central to their personalities than those of Golding's heterosexual characters. But, whatever the nature of the sexual impulse, in whatever direction it is pointed, it seems, in Golding's work, to be as much pain as it is pleasure. Moreover, sex never seems to be integrated as part of the whole man or woman. It remains something which takes over, subdues the will, and forces the subject, often against his own intention, to comply with a compulsion over which he has no control.

Sex is not the only emotion which takes over the individual. Golding has a pre-Freudian vision of man in which the notion of repression plays little part. He thinks much more in terms of dissociation and even of possession. Actual loss of consciousness is surprisingly common in the novels. Simon, the Christ figure in *Lord of the Flies,* is an epileptic. He loses consciousness, not only on his first appearance in the book, but also after the pig's head delivers its sermon to him. It is worth recalling that epilepsy was called the "sacred" malady until Hippocrates affirmed that it had natural causes. In *Darkness Visible,* Sophy suddenly loses consciousness at a party when presented with a Rorschach inkblot which everyone else sees as part of a game. She does so again after her terrifying fantasy of murdering the kidnapped boy. Earlier in the same book, Matty loses consciousness twice after his agonizing encounter with the aborigine. De Tracy passes out from alcohol in *The Pyramid.* Confronted with an image of Christ, Wilfred Barclay, the alcoholic, pursued author in *The Paper Men,* loses consciousness

and wakes up in hospital: "Surrounded, swamped, con-
founded, all but destroyed, adrift in the universal intolerance, mouth open, screaming, bepissed and beshitten, I
knew my maker and I fell down."[10] Sammy nearly faints
after his encounter with the psychotic Beatrice in *Free Fall.*
Jocelin, in *The Spire,* loses consciousness more than once,
and, when dying, has an "out-of-body" experience of the
kind often described by those who have been close to death.

Nor are faints, fits, and drink the only things to obliterate
normal consciousness. Madness is never far away. It takes
over Miss Bounce in *The Pyramid* as well as Beatrice in *Free
Fall.* It hovers round the heads of both Jocelin and Roger
Mason in *The Spire.* It is an essential ingredient in *Pincher
Martin:* "There is always madness, a refuge like a crevice in
the rock. A man who has no more defence can always creep
into madness like one of those armoured things that scuttle
among weed down where the mussels are."[11]

Golding acknowledges his belief in God, but his vision is
not that of a Christian. It is closer to that of the ancient
Greeks, in whose language and literature he is so profoundly steeped. The Greeks believed that the onslaughts of
passion which assail human beings were the work of the
gods rather than the responsibility of men themselves. Lust,
aggression, ecstasy, inspiration, and prophecy possess men
unpredictably and are not within human control. Emotions
appear from nowhere, and have to be examined and evaluated before they can be understood. In *The Inheritors,* when
Liku has been captured by "the new people," Lok "examined the feeling of heaviness in his head and body. There
was no doubt at all. The feeling was connected with Liku."[12]
Later, when Fa's tracks and scent have disappeared,

> Lok began to bend. His knees touched the ground, his
> hands reached down and took his weight slowly, and
> with all his strength he clutched himself into the earth.
> He writhed himself against the dead leaves and twigs,
> his head came up, turned, and his eyes swept round,

astonished eyes over a mouth that was strained open.
The sound of mourning burst out of his mouth,
prolonged, harsh, pain-sound, man-sound. . . . He
clutched at the bushes as the tides of feeling swirled
through him and howled at the top of his voice.[13]

Lok is not *homo sapiens,* but, in Golding's vision, although *homo sapiens* has developed language to a greater extent than Lok, he has not gained much more control over his emotions, nor integrated them as part of the totality of his being.

It is partly for this reason that, in Golding, human identity is more fluid, more easily lost or dissolved than in the work of other writers. The sense of continuing identity is, for most people, rooted in the body. There are passages in Golding's novels in which dissociation from the body is as complete as it often is in Kafka. In *Pincher Martin,* the drowning man's "mind inside the dark skull made swimming movements long after the body lay motionless in the water."[14] Later, when the sea has deposited him on the rock, "The hardnesses under his cheek began to insist. They passed through pressure to a burning without heat, to a localized pain. They became vicious in their insistence like the nag of an aching tooth. They began to pull him back into himself and organize him again as a single being."[15] This experience of dissociation from the body is like that experienced in high fever or other serious illness. Virginia Woolf describes something similar in *The Voyage Out.* Has Golding ever been seriously ill? The description of Sammy Mountjoy's mastoid in *Free Fall,* as well as Jocelin's "out-of-body" experience referred to above, suggests the possibility.

However this may be, Christopher Hadley Martin, alone on his rock in mid-Atlantic, asks himself:

How can I have a complete identity without a mirror?
That is what has changed me. Once I was a man with
twenty photographs of myself—myself as this and that
with the signature scrawled across the bottom right-
hand corner as a stamp and seal. Even when I was in the

Navy there was that photograph in my identity card so
that every now and then I could look and see who I
was.[16]

One might argue that Martin was an actor, a role player with
less than average sense of being continuously the same person, but the theme of uncertain identity recurs too often for
this to be a convincing explanation. "What is it like to be
you?" asks the adolescent Sammy in *Free Fall* of his girlfriend
Beatrice. "What is it like in the bath and the lavatory and
walking the pavement with shorter steps and high heels;
what is it like to know your body breathes this faint perfume
which makes my heart burst and my senses swim?"[17] A
natural enough inquiry for an adolescent who is still in the
business of self-discovery, but this quest for identity is persistent in other contexts. In *Darkness Visible*, Matty recurrently
confronts those dreaded questions, "What am I for? What
am I?" In *Free Fall*, the Nazi interrogator, Dr. Halde,
says:

> "There is no health in you, Mr. Mountjoy. You do not
> believe in anything enough to suffer for it or be glad.
> There is no point at which something has knocked on
> your door and taken possession of you. You possess
> yourself. Intellectual ideas, even the idea of loyalty to
> your own country, sit on you loosely. You wait in a dusty
> waiting-room on no particular line for no particular
> train. And between the poles of belief, I mean the belief
> in material things and the belief in a world made and
> supported by a supreme being, you oscillate jerkily
> from day to day, from hour to hour."[18]

A novelist who wants to write a series of books as different
from one another as possible is better off without too rigid a
set of beliefs or too fixed a sense of his own identity. One
recalls Keats's famous letter to Richard Woodhouse in which
he affirms, "A Poet is the most unpoetical of anything in
existence; because he has no Identity—he is continually in
for—and filling some other body.[19] One way of looking at
Golding's novels is to see them as a voyage through all the

contradictory possibilities he finds within himself; a quest
for some sort of coherence and consistency:

> Yet I am a burning amateur, torn by the irrational
> and incoherent, violently searching and self-con-
> demned. . . . I have hung all systems on the wall like a
> row of useless hats. They do not fit. They come in from
> outside, they are suggested patterns, some dull and
> some of great beauty. But I have lived enough of my life
> to require a pattern that fits over everything I know;
> and where shall I find that?[20]

Has Golding found such a pattern? One should not
assume that he shares the requirements of a character he
invents, and, as we have already seen, he is profoundly intolerant of those great reductionist pattern-makers Darwin,
Marx, and Freud. We know from his most revealing lecture,
"Belief and Creativity," that he believes in God, and in both
the truth and the mystery of the imagination. Golding has
one of the most powerful imaginations of any living writer,
which is why he convinces even at his most obscure. It seems
to me that he believes that imagination can sometimes penetrate what, in *Darkness Visible,* the captain who rescues the
child Matty calls "the screen that conceals the working of
things."[21] This is what gives the poet and the novelist absolute conviction, the "voice of authority, power" to which
Golding refers in his lecture.[22] It is a profoundly irrational,
anti-intellectual view of reality; and so it is not surprising
that, in the novels, it often seems to be the primitive or the
simple who come closest to it. *The Inheritors* used to be, and
may still be, Golding's own favorite among his novels. The
"pictures" which Lok and his fellow creatures share are both
precursors of thought and intimations of a reality which
thought cannot penetrate. In *Darkness Visible,* poor, ugly,
burned Matty may perform inexplicable rituals and have psychotic visions, but he finally "knows" what he is for more
clearly than do any of the more conventional characters.
Golding believes that the violence of our century is, at bot-

tom, a revolt against reductionism. Perhaps this is what he is getting at when, in *Darkness Visible,* a truth appears in the mind of Sophy: *"The way towards simplicity is through outrage."*[23]

I count myself fortunate in having known William Golding for over twenty years. He and some of his best work are still mysterious to me. He would not want this any other way, nor would I. Intimations of mystery are what the twentieth century needs.

NOTES

References are to William Golding's books unless otherwise indicated.

1. *A Moving Target* (London: Faber and Faber, 1982), p. 198.
2. Bertrand Russell, *Portraits from Memory and Other Essays* (London: Allen and Unwin, 1956), p. 82.
3. *Lord of the Flies* (London: Faber and Faber, 1954), p. 86.
4. *A Moving Target,* pp. 186–87.
5. *The Inheritors* (London: Faber and Faber, 1955), p. 175.
6. *The Standard Edition of the Complete Psychological Works of Sigmund Freud,* 24 vols., ed. and trans. James Strachey (London: Hogarth Press, 1953–64), 7:196.
7. *The Pyramid* (London: Faber and Faber, 1967), p. 79.
8. *Pincher Martin* (London: Faber and Faber, 1956), p. 149.
9. *Free Fall* (London: Faber and Faber, 1959), pp. 122–23.
10. *The Paper Men* (London: Faber and Faber, 1984), p. 123.
11. *Pincher Martin,* p. 186.
12. *The Inheritors,* p. 130.
13. Ibid., pp. 190, 191.
14. *Pincher Martin,* p. 16.
15. Ibid., p. 24.
16. Ibid., p. 132.
17. *Free Fall,* pp. 103–4.
18. Ibid., p. 144.
19. *The Letters of John Keats,* ed. M. B. Forman (Oxford: Oxford University Press, 1935), p. 228.
20. *Free Fall,* pp. 5, 6.
21. *Darkness Visible* (London: Faber and Faber, 1979), p. 16.
22. *A Moving Target,* p. 193.
23. *Darkness Visible,* p. 167.

9

Jung's Conception of Personality

ALL CONCEPTIONS OF personality are, to a varying extent, subjective. Jung's idea of the person is no exception. It was influenced by his family background, by the time at which he lived, by his reading and education, and by the fact that he was a citizen of German-speaking Switzerland. It is therefore appropriate to give a brief outline of Jung's origins.

Carl Gustav Jung was born on July 26, 1875. His father was a minister in the Swiss Reformed Church. The greater part of his early childhood was passed at Klein-Hüningen, near Basel, to which the family moved in 1879. For his first nine years, Jung remained an only child who lived primarily in his imagination and who spent much of his time in solitary play. The birth of his much younger sister did little to alleviate Jung's solitude.

He attended the local school; but, being more intelligent than most of his schoolfellows, attracted a certain amount of competitive hostility. In his eleventh year, he was moved to the gymnasium in Basel. From there, he went to Basel University. Jung originally wished to study archaeology; but there was no teacher in this subject at Basel University, and, since the family was far from rich, he was dependent upon a grant which applied only to his local university. He therefore decided to read medicine, but continued to feel that this choice was something of a compromise. However, his interest in the past found fulfillment in studying evolutionary theory and comparative anatomy. Jung came to think of the mind as having an immensely long history; as functioning along lines laid down in the remote past. I believe that this view of mind took origin from his anatomical studies. If the structures of the body had been adaptively evolved over many centuries, the same consideration might reasonably apply to the structures of the mind.

As he approached the end of his medical studies, Jung was in debt and realized that he would have to earn a living as soon as possible. At first he was inclined toward surgery. Then, he happened to read a textbook by the Viennese psychiatrist Krafft-Ebing, and at once realized in what field his future lay. In December 1900, Jung became an assistant at the Burghölzli Mental Hospital in Zürich, which was then under the direction of Eugen Bleuler, the pioneer investigator of schizophrenia. In 1902, his M.D. dissertation, *On the Psychology and Pathology of So-Called Occult Phenomena*, was published. During the winter of 1902–1903, Jung spent a term at the Salpêtrière in Paris in order to study psychopathology with Pierre Janet. This was the same famous hospital at which Freud had studied with Charcot in 1885–1886. In 1903, Jung married Emma Rauschenbach, by whom he had a son and four daughters. In 1905, Jung was promoted to senior staff physician at the Burghölzli and was also appointed as lecturer in psychiatry at the University of Zürich.

In 1907, Jung published his original study of schizophrenia, *The Psychology of Dementia Praecox*. He sent a copy to Freud, whom he met for the first time in Vienna in March of the same year. In 1909, Jung visited the United States with

Freud and Ferenczi, and was given an honorary degree by Clark University. In the same year, he gave up his post at the Burghölzli in favor of his growing private practice.

Jung's break with Freud occurred in 1913. Following this, Jung went through a period of intense personal crisis, and resigned his lectureship at the University of Zürich. He continued to write and practice at his house in Küsnacht on the Lake of Zürich until his death in 1961.

Although Jung was, for a time, strongly influenced by Freud, it is important to realize that he had carried out a great deal of original work before he even met Freud. The main ideas which coalesced to form his picture of human personality can be traced to earlier periods in his development. Jung was never an uncritical Freudian disciple. The differences between the two men were evident from the beginning.

Jung's earliest work and his later writings are linked by the theme that mental illness is characterized by disunity of the personality, while mental health is manifested by unity. Jung's doctoral thesis was a study of a fifteen-and-a-half-year-old cousin of his, Hélène Preiswerk, who, claiming to be a medium, said that she was "controlled" by a variety of different personalities. Jung interpreted these as being personifications of various unconscious parts of herself; subsidiary, incomplete personalities which could temporarily take over.

It will be recalled that, at the turn of the century, psychiatrists were fascinated by cases of so-called "multiple personality" like Morton Prince's famous case of Sally Beauchamp. Pierre Janet was particularly interested in cases of this kind, described several examples from his own practice, and had reviewed the literature. Janet believed that neurosis was due to some physiological deficiency in the nervous system which prevented cohesion of the various aspects of personality. This lack of integration resulted in aspects of consciousness becoming split off and dissociated.

Jung was as much influenced by Janet, with whom he had studied, as he was by Freud, with whose opinions he came more and more to disagree. Although Jung valued Freud's concept of repression, he continued to think of personality as being capable of dissociation into subsidiary personalities, in line with Janet's ideas. In hysteria, for example, the patient might behave like his young cousin; as if she were two or more different persons who had no cognizance of each other. It followed that the treatment of this type of neurosis depended upon making these divided selves aware of each other and thus creating a new unity of personality.

In schizophrenia, it appeared to Jung that the personality was fragmented into many parts, rather than into two or three, as in hysteria. Jung wrote:

> Whereas in the healthy person the ego is the subject of his experience, in the schizophrenic the ego is only *one* of the experiencing subjects. In other words, in schizophrenia the normal subject has split into a plurality of subjects, or into a plurality of *autonomous complexes*.[1]

Jung's next group of studies was based upon the use of word-association tests. A list of one hundred words is read out, and the subject is asked to respond to each with the first word that occurs to him. By timing the interval between stimulus and response with a stopwatch, it becomes possible to demonstrate that, unknown to themselves, subjects are influenced by words which arouse emotion. Such words have the effect of slowing down their responses. Often, groups of words are linked around a single theme; and to such a collection of associations Jung gave the name *complex,* a term which he introduced into psychiatry. These experiments were important in that they demonstrated objectively, in ways which could be measured, the dynamic effects of unconscious mental processes. Jung gives as an example the case of a normal man of thirty-five whom he himself tested:

To begin with, it was the word *knife* that caused four disturbed reactions. The next disturbance was *lance* (or *spear*) and then *to beat*, then the word *pointed* and then *bottle*. That was in a short series of fifty stimulus words, which was enough for me to tell the man point-blank what the matter was. So I said: "I did not know you had such a disagreeable experience." He stared at me and said: "I do not know what you are talking about." I said: "You know you were drunk and had a disagreeable affair with sticking your knife into somebody." He said: "How do you know?" Then he confessed the whole thing. He came of a respectable family, simple but quite nice people. He had been abroad and one day got into a drunken quarrel, drew a knife and stuck it into somebody and got a year in prison. That is a great secret which he does not mention because it would cast a shadow on his life.[2]

The group of words connected with the incident constitutes a complex, which Jung defined as

the *image* of a certain psychic situation which is strongly accentuated emotionally and is, moreover, incompatible with the habitual attitude of consciousness. This image has a powerful inner coherence, it has its own wholeness and, in addition, a relatively high degree of autonomy, so that it is subject to the control of the conscious mind to only a limited extent, and therefore behaves like an animated foreign body in the sphere of consciousness.[3]

Jung referred to complexes as being fragmentary personalities. Often, they interfere with what the person consciously wants to do. They are responsible for those slips of the tongue which Freud described in his book *The Psychopathology of Everyday Life*. Jung wrote:

They slip just the wrong word into one's mouth, they make one forget the name of the person one is about to introduce, they cause a tickle in the throat just when the softest passage is being played on the piano at a concert, they make the tiptoeing latecomer trip over a chair with a resounding crash.[4]

Jung goes on to say that complexes appear in personified form in dreams, and also as hallucinatory "voices" in schizophrenia. The extremes of dissociation and splitting were found in the psychotic; but even normal people suffered from "complexes," and in this way demonstrated some degree of dissociation within the psyche.

Jung was deeply influenced by his clinical experience within the Burghölzli mental hospital. Although he gave up his hospital post in 1909, and from that time onward was chiefly concerned with the treatment of ambulant neurotics, he remained fascinated by schizophrenia. His last paper on the subject appeared in 1957, only four years before his death. Many of the disagreements which led to the rift between Jung and Freud can be traced to the difference in their clinical experience. Freud worked in a mental hospital for only three weeks, as a *locum tenens*. His experience with psychotic patients was minimal. Although he wrote a long study of Schreber, the judge with paranoia, this was based upon the patient's own writings, not upon any actual encounter with him. Jung was the first psychiatrist to apply psychoanalytic ideas to the study of delusions and hallucinations, and to demonstrate that such phenomena, hitherto dismissed as incomprehensible, could be shown to have a psychological origin and meaning. He believed that many cases of obsessional neurosis and hysteria were really cases of latent schizophrenia, and warned against the danger of precipitating psychotic breakdown by unwise psychotherapeutic intervention. On the other hand, Jung considered that psychotherapy did have a limited part to play in the treatment of schizophrenia, and gives examples of cases which he treated with partial success.

It was Jung's experience with psychotic patients which led him to postulate a "collective" unconscious. He found that delusions and hallucinations could seldom be explained in terms of the patient's personal history. Jung's extensive knowledge of comparative religion and mythology led him to detect parallels with psychotic material which argued a common source: a myth-producing level of mind which was common to all men. Jung described the collective unconscious as consisting of mythological motifs or primordial images to which he gave the name "archetypes." Archetypes are not inborn ideas, but "typical forms of behaviour which, once they become conscious, naturally present themselves *as ideas and images,* like everything else that becomes a content of consciousness."5

The kind of observation which led Jung to this conclusion is illustrated by the case of a man in his thirties who was suffering from paranoid schizophrenia. Jung encountered him in the corridor of the hospital:

> One day I came across him there, blinking through the window up at the sun, and moving his head from side to side in a curious manner. He took me by the arm and said he wanted to show me something. He said I must look at the sun with my eyes half shut, and then I could see the sun's phallus. If I moved my head from side to side the sun-phallus would move too, and that was the origin of the wind.

Four years later, Jung came across a Greek text, thought to be a liturgy of the Mithraic cult, in which a vision is described.

> "And likewise the so-called tube the origin of the ministering wind. For you will see hanging down from the disc of the sun something that looks like a tube. And towards the regions westward it is as though there were an infinite east wind. But if the other wind should

prevail towards the regions of the east, you will in like
manner see the vision veering in that direction."[6]

Jung goes on to point out that certain medieval paintings
depict the Virgin as being impregnated from Heaven by
means of a tube down which the Holy Ghost descends. The
Holy Ghost was originally thought of as a rushing, mighty
wind: the *pneuma*.

Freud thought of the unconscious as chiefly derived from
repression; a kind of dungheap of the personally unacceptable. Jung thought that, while the unconscious certainly
contained elements of personality which the individual
might repudiate, it also contained the germs of new possibilities, the seeds of future, and possibly better, adaptation.
Freud believed that neurosis originated in early childhood;
that it derived from the patient having become fixated at
certain stages of childhood emotional development. Jung
agreed that material from childhood was often evident in
neurosis, but considered that the appearance of such material was secondary to a failure of adaptation in the present.
Jung wrote:

> The psychological determination of a neurosis is only
> partly due to an early infantile predisposition; it must
> be due to some cause in the present as well. . . .
>
> The moment of the outbreak of neurosis is not just a
> matter of chance; as a rule it is most critical. It is
> usually *the moment when a new psychological adjustment,
> that is, a new adaptation, is demanded.* . . .
>
> I no longer seek the cause of neurosis in the past, but
> in the present. I ask, what is the necessary task which
> the patient will not accomplish?[7]

In Jung's view, therefore, the development of neurotic
symptoms was not to be regarded as merely the onset of
illness, but was also to be taken as a signal for the person to
reexamine himself and his values in order to attain a new

and better adaptation. This was particularly true of certain transitional periods of life, as, for example, the passage from adolescence to adulthood. Jung was fond of saying, "Thank God he became neurotic!," meaning by this that depression or whatever symptom the person had developed had had the positive function of compelling him to look inward.

Freud and his followers were primarily concerned with the childhood determinants of neurosis. The task of psychoanalysis was to facilitate the recall of the patient's earliest memories. The older the patient, the harder this task became. Therefore, in the early days of psychoanalysis, analysts were reluctant to take on middle-aged patients. Jung, on the other hand, came to specialize in the treatment of the middle-aged. Jung's major contribution to psychology is in the field of adult development. His interest in this period of life undoubtedly originated from the years of psychological stress which he experienced after his break with Freud. This upheaval was so intense that Jung feared for his own sanity. In 1912, Jung published the first edition of what became known, in English, as *The Psychology of the Unconscious*. In his autobiography, he describes how he was unable to write the end of this book for two months because he knew that it would cost him his friendship with Freud. He was right. The sad story of the estrangement between the two men can be traced in *The Freud/Jung Letters*.[8]

In July 1913, Jung reached the age of thirty-eight; a time of life in which so-called mid-life crises often occur. Jung was the first psychiatrist to draw attention to this phenomenon, which sprang directly from his own experience. By this time, Jung had married, fathered a family, and had achieved professional recognition and a position in the world. His conscious aspiration had been that, together with Freud, he could develop a new science of the mind. But something within him forced him, against his conscious inclination, to assert his own individual point of view, even though he knew that this would be treated by Freud as a betrayal. During the years of the First World War, Jung went through a personal crisis which was extremely disturbing but which, in the end, proved to be highly rewarding. He conducted a self-analysis in which he recorded his own visions and dreams, many of which were alarming. For example, he thrice dreamt that "in the middle of summer an Arctic cold wave descended and froze the land to ice. I saw, for example, the whole of Lorraine and its canals frozen and the entire region totally deserted by human beings. All living green things were killed by frost." In a later dream this scene of desolation was relieved by the appearance of "a leaf-bearing tree, but without fruit (my tree of life, I thought), whose leaves had been transformed by the effects of the frost into sweet grapes full of healing juices.9

Jung wrote, "The years when I was pursuing my inner images were the most important in my life—in them everything essential was decided."10 It was certainly out of the experience of those years that Jung's view of the development of personality originated. His self-analysis convinced him that the most important thing in life was to discern and make manifest one's own, individual point of view. Men became neurotic when they were in some sense false to themselves; when they strayed from the path which Nature (or God) intended them to follow. By listening to the inner voice, which manifested itself in dreams, fantasies, and other spontaneous derivatives of the unconscious, the lost soul could rediscover its proper path. This is, of course, a "religious" point of view, but one which does not necessarily postulate a God "out there."

The end of Jung's mid-life crisis was signaled by his writing one of the books by which he is best known to the general public, *Psychological Types*. Jung's concepts of "extravert" and "introvert," terms which he introduced, took origin from his observation that Freud and Adler could each confront the same psychopathological material and make quite different interpretations of it. Jung wrote:

> Since both theories are in a large measure correct—that is to say, since they both appear to explain their material—it follows that a neurosis must have two opposite aspects, one of which is grasped by the Freudian, the other by the Adlerian theory. But how comes it that each investigator sees only one side, and why does each maintain that he has the only valid view?[11]

Jung points out that Adler's psychology emphasizes the importance of the subject at the expense of the object; whereas Freud's psychology sees the subject in perpetual dependence upon significant objects.

Introversion and extraversion have become familiar ideas to most people, and have been taken over by experimental psychologists like Eysenck. The importance of the dichotomy in Jung's view of personality takes us back to his days as a medical student. Since the time of the physiologist Claude Bernard, scientists have accepted the idea that the body is a self-regulating entity. Human physiology is a system of checks and balances which ensure that any tendency to go too far in one direction is compensated by an opposing swing in the other. These so-called "homeostatic mechanisms" are dependent upon negative feedback; that is, upon fluctuations in some property like blood sugar being reported to a central control, whence compensatory changes are set in motion to restore the normal balance.

Jung's delineation of extraversion and introversion made it possible for him to advance the notion of personality being distorted by what he called "one-sided development." A man could be so extraverted, so totally involved in the external world, that he lost touch with the inner world of his own psyche. On the other hand, an introverted eccentric could be so preoccupied with the workings of his own mind that he failed to adapt himself to reality. Jung postulated that the mind was self-regulating in the same way as the body. The outbreak of neurotic symptoms should be taken as a signal indicating that a compensatory process was beginning in the unconscious. When a new patient turned to Jung asking what he should do, Jung would reply: "I have no idea; but let us see what the unconscious has to say. Let us examine your dreams and fantasies."

An illustration of this procedure is given by Jung in his paper, *The Practical Use of Dream-Analysis*. He was consulted by a man in a prominent position who complained of anxiety, insecurity, and dizziness which sometimes caused nausea, heaviness in the head, and constriction of breath: symptoms which, as Jung points out, are not unlike those of mountain sickness. The patient had risen from humble origins to a leading position. His first dream was: "I am back again in the small village where I was born. Some peasant lads who went to school with me are standing together in the street. I walk past, pretending not to know them. Then I hear one of them say, pointing at me: 'He doesn't often come back to our village.'" The patient's second dream was concerned with his being in a frantic hurry to go on a journey; with his just missing a train; and with his realization that the engine driver is going too fast, with the result that the rear coaches of the train are thrown off the rails.[12]

Jung interpreted these dreams as indicating that, for the time being, the patient had reached the pinnacle of his career: that he had strayed too far from his humble origins, and that he should rest upon his laurels rather than strive after the further achievements which he was set upon pursuing. This interpretation did not convince the patient; Jung was unable to continue his treatment; and, within a short time, the patient did indeed "run off the rails" into disaster.

These dreams are simple illustrations of what Jung meant by compensation and self-regulation. If the patient had only had the sense and insight to take seriously what his unconscious was indicating, he might have been spared the disaster which finally overtook him.

The analysis of dreams became one of the most important techniques of treatment used by Jung and his pupils. The interpretation of dreams was one of the main areas in which Jung diverged from Freud. Freud, it will be recalled, treated virtually all dreams as disguised wish fulfillments. He considered that dreams represented indirect ways of expressing repressed, infantile desires which were incompatible with, or distasteful to, the dreamer's ego. Jung believed that this was far too narrow a conception of dreams. Dreams might be expressed in a symbolic language which was hard to understand; but there was no reason to suppose that dreams were invariably concealing the unacceptable. Jung wrote:

> The fundamental mistake regarding the nature of the unconscious is probably this: it is commonly supposed that its contents have only one meaning and are marked with an unalterable plus or minus sign. In my humble opinion, this view is too naive. The psyche is a self-regulating system that maintains its equilibrium just as the body does. Every process that goes too far immediately and inevitably calls forth compensations, and without these there would be neither a normal metabolism nor a normal psyche. In this sense we can take the theory of compensation as a basic law of psychic behaviour. Too little on one side results in too much on the other. Similarly, the relation between conscious and unconscious is compensatory. This is one of the best-proven rules of dream-interpretation. When we set out to interpret a dream, it is always helpful to ask: What conscious attitude does it compensate?[13]

Jung's view of personality was, in the first place, largely derived from his experience with psychotic and neurotic patients. However, as his reputation grew, he came to be consulted by a variety of people who did not necessarily

present obvious neurotic symptoms, but who were dissat-
isfied and unhappy because they could no longer find meaning and purpose in their lives. Many of these patients were
conventionally successful, highly intelligent, and well
adapted socially. The majority were middle-aged, perhaps
passing through the kind of mid-life crisis which Jung himself had experienced.

These were the people who most interested Jung; exceptional individuals whose natures compelled them to reject
convention and discover their own path. Jung said that, as
an investigator rather than as a therapist, he was concerned
with quality rather than with quantity: "Nature is aristocratic, and one person of value outweighs ten lesser ones."[14]
Since Jung considered that such individuals were the carriers of culture, aiding them to fulfill themselves became a
task of vital importance.

Jung defined personality as an achievement rather than
as a datum of genetics. He called it "the supreme realization
of the innate idiosyncrasy of a living being."[15] It is essentially an *adult* ideal, which is why I earlier made the point
that Jung's main contribution was in the field of adult development: "It is not the child, but only the adult, who can
achieve personality as the fruit of a full life directed to this
end. The achievement of personality means nothing less
than the optimum development of the whole individual
human being."[16]

This optimum development tends toward a goal called
"wholeness" or "integration"; a condition in which the different elements of the psyche, both conscious and unconscious,
are welded together indissolubly; a condition which might
be described as the opposite of the fragmentation and splitting found in schizophrenia. The person who approaches
this goal, which can never be entirely or once and for all
achieved, possesses what Jung called "an attitude that is
beyond the reach of emotional entanglements and violent
shocks—a consciousness detached from the world."[17]

This search for integration is essentially a religious quest, though not one which is concerned with any recognized creed. It is religious because it involves a change within the individual from one in which ego and will are paramount to one in which he acknowledges that he is guided by an integrating factor which is not of his own making. Jung describes people as achieving peace of mind after "long and fruitless struggles":

> If you sum up what people tell you about their experiences, you can formulate it this way: They came to themselves, they could accept themselves, they were able to become reconciled to themselves, and thus were reconciled to adverse circumstances and events. This is almost like what use to be expressed by saying: He has made his peace with God, he has sacrificed his own will, he has submitted himself to the will of God.[18]

Jung described the symbols in which this change of attitude and new unity of personality expressed itself; circular forms indicating wholeness which are comparable with the so-called "mandalas" used in Tibetan Buddhism as ritual instruments to assist meditation.

> If the unconscious can be recognized as a co-determining factor along with consciousness, and if we can live in such a way that conscious and unconscious demands are taken into account as far as possible, then the centre of gravity of the total personality shifts its position. It is then no longer in the ego, which is merely the centre of consciousness, but in the hypothetical point between conscious and unconscious. This new centre might be called the "self."[19]

The self, of which the mandala is a symbol, is the archetype of unity and totality. Jung believed that this archetype was the underlying reality manifesting itself in the various forms of monotheism. The self, therefore, is the God within;

and the individual, in seeking self-realization and unity, becomes the means through which, as Jung put it, "God seeks his goal."[20]

In the biographical sketch of Jung at the beginning of this chapter, I mentioned that he was the son of a pastor in the Swiss Reformed Church. Two of his paternal uncles were also clergymen, and there were no less than six parsons in his mother's family. However, at an early age, Jung developed serious doubts about the conventional faith in which he was brought up. He began to think of religion as a personal matter which had little to do with accepted creeds. He tried to discuss some of these doubts with his father, but found the latter unwilling to enter into argument. Jung found himself in the position of being unable to subscribe to the faith in which he had been reared, while at the same time continuing to believe that individuals could neither be happy nor healthy unless they acknowledged their dependence upon some higher power than that of the ego.

In the letters between himself and Freud, the question of whether or not they should join a new International Fraternity for Ethics and Culture is discussed:

> Is there perchance a new saviour in the I.F? What sort of new myth does it hand out for us to live by? Only the wise are ethical from sheer intellectual presumption, the rest of us need the eternal truth of myth. You will see from this string of associations that the problem does not leave me simply apathetic and cold. The ethical problem of sexual freedom really is enormous and worth the sweat of all noble souls. But 2000 years of Christianity can only be replaced by something equivalent.[21]

A critic might allege that the whole of Jung's later work represents his attempt to find a substitute for the faith which he lost when he was a child. He might go on to say that Jung substituted the analysis of dreams and fantasies for prayer.

Jung urged his patients to draw and paint their dreams and fantasies. Moreover, he encouraged them deliberately to set aside part of the day for reverie; for what, in Jungian technique, became known as "active imagination." This is a state of mind not unlike that described in some forms of meditation, in which judgment is suspended but consciousness is preserved. The patient was enjoined to notice what fantasies occurred to him. In this way, the patient might be able to rediscover hidden parts of himself as well as portray the psychological journey upon which he was embarking. The parallels with the processes of Recollection, Quiet, and Contemplation described by the mystics are striking.

The state of reverie is also one in which most creative discoveries are made. A few artists and scientists have left accounts of inspiration being directly derived from a dream. R. L. Stevenson, for example, said that the plot of *Dr. Jekyll and Mr. Hyde* came to him in a dream. But most new ideas or solutions to problems appear during states of mind intermediate between waking and sleeping which are the same as, or closely similar to, "active imagination" as described by Jung. Jung himself said that his aim was to bring about a state of mind in which the use of creative imagination would allow the subject to experiment with his own nature instead of remaining in a condition of fixed sterility.

In spite of this, Jung was particularly insistent that his patients should not regard their fantasies as anything to do with art, although some produced paintings which were worthy of display. In my paper "Individuation and the Creative Process,"[22] I discussed some of the reasons for this attitude.

Jung was apparently concerned to distinguish spontaneous, natural fantasies emanating directly from the unconscious from artistic fantasies which he regarded as arbitrary inventions. This distinction cannot ultimately be maintained. Although artists consciously apply themselves to refining and shaping their fantasies, and scientists set about trying to prove their hypotheses, both artists and scientists attribute many of their inspirations and discoveries to a source beyond conscious striving. Jung's patients, even if not gifted artistically, were often dealing with the raw material of art; the stuff from which novels or paintings are eventually constructed.

The individuation process, as described by Jung, and the creative process, as described by both scientists and artists, have much in common. We have already noted that the state of mind which Jung encouraged his patients to cultivate is the same as that in which inspiration most commonly occurs. The process of individuation is a lifetime's task which is never completed; a journey upon which the individual hopefully embarks toward a destination at which he never arrives. Jung himself wrote: "The new attitude gained in the course of analysis tends sooner or later to become inadequate in one way or another, and necessarily so, because the constant flow of life again and again demands fresh adaptation. Adaptation is never achieved once and for all."[23]

The creative quest, whether in science or in the arts, is also a journey without a final destination. No scientist or artist is ever satisfied for long with what he has discovered or accomplished. There is always a next step to be taken, a new problem demanding solution.

Jung described integration in terms of uniting opposites; of finding a new balance between extraversion and introversion, or between conscious and unconscious. As Koestler demonstrated in his book *The Act of Creation*, "bisociation," the essential creative perception, is concerned with linking situations or ideas which have hitherto been conceived as incompatible; in other words, with forming new unions between opposites.[24] In science, a new hypothesis characteristically reconciles and supersedes previously incompatible hypotheses. In the arts, balance and contrast between opposites is usually an essential part of creating an aesthetic pattern.

Jung's concentration upon changing dynamics within the

charmed circle of the individual psyche is interesting, partly because it is so unfashionable. During the last thirty years, we have witnessed the rise of the so-called "object-relations" school of psychoanalysis, dominated by Melanie Klein, Ronald Fairbairn, and Donald Winnicott, and later reinforced by John Bowlby. Whatever disagreements still divide the psychoanalytic camps, there has been a consensus of opinion that, if one wants to understand the growth and development of human beings, one must first study their interpersonal relationships. From the baby's earliest relation with its mother onwards, it has been assumed that human happiness and fulfillment depend upon interpersonal relationships, and that treatment of neurotic problems largely consists in helping patients to improve their relationships by means of understanding and improving the way in which they relate to the therapist.

Yet, here is Jung saying that what really matters is the patient's relationship with the unconscious, together with the dynamic changes which take place within the individual psyche as a consequence of the process of individuation. Jung was perfectly well aware of the significance of interpersonal relationships, but his emphasis is quite different from that of contemporary analysts. Perhaps our present elevation of interpersonal relationships into the be-all and end-all of human existence has been overdone. Jung's point of view might be a starting point for a compensatory swing of the pendulum away from object-relations.

Jung's later work is chiefly concerned with the process of individuation and the symbols in which that process is expressed. His interest in alchemy, which often seems to puzzle people, arose because he found parallels between the alchemists' description of their "work" with what seemed to be happening in his patients. Jung believed that the alchemists' quest for the Philosopher's Stone, or for means of transforming other substances into gold, was not so much a series of chemical experiments as a spiritual journey. More particularly, the alchemists were concerned with the transformation and combination of opposites, using chemical interaction as a symbol of psychic processes. Because there was nothing in alchemy scientifically, it acted as a gigantic projection test; a kind of Rorschach inkblot in which anything that was seen actually originated in the mind of the observer.

Part of Jung's rejection of conventional Christianity seems to have been based upon his impatience with what might be called the Pangloss element. He felt that orthodox Christians were disinclined to accept the reality of evil. In adolescence, therefore, it was reassuring for him to encounter Schopenhauer:

> Here at last was a philosopher who had the courage to see that all was not for the best in the fundaments of the universe. He spoke neither of the all-good and all-wise providence of a Creator, nor of the harmony of the cosmos, but stated bluntly that a fundamental flaw underlay the sorrowful course of human history and the cruelty of nature: the blindness of the world-creating Will.[25]

The problem of evil continued to preoccupy Jung throughout his life. His insistence upon the equal reality of evil and good led to an interesting series of exchanges with Father Victor White, a Dominican priest who was professor of dogmatic theology at Blackfriars, Oxford. Father White was a close friend of Jung; but the differences between them on the problem of evil led to an estrangement. Victor White maintained the Catholic doctrine of the *privatio boni,* which alleges that evil is the absence of good and has no substance or reality of its own. Jung strongly objected to this view. For him, good and evil were equally real as polar opposites.

A good deal of Jung's thought seems to be directly derived from Schopenhauer. Schopenhauer considered that individuals were the embodiment of an underlying Will which was outside space and time. Jung endorses a similar view when, at the beginning of his autobiography, he writes, "My life is a story of the self-realization of the unconscious."[26]

Jung took the term "individuation" from Schopenhauer. Schopenhauer considered that the very notion of individuality, the *principium individuationis,* is dependent upon the human categories of space and time which force us to be conscious of individual objects and which prevent us from seeing the original unity of the Will of which individuals are a manifestation.

Jung also believed in a realm outside space and time from which individuals became differentiated. Borrowing the Gnostic term, he referred to this spiritual realm transcending consciousness as the "pleroma." In the pleroma, all is one. There is no differentiation between opposites like good and evil, light and dark, time and space, or force and matter.

But, whereas Schopenhauer's philosophy is governed by the ideal of deliverance from the bonds of individuality by means of denial and asceticism, Jung's philosophy is governed by the idea of affirmation and realization of individuality.

Jung's belief in the underlying unity of all existence led him to believe that physical and mental, as well as spatial and temporal, were human categories imposed upon reality which did not accurately reflect it. Through his collaboration with the physicist Wolfgang Pauli, also his analysand, Jung came to think that the physicist's investigation of matter and the psychologist's investigation of mind might be different ways of approaching the same underlying reality. Perhaps mind and body were simply different aspects of a single reality viewed through different frames of reference.

Jung claimed that there were "sufficient reasons" for believing that "the psychic lies embedded in something that appears to be of a non-psychic nature."[27] Pauli postulated "a cosmic order independent of our choice and distinct from the world of phenomena."[28] Jung wrote: "The background of microphysics and depth-psychology is as much physical as psychic and therefore neither, but rather a third thing, a neutral nature which at most can be grasped in hints since in essence it is transcendental."[29]

Whatever one may think of the further reaches of Jung's later thought, there can be no doubt of his originality, of his creative power, of his contribution to the understanding of the development of personality, and of the value of the innovations which he introduced into the technique and practice of analytical psychotherapy.

NOTES

References are to Jung's works unless otherwise noted.

1. "Mental Disease and the Psyche," in *Collected Works,* 20 vols., trans. R. F. C. Hull (London: Routledge and Kegan Paul, 1953–79), vol. 3, para. 498 (cited hereafter as *CW,* by volume and paragraph number).
2. "The Tavistock Lectures" (Lecture 2), *CW* 18:105.
3. "A Review of the Complex Theory," *CW* 8:201.
4. Ibid., para. 202.
5. "On the Nature of the Psyche," *CW* 8:435.
6. "The Structure of the Psyche," *CW* 8:317–18.
7. "Psychoanalysis and Neurosis," *CW* 4:317–18, 570.
8. William McGuire, ed., *The Freud/Jung Letters,* trans. Ralph Manheim and R. F. C. Hull (London: Hogarth Press/Routledge and Kegan Paul, 1974).
9. *Memories, Dreams, Reflections* (London: Routledge and Kegan Paul, 1963), p. 170.
10. Ibid., p. 191.
11. "The Psychology of the Unconscious," *CW* 7:57.
12. "The Practical Use of Dream-Analysis," *CW* 16:297–300.
13. Ibid., para. 330.
14. "The Relations Between the Ego and the Unconscious," *CW* 7:236.
15. "The Development of Personality," *CW* 17:289.
16. Ibid.
17. "Commentary on 'The Secret of the Golden Flower,' " *CW* 13:68.
18. "Psychology and Religion," *CW* 11:138.
19. "Commentary on 'The Secret of the Golden Flower,' " *CW* 13:67.
20. "The Undiscovered Self," *CW* 10:588.

21. McGuire, *Freud/Jung Letters*, Letter 178J, p. 294.
22. Anthony Storr, "Individuation and the Creative Process," *Journal of Analytical Psychology* 28 (1983):329–43.
23. "The Transcendent Function," *CW* 8:143.
24. Arthur Koestler, *The Act of Creation* (London: Hutchinson, 1964).
25. *Memories, Dreams, Reflections*, p. 76.
26. Ibid., p. 17.
27. "On the Nature of the Psyche," *CW* 8:437.
28. Wolfgang Pauli, "The Influence of Archetypal Ideas on the Scientific Theories of Kepler," in *The Interpretation of Nature and the Psyche*, C. G. Jung and Wolfgang Pauli (London: Routledge and Kegan Paul, 1955), p. 152.
29. "Mysterium Coniunctionis," *CW* 14:768.

10

Why Psychoanalysis
Is Not a Science

THE PURPOSE OF this chapter is to affirm that, although Freud continued to hope that psychoanalysis was, or might become, a science, that hope was doomed to disappointment.

Although some of the hypotheses of psychoanalysis can be treated scientifically, that is, subjected to objective assessment and proved or disproved in the same fashion as scientific hypotheses in other fields, this is only true of a minority. For most of the hypotheses of psychoanalysis are based upon observations made during the course of psychoanalytic treatment, and psychoanalytic treatment cannot be regarded as a scientific procedure. Observations made during the psychoanalytic encounter are inevitably contaminated with the subjective experience and prejudice of the observer, however detached he tries to be, and cannot therefore be regarded in the same light as observations made during the course of a chemical or physical experiment.

It is certainly possible to study human beings as if they

were objects merely responding to the stimuli impinging upon them. This is the aim of experimental psychology. But it is not possible to conduct psychoanalysis or any other form of psychotherapy in this fashion, for reasons which I shall proceed to outline.

To my mind, Freud's wish to be thought a scientist, and his reluctance to admit that he abandoned this role at an early stage in his career, have had an unfortunate effect. If no one had ever claimed that psychoanalysis was a science, dispute about its status would not have been so intemperate. John Bowlby, perhaps the most influential psychoanalyst in Britain during the last three decades, once said that he thought that Freud's attitude had held up the development of psychotherapy by fifty years. Yet Bowlby would the first to acknowledge the originality of Freud's genius. In order to understand this paradox, it is necessary to glance at some aspects of the development of Freud's thought.

Freud was not only a medical man, but had also been trained in the laboratories of Ernst Brücke, a scientist who, according to his collaborator Emil du Bois-Reymond, had "pledged a solemn oath to put into power this truth: no other forces than the common physico-chemical ones are active within the organism."[1] This hardheaded, uncompromisingly deterministic point of view, which has proved so rewarding in the exact sciences of chemistry and physics, was, at that date, a departure from the vitalistic form of biology taught to Brücke and his fellows when they were students. For fifteen years, Freud conducted research, first into the nervous systems of fish, and then into the human central nervous system. Even when he had begun to formulate psychoanalytical ideas, he looked back with regret to his neuroanatomical days. As late as 1891, he published a monograph on aphasia, and a major work on childhood cerebral palsy appeared in 1897. Because Brücke's two assistants were relatively young, Freud had little prospect of advancement within that laboratory. On this account,

Brücke advised him to practice medicine. Freud's decision to do so was reinforced by his having fallen in love with Martha Bernays, whom he could not marry without increasing his earnings. Freud reluctantly took his medical degree in 1881, and was then appointed a demonstrator in Brücke's Physiological Institute.

With so much "hard" science behind him, it was natural enough that Freud's approach to the study of neurotic symptoms should derive from his medical and scientific training. That is, he approached neurotic symptoms as if they were phenomena of the same order as the physical symptoms of organic disease, and at first treated them with the physical methods of treatment then available: hydrotherapy, electrotherapy, and massage. But, in the summer of 1885, Freud applied for, and won, a traveling fellowship, which enabled him to spend the winter of 1885–1886 studying in Paris with the famous neurologist Charcot.

Charcot had, for some years, been investigating hypnotism, with the object of finding a way of distinguishing between organic and hysterical paralyses. Charcot demonstrated to Freud that *ideas*, although intangible, could nevertheless be causal agents in neurosis. For when a patient developed an hysterical paralysis, the form which the paralysis took was not determined by the facts of anatomy, but by the patient's faulty *idea* of anatomy. Instead of developing a paralysis which could be explained by a lesion of a particular peripheral nerve, he exhibited a paralysis of a limb which corresponded to his *idea* of where his leg began and ended. Moreover, Charcot demonstrated that hysterical paralyses could be artificially produced by means of hypnosis.

If ideas could cause hysterical symptoms, then ideas might also bring about cures. By means of hypnosis, ideas of health could be forcibly implanted; and Freud found that hypnosis could indeed relieve a number of hysterical symptoms. Freud therefore began to employ hypnosis as his main method of treatment for neurotic disorders, and continued to do so until 1896.

Hypnosis came to have two aspects. The first was the implantation of ideas of health into the mind of the patient; positive suggestions designed to counteract the negative ideas which were causing the symptoms. The second and more important aspect derived from the work of Freud's friend and collaborator Josef Breuer. When treating his famous case, Anna O. (Bertha Pappenheim), with hypnosis, Breuer discovered that if she could be persuaded to recall the very first moment of the appearance of each hysterical symptom, the symptom disappeared. Breuer named this method of treatment "catharsis." Hypnosis, therefore, came to be used as a method of getting the patient to recall forgotten origins. Instead of being used as a positive, direct attack upon neurotic symptoms, it became a method of investigation.

Freud and Breuer came to hope that all neurotic symptoms could be abolished in this laborious, although essentially simple, way. In their first paper in *Studies on Hysteria*, they wrote:

> For we found, to our great surprise at first, that *each individual hysterical symptom immediately and permanently disappeared when we had succeeded in bringing clearly to light the memory of the event by which it was provoked and in arousing the accompanying affect, and when the patient had described that event in the greatest possible detail and had put the affect into words.*[2]

Later, the same technique was applied to obsessional symptoms. In another paper, we read of a girl

> who had become almost completely isolated on account of an obsessional fear of incontinence of urine. She could no longer leave her room or receive visitors without having urinated a number of times. *Reinstatement:* it was an obsession based on temptation or mistrust. She

did not mistrust her bladder, but her resistance to erotic impulses. The origin of this obsession shows this clearly. Once, at the theatre, on seeing a man who attracted her, she had felt an erotic desire, accompanied (as spontaneous pollutions in women always are) by a desire to urinate. She was obliged to leave the theatre, and from that moment on she was a prey to the fear of having the same sensation, but the desire to urinate had replaced the erotic one. She was completely cured.3

We can see from this account that, although neurotic symptoms differed from those of physical disease in originating from unpleasant memories or unwelcome or unadmitted emotions, it was nevertheless possible to regard them in much the same light. Just as pneumococci might be regarded as the "cause" of pneumonia and abolished by suitable medication, so neuroses were "caused" by repressed emotions or traumas, and could be abolished by recall and abreaction.

Moreover, while hypnosis remained the technical method for enabling the patient to recover the repressed memories and the unpleasant emotions which had accompanied them, it was possible to teach it in the same way that one could teach the technique of removing an appendix. The psychotherapist could therefore assume the traditional medical role of a skilled professional; a benign authority, giving the patient the benefit of his superior knowledge; benevolent, considerate, but essentially detached.

So long as this view of neurosis could be maintained, it also followed that the patient could be treated as an isolated individual, without reference to his present circumstances or current interpersonal relationships. For, if the cause of neurosis lay in the past, the task of the therapist was merely to facilitate remembrance of things past. Psychoanalysts have often been criticized for only attempting to understand their patients when the latter have been put into an isolated, artificial situation which is remote from ordinary life, and which precludes access to those who know them best, their relatives and friends. But, if it is assumed that neurosis is caused by repressed emotions originating in the past, more particularly in the earliest years of the patient's childhood, it is not unreasonable to disregard current relationships and to create a situation in which the recall of the past is facilitated. If a patient's illness is due to an inflamed appendix, the surgeon's task is to locate the appendix and remove it. Relatives' descriptions of the patient's reactions to pain and illness are unlikely to be relevant.

The case history of the girl with the obsessional fear of incontinence of urine is not given in any detail. There are many questions about her to which any psychiatrist practicing today would like to have answers. But, as Freud presents the case, we are told that she was completely cured; and this was probably good enough for her as it must be good enough for us. Freud's attitude toward his patient, at this period of history, is similar to that advocated by behavior therapists today. Although behavior therapists think of neurotic symptoms as learned, maladaptive habits rather than as being caused by repressed emotions, their attitude toward the patient resembles that adopted by a physician toward a patient suffering from a physical illness; and this was also Freud's attitude when he began treating such patients. The physician has as his aim the understanding of the underlying cause of whatever symptoms the patient presents, and the abolition of those symptoms by appropriate techniques of treatment. This is entirely proper. There is no need for the physician to get to know his patient as a person, and still less for him to examine his own personality and motives. The physician's ideal is to discover ways of treating disease by methods which can be learned and applied by any other doctor; methods to which the personality of the doctor is irrelevant. In similar fashion, Eysenck has been heard to say that behavior therapists should be like dentists: considerate and kind, no doubt; but essentially skilled technicians who apply techniques of treatment which can be learned by any intelligent person, and which can be evaluated by the ordinary methods of science.

This objective, scientific approach is perfectly all right as far as it goes, both in physical disorders and in certain defined types of neurotic disorder. If I consult a physician for asthma, what I want is that he shall be an expert in respiratory disease, and that he shall be able to prescribe what drugs are necessary. If he happens to be skilled in interpersonal relationships and comes to understand me as a person, this an unsought bonus for which I may be grateful, but which is a secondary gain rather than a prime objective.

Behavior therapists score their greatest successes with specific phobias, especially with those which take origin from defined traumatic incidents, and I am the last person to question their achievements. Indeed, I have considerable sympathy with their point of view. It would be admirable if all forms of neurosis could be treated by objective, scientific techniques which anyone could learn. This was certainly Freud's hope in the early days, and one which he never completely abandoned. However, subjective factors began to interfere with this aspiration, even before the close of the nineteenth century. In his paper "The Aetiology of Hysteria," published in 1896, Freud states that, having treated eighteen cases, "whatever case and whatever symptom we take as our point of departure, *in the end we infallibly come to the field of sexual experience.* So here for the first time we seem to have discovered an aetiological precondition for hysterical symptoms."[4]

Freud goes on to point out that, in cases in which the onset of hysterical symptoms seems to have been triggered by something trivial, psychoanalytic investigation reveals that "at the bottom of every case of hysteria there are *one or more occurrences of premature sexual experience,* occurrences which belong to the earliest years of childhood but which can be reproduced through the work of psycho-analysis in spite of the intervening decades."[5]

Roger Brown has drawn attention to the fact that this was Freud's last attempt to give figures concerning etiology, and that, even in this instance, there were no controls. Brown suggests that there were two reasons for Freud's change of attitude. First, he came to believe that some of his patients were telling him fantasies, not facts, about their pasts. Second, Freud had embarked upon his own self-analysis. Freud knew that, in his own case, the case of the nineteenth patient, the Oedipus complex had bulked large in childhood. But he also knew that he had not experienced actual sexual seduction. Accordingly, Freud transferred his interest from so-called traumatic incidents, of which sexual seduction had seemed to be the most important variety, to an examination of the patient's inner world of fantasy. Psychoanalysis changed from what might be called a scientific attempt to disclose a causal series of events culminating in the outbreak of a neurosis, to an exploration of the patient's imaginative world which could not be categorized as scientific.[6]

These were not the only reasons for supposing that Freud's ideal of establishing psychoanalysis as a true science of the mind was doomed to failure. Freud's original hypothesis concerning precocious sexual arousal was based on dramatic cases of "conversion hysteria" which are hardly ever seen today. Why this is so is uncertain; but it has been suggested, rather convincingly, that it may be connected with the fact that women, however incomplete their freedom, are at least more emancipated than they were in the days of Freud. In the nineteenth century, life had very little to offer an intelligent woman who did not get married, or who was unhappily married. Condemned to social, as well as to sexual, frustration, and either despised for not achieving the status of marriage or locked into a situation from which there was no escape, such women expressed their dissatisfaction in dramatic fashion, developing symptoms which, if they did not get them what they wanted, at least ensured that they were paid attention.

The kind of hysterical symptoms produced by Anna O. and her sisters could, in many instances, be traced to a defined origin and abolished in much the same fashion as could symptoms of physical disorders. But the majority of neurotic symptoms are not like this. If a patient complains of headache, it is legitimate to think of this symptom as an alien intruder. The same is true of a limited range of neurotic symptoms, of which specific phobias are the best examples. But most neurotic symptoms are much more intimately connected with the patient's personality as a whole, and cannot be understood unless the patient's whole personality is taken into account.

Consider, for example, the common symptom of agoraphobia. In some instances, agoraphobia may take origin from a frightening experience, a so-called traumatic incident. For instance, one may expect that a girl who has been sexually assaulted in the street will be reluctant to venture out alone for a while. But, in most cases, it will be found that agoraphobia originates from what Bowlby calls a disturbance in "attachment behavior." That is, inquiry into the patient's early emotional development will reveal that, during childhood, attachment figures were unreliable or absent, with the consequence that, instead of developing increasing confidence, the child came to regard the world as a frightening and unpredictable place into which it was not safe to venture alone without a supporting arm.

Or consider recurrent depression. People who are prone to depression tend to feel both helpless and hopeless in the face of any form of adversity. If one is to understand the reasons why anyone habitually reacts with severe depression to disappointment, loss, or challenge, it is necessary to investigate the emotional climate in which the patient was reared. Although a specific attack of depression may be relieved by physical methods of treatment, the tendency to become severely depressed cannot be understood without taking the whole personality into account; nor can the person be expected to learn to deal better with this tendency because his symptom has been directly attacked with antidepressant drugs or electroconvulsive therapy.

As time went on, patients seeking psychoanalysis presented symptoms which were even less defined than agoraphobia or recurrent depression. Today, many patients asking for psychotherapy are not suffering from any definable neurosis but from generalized unhappiness, from tensions at work, or from difficulties in interpersonal relationships. They bring to the psychoanalyst what Thomas Szasz has accurately called "problems in living,"[7] and therefore demand to be understood as persons rather than treated for particular symptoms. Since its inception in the 1890s, psychoanalysis has moved farther and farther away from the medical model.

Another important reason for psychoanalysis becoming more concerned with persons as a whole rather than with neurotic symptoms springs from Freud's change in technique. I mentioned earlier that Freud continued to use hypnosis until 1896. I should rather have written that he finally abandoned its use in 1896. From 1892 onward, he was gradually modifying his technique. Freud's substitution of free association for hypnosis was, I believe, his most momentous therapeutic innovation. The employment of free association compels the psychotherapist to assume a much more passive, less authoritarian role than that conventionally expected of the doctor, and makes the patient take the initiative. Hypnosis is a treatment which is principally dependent upon the doctor's authority and the patient's compliance. The hypnotized patient recovers because the hypnotist tells him that he will; or recalls the remote past because the hypnotist urges him to do so. The adoption of free association means that the patient retains his or her autonomy, instead of being automatically placed in a submissive or childish relation to the therapist. Instead of looking to the therapist for direct advice or specific instructions, the patient learns to use psychoanalysis as a means of understanding himself better and, through this, begins to learn to solve his own problems.

This change toward greater autonomy for the patient is the most important consequence of adopting free association, but it is not the only one. If a person is encouraged to say everything which comes into his mind without censorship, he will talk not only about his symptoms but also about his hopes and fears, his aspirations and disappointments, his successes and failures, and everything else which preoccupies him and which constitutes him as a unique person. Once again, we observe that the emphasis in psychoanalytic treatment has shifted from a direct attack upon neurotic symptoms to the consideration of the whole person.

A further reinforcement of this shift was Freud's discovery of transference. As he proceeded with his psychoanalytic work, he found that he became emotionally important to his patients in a way he did not welcome but reluctantly came to realize was a vital part of psychoanalytic procedure. Freud at first thought of transference as an erotic attachment to the psychoanalyst, as indeed it can be. However deplorable this might be, it was, so Freud considered, a useful way of overcoming resistance. Later Freud came to think of transference as an artificially induced neurosis in which the patient repeated all the attitudes which he had held toward his parents. By means of interpretation, Freud strove to convert this repetition into recollection, thus reducing the intensity of the patient's present emotions by affirming that they really belonged to the past. Freud wrote:

> The patient, that is to say, directs toward the physician a degree of affectionate feeling (mingled, often enough, with hostility) which is based on no real relationship between them and which—as is shown by every detail of its emergence—can only be traced back to old wishful phantasies of the patient's which have become unconscious.[8]

In other words, Freud was striving to discount any possibility that his patients might be experiencing genuine emotional feelings toward him in the here and now.

In fact, it is perfectly natural that patients should genuinely value the psychoanalyst in a special way, however much their picture of him or her may be distorted by past experience. Many patients in analysis have never experienced the kind of long-term concern that a psychoanalyst gives them. There is no other situation in life in which one can count upon a devoted listener for so many hours. In June 1910, Freud wrote to Pfister, "As for the transference, it is altogether a curse."9 One can understand why Freud felt this. Instead of his patients accepting him merely as a trained and skilled operator who could, by means of his technique, expose the origins and abolish the symptoms of their neuroses, they made him into a savior, an idealized lover, or a father figure. What they wanted was not his science but his love.

Freud's recognition of the phenomena of transference, however interpreted or explained, once again deflected interest from neurotic symptoms as such, and steered it in the direction of interpersonal relationships. Moreover, it soon became obvious that the psychoanalyst was not and could not be the kind of detached observer who was no more affected by his patient than if the latter were a chemical solution. Jung was the first of the early psychoanalysts to insist that the analyst must himself be analyzed. Analysts, ideally, were supposed to be freed from their own emotional blocks and prejudices if they were to be able to treat their patients satisfactorily. However, Jung insisted, they must always remain open to influence and to change themselves. The analyst must allow himself to be affected by his patient if he was to be able to help him. He must monitor his own emotional responses by means of introspection, since his own, subjective response to what the patient was saying was a vital means toward understanding him.

This is a far cry from the mental set demanded of a scientist. In conducting an experiment, the scientist must take pains to ensure that his own emotions do not in any way affect the objectivity of his observations. Perhaps his hopes and fears are deeply aroused by a particular experiment. Perhaps a Nobel Prize depends upon whether a solution turns red or blue. But the scientist's hopes and fears must not be allowed to influence the detachment with which he notes his results; nor does his own knowledge of himself affect his understanding of the interacting chemicals.

In psychoanalysis, the analyst must, to some extent, regard his patient objectively. But, if he is to understand the patient, he must at the same time take into account his own feelings and his own reactions to the patient's feelings. If he treats the patient in the way in which a scientist treats a chemical solution, the psychoanalyst cuts himself off from the sources of information which we all habitually use in understanding one another.

So, in the various ways expounded, it came to pass that psychoanalysis became less and less concerned with a direct attack upon neurotic symptoms, and more and more concentrated upon understanding persons and interpersonal relationships. Neurotic symptoms have become an entry ticket for embarking upon psychoanalysis, and are often largely disregarded once the analysis is under way. Not long ago, I was talking to a senior member of the staff of London's Tavistock Clinic, which is entirely staffed by psychoanalysts. He told me that they were thinking of appointing a behavior therapist to the staff. I was at first surprised that so apparently alien a figure should be introduced into a Freudian stronghold. Then the light dawned. "You want the behavior therapist to get rid of the symptoms," I said. "Then you can get on with what really matters—the analysis."

If one is to understand persons, one is compelled to try to understand their interpersonal relationships. For what we call a person is defined by comparison with, and interaction with, other persons. As John Macmurray put it: "Persons, therefore, are constituted by their mutual relation to one another. 'I' exists only as one element in the complex 'You and I.' "[10]

The growth of what is now known as the "object-relations" school of psychoanalysis bears witness to the change from regarding the patient as a closed system whose difficulties are explained in terms of repression and instinctual fixation to looking upon him as someone whose interpersonal relationships have gone awry at an early stage in his development. This change in emphasis has reached its zenith in the work of John Bowlby, whose massive three-volume work, *Attachment and Loss,* was completed in 1980.[11] Bowlby's conception of neurosis is couched entirely in terms of disturbed relationships with significant others rather than in terms of instinctual fixation.

Treating symptoms and treating persons are two different exercises. It is possible to sustain an objective, scientific approach to neurotic symptoms, but it is not possible to do so in understanding persons. Because Freud tried to maintain the notion that psychoanalysis was a science and that he was a scientist, this difference has not been made as clear as it should have been, and this has given rise to unnecessary misunderstanding. Eysenck was perfectly right in asserting that psychoanalysis is unscientific, but his attack would never have been made if Freud and his followers had not tried to claim that psychoanalysis was a science. Their efforts to do so sprang partly from Freud's original training, and partly from a general overvaluation of the exact sciences which we are only now beginning to correct. Other forms of human endeavor, like history and literature, are equally valuable in an entirely different way. One can hardly imagine that Eysenck would attack poetry for being unscientific, since no one supposes that poetry has anything to do with science.

Why is it that the objective, scientific approach to human

beings is insufficient? The behaviorists, of whom B. F. Skinner is the most famous modern example, argue that this is not the case. The original behaviorists tried to adopt a purely determinist, objective approach to human beings, and therefore discarded anything derived from introspection, confining themselves to examining only overt behavior. This approach demands that human beings be studied as if their behavior was entirely determined by external forces; as if they were billiard balls possessing no inner life, neither will nor intention. Skinner's view of man is precisely that. His notion of Utopia is one in which the environment is so controlled that appropriate "contingencies of reinforcement" will automatically produce socially desirable behavior and general happiness. Skinner writes:

> What is being abolished is autonomous man—the inner man . . . the man defended by the literature of freedom and dignity. . . . A scientific analysis of behavior dispossesses autonomous man and turns the control he has been said to exercise over to the environment. . . . What is needed is more control, not less. . . . The problem is to design a world which will be liked not by people as they now are but by those who live in it. . . . It is science or nothing.[12]

Is it? I do hope not. Someone, presumably Skinner, has to decide what kind of world is wanted, and has to design the contingencies of reinforcement which will bring this world into being. I have met Skinner, and I reviewed the first volume of his autobiography. Although he is an agreeable enough person to meet, I would not want to live in a world designed by him. It is because the behaviorists have taken this strictly deterministic attitude toward human beings that what they have been able to tell us about ourselves has proved to be of so remarkably little interest.

As already indicated, it is just possible to sustain a more or less deterministic attitude toward neurotic symptoms, but the philosophers have always realized that such an attitude cannot be sustained when there is any question of day-to-day interpersonal relationships. For example, P. F. Strawson points out that the psychoanalyst may temporarily or partially adopt an objective, impersonal stance toward those parts of his patient's behavior which are at first incomprehensible or which the patient cannot control. But, once those parts have been understood and brought into relation with the rest of the patient's behavior, such an attitude is no longer appropriate. Strawson takes as his example the kind of psychoanalyst which Freud originally attempted to be. Strawson writes:

> His objectivity of attitude, his suspension of ordinary moral reactive attitudes, is profoundly modified by the fact that the aim of the enterprise is to make such suspension unnecessary or at least less necessary. Here we may and do naturally speak of restoring the agent's freedom. But here the restoring of freedom means bringing it about that the agent's behaviour shall be intelligible in terms of conscious purposes rather than in terms only of unconscious purposes. This is the object of the enterprise; and it is in so far as this object is attained that the suspension, or half suspension of ordinary moral attitudes is deemed no longer necessary.[13]

In other words, once the psychoanalyst has traced the origin of the symptoms and brought their meaning and the affects connected with them into consciousness, he is bound to revert to treating the cured patient as possessing will and intention; as a being who has the power of choice; not as a being whose behavior is determined either by factors of which he is unconscious, or by factors external to him, "contingencies of reinforcement," as Skinner would call them.

In his introduction to a collection of essays on psychoanalysis, Charles Rycroft has charted his own progress from considering psychoanalysis as a causal theory to regarding it as a semantic theory. That is, he no longer sees the main task of psychoanalysis as uncovering the causes of symptoms, but rather as a means of understanding and making sense of the communications and personalities of his patients. If a patient's symptoms are entirely the consequence of unconscious wishes or repressed traumatic incidents, then making the patient conscious of these determinants should, and sometimes does, result in the disappearance of these symptoms, as in the early cases Freud describes. But, as Rycroft points out:

> Firstly, symptoms are not solely an individual matter, they have a social nexus and function and change in one person may be contingent on change in others. Secondly, in patients other than straightforward psychoneurotics, analysis involves consideration of the whole personality including his conscious values. And thirdly, conscious as well as unconscious motives play a part in the maintenance of neuroses.[14]

Modern psychoanalysts, therefore, are not merely concerned with making what is unconscious conscious, but with understanding persons. If we are to understand persons, we must assume that which Skinner and his followers try to eliminate, an inner life which is only revealed through introspection; a life concerned with conscious intention, will, motives, beliefs, and values.

There really is a sense in which understanding a person is a different enterprise from understanding a disease, an animal, a tree, or even a neurotic symptom. Isaiah Berlin puts it clearly:

> Understanding other men's motives or acts, however imperfect or corrigible, is a state of mind or activity in principle different from learning about, or knowledge of, the external world. . . .

> Just as we can say with assurance that we ourselves are not only bodies in space, acted upon by measurable natural forces, but that we think, choose, follow rules, make decisions, in other words possess an inner life of which we are aware and which we can describe, so we take it for granted—and, if questioned say that we are certain—that others possess a similar inner life, without which the notion of communication, or language, or of human society, as opposed to an aggregate of human bodies, becomes unintelligible.[15]

This kind of understanding, as Isaiah Berlin implies, is a refinement and deepening of the kind of understanding which, every day, we employ in our social lives. To adopt an impersonal, scientific attitude toward human beings tells us only about their behavior. It is to treat others as not possessing an inner life; more particularly, as not possessing will or intention. D. C. Dennett, in one of his essays, refers to "intentional explanations" which "cite thoughts, desires, beliefs, intentions, rather than chemical reactions, explosions, electric impulses, in explaining the occurrence of human motions."[16]

The impersonal stance, referred to by Dennett as "mechanistic," can only inform us about another person's behavior. Although, by adopting this attitude, we may be able to discern *causes* for this behavior, our explanation cannot be in terms of intention, nor can we determine what this behavior means to the individual concerned.

In our ordinary day-to-day encounters with individuals, we are bound to adopt the intentional stance. I cannot but assume that I myself have feelings, thoughts, desires, beliefs, and intentions; and I must, in the ordinary way, assume that others are similarly constituted. The mechanistic stance is the exception; the intentional stance must be the rule. Anatol Rapoport has pointed out that, when playing a game, we are bound to make what he calls "the assumption of similarity" about our opponent. Playing a game is impossible unless one can assume that one's opponent intends to win if he can, and that, in trying to achieve this, he will be influenced by the same kind of considerations, and have in mind the same kinds of strategy, as one does oneself.[17]

Adopting the objective, mechanistic stance toward human beings actually deprives the observer of an important source of understanding. In our exchanges with others, we are bound to rely upon our own subjective experience if we wish to grasp what others are thinking and feeling. We observe behavior; the signals which others give us. But we interpret those signals, at least in part, in terms of what we ourselves feel or have felt in the past. This is why it is often difficult to understand patients or others who come from different cultures. It is easy to misinterpret the signals with which we are presented.

In contrast, persons who are particularly close to one another, like husband and wife, often develop sensitive antennae which tell each what the other is feeling, not just because the other provides evidence of happiness, sorrow, fatigue, or zest, but because the emotional state of the other has an immediate influence. We care about how those who are close to us are feeling, in some degree because we possess a measure of altruism, but more especially because their happiness or unhappiness has a direct effect upon our own. Psychoanalysts need to be affected by their patients if they are to understand them, which is one reason why psychoanalysis is an emotionally demanding profession.

Although psychoanalysis which goes beyond a concern with isolated neurotic symptoms is not, and can never be, scientific in the sense in which the "hard" sciences are scientific, this does not mean that it should be dismissed as hopelessly subjective. Psychoanalysis is a professional discipline: a skill which ought only to be practiced by people who have been properly trained. The potential psychoanalyst must use his own emotional reactions in understanding his patient, but he must also learn to control those emotional reactions and not permit them to interfere with the patient's discourse. Psychoanalysis is a long way removed from ordinary social interaction. Although the skills used by the psychoanalyst are refinements of those which we all employ in understanding others, the analyst must learn to be self-effacing. He must not respond to his patient in the same way that he would in ordinary social intercourse, but must suppress all responses of his own that do not further the patient's understanding of himself. Psychoanalysis is bound to be one-way traffic, in that the enterprise is designed to benefit the patient without providing any gratification for the analyst other than that of exercising, and being paid for, a professional skill. But the practice of psychoanalysis demands of the analyst all the intuitive, empathic understanding which he can muster. Because such understanding must be derived from his own subjective, human experience, the analyst can never employ the detached, cold objectivity which is a mandatory requirement of the experimental scientist, and psychoanalysis itself can never become an exact science.

NOTES

1. Quoted in Frank J. Sulloway, *Freud, Biologist of the Mind: Beyond the Psychoanalytic Legend* (New York: Basic Books, 1979), p. 14.
2. *The Standard Edition of the Complete Psychological Works of Sigmund Freud,* 24 vols., ed. and trans. James Strachey (London: Hogarth Press, 1953–64), 2:6.
3. Freud, *Standard Edition,* 3:77.
4. Ibid., 3:199.
5. Ibid., 3:203.
6. Roger Brown and Richard J. Herrnstein, *Psychology* (Boston: Little, Brown, 1975), p. 583.
7. Thomas S. Szasz, *The Ethics of Psychoanalysis* (New York: Basic Books, 1965), p. 71.
8. Freud, *Standard Edition,* 11:51.
9. Quoted in Ernest Jones, *The Years of Maturity, 1901–19,* vol. 2 of *Life and Work of Sigmund Freud* (London: Hogarth Press, 1955), p. 497.

10. John Macmurray, *Persons in Relation,* vol. 2 of *The Form of the Personal* (London: Faber and Faber, 1961), p. 24.

11. John Bowlby, *Attachment and Loss,* 3 vols. (London: Hogarth Press/ Institute of Psycho-Analysis, 1969, 1973, 1980).

12. B. F. Skinner, *Beyond Freedom and Dignity* (New York: Knopf, 1971), pp. 200, 205, 177, 164, 160.

13. P. F. Strawson, *Freedom and Resentment and Other Essays* (London: Methuen, 1974), pp. 19–20.

14. Charles Rycroft, ed., *Psychoanalysis Observed* (New York: Coward-McCann, 1967), p. 11.

15. Isaiah Berlin, *Vico and Herder: Two Studies in the History of Ideas* (London: Hogarth Press, 1976), pp. 28, 23.

16. D. C. Dennett, "Mechanism and Responsibility," in *Essays on Freedom of Action,* ed. Ted Honderich (London: Routledge and Kegan Paul, 1973), p. 161.

17. Anatol Rapoport, *Fights, Games and Debates* (Ann Arbor: University of Michigan Press, 1960), pp. 306ff.

11

The Psychology of Symbols: Symbols of Unity and Integration

THE PSYCHOLOGY OF symbols is a vast subject. I have therefore given this chapter a subtitle, to indicate the part of the subject upon which I chiefly wish to comment.

A symbol may be defined as "whatever stands for something, or has representative function." A banal example is a national flag. When planted on a particular piece of land, it serves to indicate or symbolize possession of that piece of land by the country it represents. The Cross is the central symbol of the Christian religion. Everyone seeing the Cross knows that it stands for, or symbolizes, Christianity, just as the crooked cross or swastika, personally selected by Hitler, became the symbol of Nazi Germany.

Why do we use symbols at all? What is the place of symbolism in the human mental economy? What function do symbols serve? It is clear that symbolization belongs with the higher reaches of human mental activity; with the ability to conceptualize and to think in abstract terms rather than with reflex responses or emotional outbursts. We know that higher animals dream. Perhaps they are also capable of appreciating or forming symbols; but it is difficult to believe that this capacity can be found very far down the evolutionary scale. It seems probable that the development of the capacity to use symbols is closely linked with the development of intelligence and thinking, and also with the development of an "inner world" of the psyche which does not necessarily correspond closely with the reality of the external world.

Let us imagine an animal which is nearly perfectly adapted to its environment. The food it needs for survival is plentiful and easily obtained. There are sufficient potential mates in the neighborhood for reproduction to be assured, and no serious threat from predators against which it need take precautions. For such an animal to survive and prosper, all that is required is that the environment remain constant. So long as this state of affairs obtains, the animal's behavior can be governed by preprogrammed, automatic responses. It need not think or plan, let alone make use of symbols. As we know from observation of insects, complex sequences of behavior like those concerned with catching prey or digging burrows are enshrined within the creature's nervous system. Some of these patterns of behavior are so elaborate that, at first sight, it is difficult to believe that they are not the product of conscious deliberation. Yet, if the sequence is interfered with experimentally, the rigidity of the pattern is made manifest. The animal has to "go back to the beginning." It cannot vary the pattern.

More importantly, it cannot adapt if circumstances change. Such animals are at the mercy of the environment. Koala bears live, very selectively, on the leaves of the eucalyptus tree. Their internal economy is perfectly designed to cope with daily ingestion of huge quantities of eucalyptus leaves. But, if forest fires rage, or a blight hits the eucalyptus, the koala bear is at risk of extinction.

This can even happen in man. In the 1840s, when Ireland

suffered from a blight which destroyed the potato crop, the peasant population died in the thousands, in spite of the fact that the seas around the island were teeming with fish. If the peasants had been sufficiently educated to make use of their human potential, instead of being both ignorant and exploited, the Great Hunger need never have happened. As it was, as many as possible fled from Ireland and emigrated to the United States. Britain is still suffering from the incompetence of the British government in dealing with the famine. The Irish have never forgiven us, and the descendants of those Irish emigrants send funds across the Atlantic to support the terrorist activities of the Irish Republican Army. The example of the Irish peasants illustrates the point that behavioral rigidity is the enemy of survival, except in a world in which the environment remains entirely stable. This may be the case in the Isles of the Blessed, but is not a feature of the world as we know it.

The success of the human species is in part due to behavioral flexibility. Konrad Lorenz calls man "the specialist in non-specialization." We are not rigidly programmed for adaptation to one particular environment or dependent upon one type of diet. Because of this, man has been able to survive both at the equator and in the Arctic; to live at the level of the Dead Sea or high amid the peaks of the Andes. Man can exist on a diet which is largely protein or on one which is mostly vegetable. Although there are certain needs which must be fulfilled, for oxygen, water, and protection against extremes of temperature, the limits imposed by Nature are wide indeed.

It can, however, be argued that the price of flexibility is a less than perfect adaptation to the external world, and hence some degree of dissatisfaction. Consider the more or less perfectly adapted animal which was postulated earlier. So long as the environment remains constant, all its needs are met. Satisfied, content, and at peace with itself and the world, the animal, we may suppose, lives in a state of Boeotian bliss. For man, however, such peace belongs to fantasy rather than to reality.

"Call no man happy till he dies, he is at best but fortunate," said Solon.[1] Although we may experience moments of utter content, such moments are always transient. The achievements of man are based upon a restless hunger which drives him to entertain utopian fantasies, to seek new conquests, to search for new ways of living, to venture even beyond this planet in the fearsome expanses of space.

The fact that there is no close fit between man and his environment has been one factor determining the development of human imagination.

> Ah, but a man's reach should exceed his grasp,
> Or what's a heaven for?[2]

The development of an inner world of the imagination and the development of symbolization march hand in hand. Since the inner world of the imagination and the external world are discrete entities, bridges between the two are needed if man is to be able to relate one with the other. One function of symbols is to form such bridges.

Donald Winnicott, a British psychoanalyst of considerable originality, made a study of what he called "transitional objects."[3] Many very young children develop powerful attachments to inanimate objects from which they are reluctant to be parted. Such objects may be teddy bears or dolls, but can equally well be blankets or even diapers. Because such an object provides comfort and security for the child, it is invested with such emotional significance that he or she may be unable to sleep without it. It is clear that such an object has become a symbol. It symbolizes what the mother provides and therefore acts in some degree as a substitute for her. This kind of object cannot be dismissed as merely imaginary, for it does have a real existence in the external world. Yet the child's imagination is what renders it significant. In this way, a symbolic object acts as a bridge between the child's imagination and the external world. It belongs wholly to neither world, but partakes of both.

Because symbols bridge the gap between subjective and objective, they give meaning to the external world. Symbols and symbolic activities play a part in changing one form of psychic energy into another. Jung gives as an example the fertility rites of the Wachandi of Australia. When spring comes, they dig a hole in the ground, shaping it and setting it round with bushes so that it resembles the female genitals. Then they dance round the hole all night, thrusting their spears into it and shouting, "Not a pit, not a pit, but a cunt." By means of these symbolic activities, the primitive sexual drive is redirected toward agriculture, and emotional meaning is given to an activity which might otherwise seem no more than exhausting toil. Jung also notes the old custom of the "bridal bed" in the field, set there to make the field fruitful. He comments: "As I make this woman fruitful, so I make the earth fruitful. The symbol canalizes the libido into cultivating and fructifying the earth."[4]

When the symbolic function fails, or the gap between inner and outer becomes too wide to be bridged, the external world loses all significance. Something of this kind appears to happen in schizophrenia. In some varieties of this mental illness, the sufferer turns away from an external reality which has brought him no satisfaction, and retreats into his own inner world of fantasy. Because this inner world is no longer linked with reality by means of commonly used symbols, it becomes less and less comprehensible to others. We call the sufferer "mad." We do not yet understand all the factors which cause schizophrenia, but, in this context, it is worth noting that, in many cases, it is possible to demonstrate that the patient's capacity to use language in a metaphorical or symbolic way is defective. Thus, if one asks a schizophrenic the meaning of a proverb—"A rolling stone gathers no moss," for example—he is likely to reply, "If a stone is rolling downhill, there isn't time for moss to grow on it."

If one is tied to the literal, one cannot make use of symbols. In some cases of schizophrenia, the patient reports dreams of being in a colorless, featureless, perhaps ice-bound landscape. This aptly reflects his inability to bridge the gap between inner and outer; to invest the world with his own feelings. Schizophrenia is also characterized by loss of cohesion within the personality. In chronic cases, cohesion may be so severely impaired that the person no longer seems to exist as an entity, but appears to the observer as a series of disconnected egos, each governed by the emotion of the moment, with nothing to connect one with the other.

But all men are, in varying degree, "divided selves." We are creatures of conflict, the prey of wishes and impulses which are often incompatible with one another. This is connected with the flexibility with which Nature has endowed us. Our imaginary, perfectly adapted animal would be at peace with itself as well as at peace with its environment. Perhaps, at times, there might be temporary conflict; for example, between its reproductive urge and its need for food. But one cannot imagine that, in such a creature, conflict would persist for long. When one need was satisfied, the animal would turn to seek fulfillment for the other.

Man, or at least Western man, seldom seems able to find entire fulfillment. Recurrent dissatisfaction with what is seems part of the human condition: perhaps the spur which has impelled man to new invention and ever increasing mastery of the environment. Even sex brings only transient satisfaction. Freud once wrote, "It is my belief that, however strange it may sound, we must reckon with the possibility that something in the nature of the sexual instinct itself is unfavourable to the realization of complete satisfaction."[5]

If this is so, it is not surprising that men seem compelled to seek a fusion or unity which perpetually eludes them. Plato, in the *Symposium,* assigns to Aristophanes the speech in which it is supposed that men and women are merely halves of what were originally wholes. These wholes were of three sexes; male, female, and hermaphrodite. Because of their *hubris,* they were bisected by Zeus. As a consequence, each is compelled to seek the lost half, in order to regain a pristine unity. Love is, therefore, "the desire and pursuit of the whole." Aristophanes says, "The way to happiness for our race lies in fulfilling the behests of Love, and in each finding for himself the mate which properly belongs to him; in a word, in returning to our original condition."[6]

The conciseness with which this myth expresses a truth about human nature in symbolic language points to another function of symbols. Because their meaning is not precise but diffuse, symbols can convey ideas with an economy which prosaic statements cannot rival.

The desire and pursuit of the whole can be sought in ways other than physical unity with a beloved person. The psychologist who has paid most attention to this quest for internal unity is Jung, whose conception of personality is examined in Chapter 9. Jung postulates a quest for integration within the psyche of the single individual which he calls "the process of individuation." Jung found that if he could enable the subject to experiment with different sides of his own nature, by paying attention to his dreams and fantasies, a process of psychological development could be initiated which went far beyond conventional methods of reductive psychotherapy.

As indicated in Chapter 9, the newfound unity which signaled the patient's progress was expressed in symbolic, circular forms which Jung compared with the mandalas used to assist meditation by Tibetan Buddhists. Jung wrote of these mandalas: "As psychological phenomena they appear spontaneously in dreams, in certain states of conflict, and in cases of schizophrenia. Very frequently they contain a quaternity or a multiple of four, in the form of a cross, a star, a square, an octagon etc."[7] For Jung, the quaternity, like the circle, was a symbol of wholeness or unity.

The fact that mandala forms tend to appear spontaneously both when the patient is making progress toward a new unity and also in the fragmented state of schizophrenia may appear paradoxical. In fact, the phenomenon illustrates another important feature of symbols. Symbols both express states of mind and tend toward inducing them. The patient who is progressing toward integration produces these symbols as evidence of a new attitude of mind. The schizophrenic produces them as desperate attempts to recapture the integrated state of mind which is eluding him.

The same dual function can be discerned in those symbolic statements which we call "works of art." A work of art, even when it is no more than a commission specified by, and undertaken to satisfy, a patron, necessarily expresses something of the inner world, the state of mind, of the artist. But, when we contemplate the artist's work, we are ourselves affected by whatever order or harmony he has imposed upon his material. Harrison Gough expressed this effect succinctly when he wrote, "The work of art, for example, reorders and brings into balance the tensions of form and space, and in doing so moderates the inner tensions of the observer, giving him a sense of encounter and fulfilment."[8]

Mandalas occur in various cultures, and date back at least to the paleolithic. They also occur spontaneously in the drawings of children. Between the ages of two and three, according to Rhoda Kellogg, children begin to superimpose forms one upon another, thus creating what Kellogg calls "combines." One of the most frequent combines is a circle enclosing other forms like squares or triangles.[9] In his book on children's drawings, the Harvard psychologist Howard Gardner writes:

> Mandalas are the examples, *par excellence,* of a combine. Not only are mandalas visible in many combines but, more important, mandalas seem to represent a central tendency of "combining behavior": the simplest and

most balanced diagrams, when combined with one
another, produce mandala-like forms.[10]

What Howard Gardner terms "combining behavior" is
characteristic of man. It is a process which constantly goes
on, both subjectively and objectively. The recurrent synthesis of opposites which Jung describes as going on within
the personality as a process of individual development is
also characteristic of the creative process, whether in the arts
or in the sciences. I noted earlier that one function of symbols is to provide bridges between the inner world of the
imagination and the outer world of fact. A famous example,
quoted in most books and papers on the creative process, is
furnished by Friedrich August Kekulé von Stradonitz, professor of chemistry in Ghent. One afternoon in 1865, he was
dozing in front of the fire. Visions of atoms combining in
various structures played before his eyes:

> My mental eye, rendered more acute by repeated
> visions of this kind, could now distinguish larger struc-
> tures, of manifold conformation; long rows, sometimes
> more closely fitting together; all twining and twisting
> in snake-like motion. But look! What was that? One of
> the snakes had seized hold of its own tail, and the form
> whirled mockingly before my eyes. As if by a flash of
> lightning I awoke.... Let us learn to dream, gentle-
> men.[11]

Kekulé's vision enabled him to formulate the structure of
the benzene ring, and thus lay a foundation of modern
organic chemistry. It also happens that the snake eating its
own tail is an ancient symbol, the uroborus, which Jung
describes as often to be found coiled about the center of
mandalas painted by his patients. This is a striking instance
of a symbol partaking of both worlds: the world of the
psyche and the world of external reality.

The process of creation in both the arts and the sciences is
often characterized by making a new synthesis between

ideas which had previously appeared to be distinct or widely separated. Solutions to problems, whether artistic or scientific, come about by discovering how apparently discrepant themes or facts can be linked to form greater wholes. The differences between scientific and artistic creativity are explored in Chapter 7, "Psychoanalysis and Creativity." But, although differences certainly exist, the sciences and the arts share the aim of seeking order in complexity and unity in diversity. The intense pleasure described as the "eureka" experience which scientists enjoy when they have made a discovery is paralleled by the pleasure described by painters and musicians upon solving an aesthetic problem. Each type of solution has both an external and an internal validity. Nature has so framed our mental processes that we rejoice in bringing together things which have previously appeared to be incongruous or widely separated. The desire and pursuit of the whole is not confined to love.

Newton's formulation of the law of universal gravitation, described in Chapter 3, is a typical example of a new scientific hypothesis uniting and transcending discoveries which had previously been regarded as unconnected. Kepler had described the laws governing the motions of the planets; Galileo had discovered the laws governing the motion of objects upon earth. Newton's hypothesis of universal gravitation demonstrated that bodies in the heavens and bodies upon earth obeyed the same laws.

Painting is very often concerned with balancing contrasting masses and colors in such a way as to create a new and satisfying unity. So is music. In Chapter 7, I referred to Beethoven's "Grosse Fuge" as an example of combining and transcending themes which at first hearing appear widely discrepant. This is an extreme example. Even the simplest kind of music is composed of contrasting elements. A single line of melody leaves the tonic, ventures forth, and then returns home from whence it came: two steps in opposite directions brought together by the form of the melody.

Music, it seems to me, is *par excellence* a symbolic activity. It is often declared to be the most abstract of the arts. Perhaps this is why Walter Pater wrote his famous sentence "All art constantly aspires towards the condition of music."[12]

Music has no obvious biological utility. It is possible to argue that drawing and painting, by sharpening man's perception of the external world, were originally adaptive rather than purely aesthetic activities. No such claim can be made for music. We might guess that literature derives from the art of the primitive storyteller. By passing on to his listeners a tradition of their origins, he might be said to be enhancing their sense of their own identity; and, by providing a framework of conventional ways of behavior, might be thought to be aiding their adaptation to the world. It is impossible to regard music in this light.

Although some music imitates natural sounds, like the song of the cuckoo or the surge of the sea, musical sounds are not very common in nature, and most music is not representational. Even the origin of music is disputed. Herbert Spencer believed that music was developed from speech; Darwin that speech was derived from music. There are only two utilitarian functions which can be assigned to music. The first is the promotion and enhancement of rhythmical bodily motion. Music lightens the fatigue of marching and other repetitive physical actions. Music can also enhance crowd solidarity by making people experience similar emotions concurrently; a function which, although abused by demagogues, may be useful on ceremonial and other occasions.

But biological and linguistic theories fail to explain the pleasure we get from music, or why we feel great music to be so important. Some musicians maintain that music has no meaning outside itself. Stravinsky, for example, says that "music expresses itself." He describes music as "supra-personal and supra-real and as such beyond verbal meanings and verbal descriptions." Although Stravinsky agrees that a composition has its origins in the emotions of the composer and may therefore be considered as symbolizing them, he goes on to state: "More important is the fact that the composition is something entirely *beyond* what can be called the composer's feelings. . . . A new piece of music *is* a new reality."[13]

Formalists like Stravinsky not infrequently compare music with mathematics. They believe that the meaning of music is to be found in the perception of the musical relationships within a particular work, and that such appreciation is primarily intellectual rather than emotional. No one with any understanding of either music or mathematics will deny the beauty of pattern and structure. But, as G. H. Hardy pointed out in his classic account of a mathematician's life, "Music can be used to stimulate mass emotion, while mathematics cannot."[14] It is clear that the appeal and the effects of music cannot be entirely cerebral.

While still affirming that music is nonreferential, and that its meaning is to be sought solely within the work of music itself, other theorists do admit that particular musical relationships and structures excite emotion rather than a purely intellectual response. However, some musical authorities question whether such emotions are genuine. Hindemith, for example, states, "The reactions music evokes are not feelings, but they are the images, memories of feelings."[15] Hindemith does not believe that music expresses the composer's feelings, and affirms that the composer is simply a skilled manipulator of the feelings of others.

> Here is what he really does: he knows by experience that certain patterns of tone-setting correspond with certain emotional reactions on the listener's part. Writing these patterns frequently and finding his observations confirmed, in anticipating the listener's reaction he believes himself to be in the same mental situation.[16]

Hindemith goes on:

Thus a composer can never be absolutely sure of the
emotional effect of his music on the listener when using
complex material, but by experience and clever distri-
bution of this material, moreover with frequent references to those musical progressions that evoke the
uncomplicated feeling-images of sadness or gaiety in
an unambiguous form, he can reach a fairly close
approximation to unanimity of all listeners' reactions.[17]

Perhaps it is arrogant of a mere listener to take issue with
the statements of a distinguished composer, but I must
confess that I find Hindemith's theories unconvincing.
Although Hindemith recognizes that "music touches both
the intellectual and the emotional parts of our mental
life,"[18] he underestimates the compelling power of the satisfaction which a symbolic union between these two different
aspects of our being affords us. Man's greatest intellectual
achievements depend upon being able to separate intellect
from emotion. Perhaps his greatest satisfactions come from
being able to reunite them. It seems probable that the great
composers are not so much adept manipulators of the emotions of others, as Hindemith suggests, but rather individuals who are particularly skilled at making new syntheses
within their own psyches. These gifted people command
our admiration because they have been able to realize, in
their own achievements, what we would all like to be able to
do: to make a coherent whole out of the disparate elements
which make up our personalities.

In his biography of Elgar, Jerrold Northrop Moore
expresses exactly what I mean. He prefaces his biography by
deploring the traditional division between "life" and
"works." As he says:

A creative life can have no general significance apart
from its works, and works have no cumulative significance outside the worker's life. What I wanted was some
means of combining the two modes, so that each new

adventure in theme and form could be understood as a chapter in the spiritual biography of the whole man. Such a book would seek its goal neither in musicology nor in the sensual man: rather it would seek the influence of each on each.

Thus I have tried to understand what it is to look at the world through creative eyes, to listen through creative ears. The artist, like the rest of us, is torn by various desires competing within himself. But unlike the rest of us, he makes each of those desires into an element for use in his art. Then he seeks to synthesize his elements all together to form a style. The sign of a successful synthesis is a unified and unique style plain for all to recognize. So it is that a successful style can seem to its audience full of indefinably familiar things—and at the same time invested with godlike power of "understanding" that is far indeed from the daily round. The process by which a man has forged such a unity is the most profound and most exalted of human stories.[19]

So style, in the case of the creatively gifted, is the cement which holds the differing parts of the personality together, and which makes manifest to others the unity which the artist has achieved. It is interesting that, today, we value this evidence of individuality so highly. Works "in the style of" count for far less, both aesthetically and in the marketplace, than those which are recognized as authentic products of a single individual. This is a modern development. Prior to the Renaissance, artists were treated as more or less anonymous craftsmen who executed the orders of their patrons, or who served communal, rather than individual, interests. It is only since the middle of the thirteenth century that the names of individual painters began to be recorded; and the idea that any of the arts could be used to further the psychological development and self-realization of the individual did not take hold until the seventeenth century or later.

The style of a writer, composer, or painter may be easily

recognizable without any implication that the artist himself feels that any ultimate goal of unity has been attained. Although the forging of a personal style is "a sign of a successful synthesis," style continues to change and develop throughout an artist's life, just as the works themselves do. Psychologists who have paid especial attention to psychological development in later life, like Jung, have always affirmed that individuation, or self-realization, is never permanently or completely achieved. Life always demands new adaptation. In the creatively gifted, the development of personality is made manifest in the works which they produce. Aaron Copland demonstrates his understanding of the relation between the creative process and the development of personality in his Charles Eliot Norton lectures:

> The serious composer who thinks about his art will sooner or later have occasion to ask himself: why is it so important to my own psyche that I compose music? What makes it seem so absolutely necessary, so that every other daily activity, by comparison, is of lesser significance? And why is the creative impulse never satisfied; why must one always begin anew? To the first question—the need to create—the answer is always the same—self-expression; the basic need to make evident one's deepest feelings about life. But why is the job never done? Why must one always begin again? The reason for the compulsion to renewed creativity, it seems to me, is that each added work brings with it an element of self-discovery. I must create in order to know myself, and since self-knowledge is a never-ending search, each new work is only a part-answer to the question "Who am I?" and brings with it the need to go on to other and different part-answers.[20]

Perhaps I can now explain why I earlier referred to music as *par excellence* a symbolic activity. First, music is a temporal art. The patterns of music exist in time, and require time for their development and completion. Susanne Langer refers to music as "a thoroughgoing symbol, an image of subjective time."[21] Although painting and architecture and sculpture make symbolic statements about relationships, these relationships are static. Music, like life, is in constant motion.

Second, music symbolizes typical patterns in the emotional life of human beings. Leonard Meyer suggests that "music activates tendencies, inhibits them, and provides meaningful and relevant resolutions."[22]

Anyone who has been reared in the Western diatonic tradition recognizes that the resolution afforded by a final return to the tonic is analogous to "returning home," winding "somewhere safe to sea," or, at a more mundane level, resembles the familiar patterns of physical need and desire followed by release of tension and fulfillment. As Meyer points out, one of the ways in which composers arouse our emotions and excite our interest is by postponing completion and return. He gives as an example the fifth movement of Beethoven's C-sharp minor quartet, opus 131. Beethoven denies the listener's expectation by the progressive fragmentation of the rhythmic and melodic pattern:

> But at the very moment when rhythm, harmony, texture, and even melody in the sense of pattern seem all but destroyed, the little figure which opens the movement and the first phrase raises our hopes and redirects our expectations of completion and return. Now we are certain what is coming.[23]

Meyer's description is very close to the theory of music advanced by Hans Keller. Keller contrasts what he calls "background" and "foreground" in music:

> The background of a composition is both the sum total of the expectations a composer raises in the course of a piece without fulfilling them, and the sum total of those unborn fulfilments. The foreground is, simply, what he does instead—what is actually in the score. . . .

> Musical meaning . . . depends for its sheer existence on the clearly implied conflict between that which you hear and that which is being contradicted by what you hear. It is this tension, varying in intensity according to the structural juncture a composition has reached, between what the composer does and what he makes you feel he was expected to do that constitutes musical logic. The clearer the tension, the more logical the music—and the clearest tension is that which combines a maximum of contradiction with a maximum of unity between the contradicting elements.[24]

Once again, in a different context, we encounter the idea that combining elements which are widely separated or dis-crepant is a profound and satisfying experience.

This is not the only way in which music can be described as a form of "combining behavior." Music integrates a variety of differing elements to form a whole. As Yehudi Menuhin writes, "Music creates order out of chaos; for rhythm imposes unanimity upon the divergent; melody imposes continuity upon the disjointed, and harmony imposes compatibility upon the incongruous."[25]

Music, therefore, symbolizes man's attempts to make sense out of existence by discovering or imposing order upon it; and, because music is, for the most part, nonrepresentational, it is "purely" symbolic in a way which representational arts are not. This is the reason why Schopenhauer regarded music as the direct representation of the Will. "The composer reveals the innermost nature of the world, and expresses the profoundest wisdom in a language that his reasoning faculty does not understand." After detailing various analogies between human emotions and different types of music, Schopenhauer continues:

> But we must never forget when referring to all these analogies I have brought forward that music has no direct relation to them, but only an indirect one; for it never expresses the phenomenon, but only the inner

nature, the in-itself, of every phenomenon, the will itself.[26]

Schopenhauer here touches upon another feature of music which is explored by Susanne Langer. To express the essence of feelings, rather than the feelings themselves directly, requires abstraction. Aaron Copland, discussing his need to compose, referred to "self-expression." But, as Susanne Langer observes, "Sheer self-expression requires no artistic form."[27]

We can all abreact our feelings of grief by howling. To reach the essence of grief, as does Purcell in Dido's lament, requires not only the composer's skill, by which he transmutes emotions into music, but the capacity to stand back from such emotions and, by imposing form upon them, universalize them. The notion of "psychical distance," elaborated by Edward Bullough[28] and used by Susanne Langer, is significant. So long as a composer is possessed by an intense emotion, he will not be able to symbolize it in music. Psychical distance, the ability to detach oneself from immediate experience, is characteristically human. Without this capacity, there would be no scientific discoveries, no mathematics, and, though this is not always appreciated, no works of art. Wordsworth said that poetry "takes its origin from emotion recollected in tranquillity." It is only when psychical distance has been achieved that symbolization can occur. What we admire about the works of great composers and other artists is not only the evidence which they provide of the artist's capacity for deep feeling, but also the proof which they afford of the artist's power to master and integrate such feelings.

Man's quest for integration and unity seems to be an inescapable part of the human condition. Because of its ability to make new wholes out of contrasting elements, music is the art which most aptly symbolizes this quest. It is interesting that so many scholars have reached the same conclusion. For example, Susanne Langer quotes a sentence

by Hans Mersmann: "The possibility of expressing opposites simultaneously gives the most intricate reaches of
expressiveness to music as such, and carries it, in this
respect, far beyond the limits of the other arts."[29] Edmund
Gurney writes of music as seeming

> like a fusion of strong emotions transfigured into a
> wholly new experience, whereof if we seek to bring out
> the separate threads we are hopelessly baulked: for
> triumph and tenderness, desire and satisfaction, yield-
> ing and insistence, may seem to be all there at once, yet
> without any dubiousness or confusion in the result; or
> rather elements seem there which we struggle dimly to
> adumbrate by such words, thus making the experience
> seem vague only in our own attempt to analyse it, while
> really the beauty has the unity and individuality per-
> taining to clear and definite form.[30]

Victor Zuckerkandl, discussing the function of music as
opposed to language, writes: "Words divide, tones unite.
The unity of existence that the word constantly breaks up,
dividing thing from thing, subject from object, is constantly
restored in the tone."[31] In a later passage, he states:

> Musicality is not an individual gift, but one of man's
> basic attributes; man's very nature predisposes him to
> music. In music, man does not give expression to some-
> thing (his feelings, for example), nor does he build
> autonomous formal structures: he *invents himself*. In
> music, the law by which he knows himself to be alive is
> realized in its purest form.[32]

If there be anyone who doubts the importance of symbolism in human life, let him meditate upon this passage.

NOTES

1. Herodotus, *Histories*, i.32.
2. Robert Browning, *Andrea del Sarto*, lines 97–98.
3. D. W. Winnicott, "Transitional Objects and Transitional Phenomena"

(1951), in *Through Paediatrics to Psycho-Analysis* (London: Hogarth Press, 1975), pp. 229–42.

4. C. G. Jung, "Symbols of Transformation," in *Collected Works*, 20 vols., trans. R. F. C. Hull (London: Routledge and Kegan Paul, 1953–79), vol. 5, para. 214, n. 22.

5. *The Standard Edition of the Complete Psychological Works of Sigmund Freud*, 24 vols., ed. and trans. James Strachey (London: Hogarth Press, 1953–64), 11:188–89.

6. Plato, *Symposium*, trans. William Hamilton (Harmondsworth: Penguin, 1951), p. 65.

7. Jung, "Mandalas," in *Collected Works*, vol. 9, part 1, para. 713.

8. Harrison Gough, "Identifying the Creative Man," *Journal of Value Engineering* 2, no. 4 (August 1964):5–12.

9. Rhoda Kellogg, *Analyzing Children's Art* (Palo Alto, Calif.: National Press Books, 1969).

10. Howard Gardner, *Artful Scribbles* (New York: Basic Books, 1980), pp. 41–43.

11. Quoted in Alexander Findlay, *A Hundred Years of Chemistry*, 2d ed. (London: Duckworth, 1948), pp. 36–38.

12. Walter Pater, "The School of Giorgione," in *The Renaissance* (Oxford: Oxford University Press, 1986), p. 86.

13. Igor Stravinsky and Robert Craft, *Expositions and Developments* (London: Faber and Faber, 1962), pp. 101–2.

14. G. H. Hardy, *A Mathematician's Apology* (Cambridge: Cambridge University Press, 1940), p. 26.

15. Paul Hindemith, *A Composer's World* (Garden City, N.Y.: Doubleday, 1961), p. 45.

16. Ibid., p. 42.

17. Ibid., p. 51.

18. Ibid., p. 48.

19. Jerrold Northrop Moore, *Edward Elgar* (Oxford: Oxford University Press, 1984), p. vii.

20. Aaron Copland, *Music and Imagination*, Charles Eliot Norton Lectures, 1951–52 (Cambridge: Harvard University Press, 1952), pp. 40–41.

21. Susanne K. Langer, *Feeling and Form* (London: Routledge and Kegan Paul, 1953), p. 118.

22. Leonard B. Meyer, *Emotion and Meaning in Music* (Chicago: University of Chicago Press, 1956), p. 23.

23. Ibid., p. 155.

24. Hans Keller, "Towards a Theory of Music," *The Listener*, June 11, 1970, p. 796.

25. Yehudi Menuhin, *Theme and Variations* (New York: Stein and Day, 1972), p. 9.

26. Arthur Schopenhauer, *The World as Will and Representation*, vol. 1, trans. E. F. J. Payne (New York: Dover, 1969), pp. 260–61.
27. Susanne K. Langer, *Philosophy in a New Key* (Cambridge: Harvard University Press, 1960), p. 216.
28. Edward Bullough, " 'Psychical Distance' as a Factor in Art and as an Aesthetic Principle," *British Journal of Psychology* 5, part 2 (1912):87–118.
29. Quoted in Langer, *Philosophy in a New Key*, p. 243.
30. Quoted in Terence McLaughlin, *Music and Communication* (London: Faber and Faber, 1970), pp. 101–2.
31. Victor Zuckerkandl, *Man the Musician*, vol. 2 of *Sound and Symbol*, trans. Norbert Guterman, Bollingen Series 44 (Princeton: Princeton University Press, 1973), p. 75.
32. Ibid., p. 350.

12

Sanity of True Genius

THE TITLE OF this essay is taken from one of Lamb's *Essays of Elia*. Lamb begins with the following words:

> So far from the position holding true, that great wit (or genius, in our modern way of speaking) has a necessary alliance with insanity, the greatest wits, on the contrary, will ever be found in the sanest writers. It is impossible for the mind to conceive a mad Shakespeare. The greatness of wit, by which the poetic talent is here chiefly to be understood, manifests itself in the admirable balance of all the faculties. Madness is the disproportionate straining or excess of any one of them.
>
> "So strong a wit," says Cowley, speaking of a poetical friend,
>
>> "did Nature to him frame,
>> As all things to his judgment overcame;
>> His judgment like the heavenly moon did show,
>> Tempering that mighty sea below."
>
> The ground of the mistake is, that men, finding in the raptures of the higher poetry a condition of exaltation, to which they have no parallel in their own experi-

ence, besides the spurious resemblance of it in dreams and fevers, impute a state of dreaminess and fever to the poet. But the true poet dreams being awake. He is not possessed by his subject, but has dominion over it.[1]

Throughout history, there have been two opposing schools of thought about men and women of genius. The one portrays the genius as exceptionally well balanced; the other affirms a close connection of genius with insanity, or at any rate with mental instability. How is it that such discrepant opinions have arisen, and is any reconciliation between the two opposing views possible?

As an example of the first school of thought, let us take a quotation from Jonathan Richardson's *An Essay on the Theory of Painting* of 1715:

> The way to be an Excellent Painter is to be an Excellent Man. . . . A Painter's Own Mind should have Grace, and Greatness; That should be Beautifully and Nobly form'd. . . . A Painter ought to have a Sweet, and Happy Turn of Mind, that Great, and Lovely Ideas may have a Reception there.[2]

Vasari, writing of Raphael, said that he

> was endowed by nature with all that humility and goodness which one sometimes meets in those who, more than others, add to their humane and gentle nature the most beautiful ornament of felicitous affability. This made him show himself sweet and agreeable to everybody and under any circumstances.[3]

The artist Peter Paul Rubens, hardworking, methodical, and immensely wealthy, was gifted with such clear judgment that he was employed as a diplomat both by the Duke of Mantua and also by the Infanta Isabella. In the face of personal bereavement and political obstruction, he remained serene. No one could be further removed from the notion that artists are necessarily tormented beings.

Characters such as these make it comprehensible that, in some periods of history, it has been believed that the greater the genius, the more likely is it that he will be an exalted type of human being; noble, lofty, and harmonious; displaying in his life, as in his works, both exquisite sensibility and perfect control. To this way of thinking, the greatest works of art could only be produced by people of the highest character. The noblest works mirror the nobility of the artist's soul.

By the middle of the nineteenth century, a less exalted notion of genius was promulgated, perhaps in the wake of Samuel Smiles's *Self-Help*, first published in 1859. Carlyle remarked, " 'Genius' (which means transcendent capacity of taking trouble, first of all)."[4]

Galton, introducing the second edition of his book *Hereditary Genius*, wrote, "At the time when the book was written (1869), the human mind was popularly thought to act independently of natural laws, and to be capable of almost any achievement, if compelled to exert itself by a will that had a power of initiation."[5] Galton believed that great achievement was dependent upon three gifts, all of which he considered were inherited. These gifts were named as "ability," "zeal," and "a capacity for hard work." He entirely repudiated the notion that anything approaching mental instability was part of creative achievement.

> If genius means a sense of inspiration, or of rushes of ideas from apparently supernatural sources, or of an inordinate and burning desire to accomplish any particular end, it is perilously near to the voices heard by the insane, to their delirious tendencies or to their monomanias. It cannot in such cases be a healthy faculty nor can it be desirable to perpetuate it by inheritance.[6]

In 1904, Havelock Ellis published a book entitled *A Study of British Genius*. Ellis selected from *The Dictionary of National Biography* 1,030 names of particularly eminent people, of whom 975 were men and 55 were women. He found that only 4.2 percent were demonstrably psychotic. He wrote of this finding:

> It is perhaps a high proportion. I do not know the number of cases among persons of the educated classes living to a high average age in which it can be said that insanity has occurred once during life. It may be lower, but at the same time it can scarcely be so very much lower that we are entitled to say that there is a special and peculiar connection between genius and insanity. The association between genius and insanity is not, I believe, without significance, but in face of the fact that its occurrence is only demonstrable in less than five per cent of cases, we must put out of court any theory as to genius being a form of insanity.[7]

The apparent incompatibility of insanity with creativity is further supported by the fact that creative people, when they do become insane, generally show a decline both in the quality and quantity of their productions. Schizophrenic painters, for example, often show a shift in their paintings toward subjects reflecting their own personal disturbance which have little relevance to the perceptions of the normal person. Not infrequently, they deteriorate to the point of endlessly repeating stereotyped patterns. The Dutch psychiatrist J. H. Plokker, in his book *Artistic Self-Expression in Mental Disease*, acknowledges that, at the onset of a schizophrenic breakdown, an artist may be stimulated to record something of his new way of perceiving the world, but the impulse is usually short-lived:

> Everyone who knows anything about art sees the difference between the normal and the pathological when he looks at a series of works by one patient, and soon becomes bored on seeing psychotic creations, once the first moment of surprise has passed. The arid, stereotyped and fixed elements in the content and particularly in the shapes soon show the mental stagnation.[8]

Nor is it only schizophrenia, among mental disturbances, which interferes with creative production. Severe depression, so long as it persists, usually prevents the process of creation, although susceptibility to recurrent depression is often associated with creative potential. Robert Schumann was manic-depressive. Eliot Slater and Alfred Meyer have charted Schumann's known periods of elation and periods of depression in relation to his compositions. They have clearly demonstrated that elation facilitated production, while depression inhibited it.[9]

There were probably a variety of reasons for Rossini abandoning the composition of operas in 1829, at the age of only thirty-seven. However, from 1839 onward, Rossini suffered from such severe episodes of depression, partly determined by physical ailments, that he contemplated suicide. After finishing the *Stabat Mater* in 1832, he composed no major work for many years. But, at the age of sixty-five, a renaissance occurred. He began composing once more, and, in addition to a prolific output of shorter pieces, composed a major religious work, the *Petite Messe Solennelle*.[10]

From these and many other similar accounts, it might appear self-evident that mental illness and the capacity to create are incompatible. Yet, from antiquity onward, a link between genius and madness has been recurrently affirmed. Seneca, in his dialogue *De tranquillitate animi*, wrote, "Nullum magnum ingenium sine mixtura dementiae fuit." That is, "There has never been great talent without some admixture of madness."[11] This belief is echoed by Dryden:

> Great wits are sure to madness near allied,
> And thin partitions do their bounds divide.[12]

Throughout the nineteenth century, the belief that genius and madness were closely related appears to have become more common. The French psychiatrist Moreau de Tours, a disciple of Esquirol, compared genius with insanity, believ-

ing that both states resulted from overactivity of mind.[13]
The German psychiatrist P. J. Moebius (1853–1907) of
Leipzig adopted the concept of the "superior degenerate,"[14]
a label which, in our own time, was converted into "creative
psychopath," and was applied to such characters as T. E.
Lawrence. Wilhelm Lange-Eichbaum, whose book *Genius,
Insanity and Fame* was still being reprinted in 1956, stated
that most geniuses were psychopathically abnormal.[15] Even
if it was not possible to demonstrate that all geniuses were
psychopathic or psychotic, it became commonplace to
allege, as did no less a figure than Proust, that "everything
great comes from neurotics. They alone have founded religions and composed our masterpieces."[16]

The number of poets who have suffered from recurrent
episodes of depression which were severe enough to rate as
mental illness is certainly striking. William Collins, John
Donne, William Cowper, Thomas Chatterton, John Clare,
Christopher Smart, Edgar Allan Poe, Gerard Manley Hopkins, Sylvia Plath, John Berryman, Anne Sexton, Hart
Crane, Theodore Roethke, Delmore Schwartz, Randall Jar-
rell, and Robert Lowell all suffered from well-authenticated
periods of severe depression. Clare, Collins, and Smart were
all admitted to "madhouses." Lowell was in and out of hospitals for both mania and depression. Five of these poets committed suicide.

Among prose writers, Charles Lamb (who was in an asy-
lum during 1795–96), Samuel Johnson, Goethe, Balzac,
Tolstoy, Conrad, Ruskin, Jack London, Ernest Hemingway,
and Virginia Woolf were similarly afflicted. Hemingway,
Jack London, and Virginia Woolf all killed themselves.

In a recent study of forty-seven British writers and artists,
selected for eminence by their having won major awards or
prizes, Jamison found that 38 percent had actually received
treatment for affective illness. Poets were particularly subject to severe mood swings.[17]

An investigation of a group of writers at the University of

Iowa's Writers' Workshop showed that 67 percent of the writers interviewed had suffered from affective illness compared with only 13 percent of controls. Moreover, among the relatives of the writers, 21 percent had definable psychiatric disorder, whereas only 4 percent of the relatives of the controls did.[18]

Boswell's account of Dr. Johnson is a vivid picture of a writer who was plagued with recurrent depression throughout life:

> He felt himself overwhelmed with a horrible hypochondria, with perpetual irritation, fretfullness and impatience and with a dejection, gloom and despair which made existence misery. From this dismal malady he never afterwards was perfectly relieved and all his labour and all his enjoyments were but temporary interruptions of its baleful influence.[19]

Johnson tried to ward off depression by all manner of obsessional rituals. He was terrified both of death and of insanity; and, like many other sufferers from depression, hated going to bed because of the morbid thoughts which tormented him.

Recurrent depression is not the only type of mental disorder to affect creative people. Newton, when he became mentally ill in middle life, was not only depressed, but also paranoid; and accused his friends of maligning him and plotting against him. Many creative people have had abnormal personalities, even if they were not overtly mentally ill. Kafka, for example, was certainly schizoid; and many of the greatest philosophers seem to have been unable, or unwilling, to form close personal relationships or embark on raising a family. I am purposely omitting the consideration of writers like Dostoyevsky, de Maupassant, and Nietzsche, who are known to have suffered from epilepsy, cerebral syphilis, or other forms of organic brain disease.

It might well be argued that, because we know so much

about these interesting people, we have gained a false impression. If less gifted, more ordinary people had been subjected to the scrutiny of biographers, might it not be found that they too exhibited as much psychopathology? It is a possibility not wholly to be discounted. The more we know about anyone, the more are we able to discern neurotic traits, mood disorders, and other aspects of personality which, when emphatically present, we label neurotic or psychotic. The famous and successful are less able to conceal their vagaries of character because biographers or earnest students in search of Ph.D.'s will not let them rest in peace. Or if, as in the cases of Freud and T. S. Eliot, their papers are guarded by watchdogs until any chance of offending the living is over, speculation often attributes to them the most improbable vices. It should be remembered that psychiatrists, and perhaps especially psychoanalysts, have very little idea of what the average, "normal" man or woman is like, and may therefore tend to call "neurotic" all kinds of people who are actually within the normal range. As one of my psychoanalytic teachers used to remark, "The normal man is a very dark horse."

There is another, more compelling reason why genius and madness have been associated. The word "genius" seems originally to have been the Roman equivalent of the Greek "psyche." According to R. B. Onians, it was "the life-spirit active in procreation, dissociated from and external to the conscious self that is centred in the chest." The genius, like the psyche, was identified as that part of the person supposed to survive death. Both genius and psyche were located in the head. Onians continues:

> The idea of the genius seems to have served in great part as does the twentieth-century concept of an "unconscious mind," influencing a man's life and actions apart from or even despite his conscious mind. It is now possible to trace the origin of our idiom that a

man "has" or "has not genius," meaning that he possesses a native source of inspiration beyond ordinary
intelligence.[20]

So, even in antiquity, it was assumed that the creative process
involved two aspects of mind, one which was presumably
under the conscious control of the subject, perhaps equivalent to the Freudian "ego"; the other something which had
to be wooed or summoned, like one of those spirits from the
vasty deep which Owen Glendower so boastfully asserted
would obey his call.

It is surely the notion of *inspiration* which has been most
closely linked with, and responsible for, the idea that creative people are unstable. The insane were once considered
to be possessed by devils or other spirits. In similar fashion
the inspired were believed to be transported into a state of
divine madness. Although Plato distinguished insanity from
inspiration, Iris Murdoch, in her Romanes Lecture of 1976,
The Fire and the Sun, tells us that Plato "speaks more than
once of the artist's inspiration as a kind of divine or holy
madness from which we may receive great blessings and
without which there is no good poetry."[21]

In later periods, the distinction between ordinary madness and divine madness became blurred. I earlier quoted
Seneca's remark to the effect that great talent always contains some admixture of madness. The word "dementia,"
which is here translated as "madness," may, according to
some scholars, have been used by Seneca as indicating
divine inspiration rather than insanity. Seneca was writing
in the first century A.D. (he was forced to commit suicide in
65). There has been some confusion between inspiration
and insanity ever since. In our own day, the confusion has, as
it were, been reversed. Instead of artists being considered
mad, the insane are thought to be inspired. R. D. Laing and
his followers have so idealized the schizophrenic condition
that those who have so far avoided this mental illness some-

times feel (wrongly, in my view) that they may have missed some startling insights into the nature of reality which are granted to the insane but not to the normal person.

When one comes to consider the accounts given by creative people of the appearance of inspiration, the confusion between inspiration and madness appears less surprising. Being inspired is often accompanied by feelings of being possessed and compelled by something beyond the ego. J. W. Cross records that George Eliot told him "that, in all she considered her best writing, there was a 'not herself' which took possession of her, and that she felt her own personality to be merely the instrument through which this spirit, as it were, was acting."[22] Thackeray recorded: "I have been surprised at the observations made by some of my characters. It seems as if an occult Power was moving the pen. The personage does or says something, and I ask, how the dickens did he come to think of that?"[23]

Sometimes, but far from invariably, the state of being inspired is accompanied by emotional exaltation of an extreme kind. An observer reported that Swinburne, uttering poetry, paced up and down the room in a passionately excited state, apparently unaware of his surroundings and oblivious of a thunderstorm which was raging at the time.[24] Tchaikovsky wrote:

> It would be vain to put into words that immeasurable sense of bliss which comes over me directly a new idea awakens in me and begins to assume a definite form. I forget everything and behave like a madman. Everything within me starts pulsing and quivering. Hardly have I begun the sketch ere one thought follows another.[25]

There seems to be general agreement that inspiration cannot be willed, although it can be wooed. When it does appear, it is usually accompanied by feelings of joy, relief, or satisfaction; but the person experiencing such feelings does not necessarily display them overtly. Tchaikovsky and Swinburne were both emotional characters. Moreover, they were living at a time when the romantic notion of the artist was paramount, and no doubt felt that tempestuous emotions and uninhibited displays of feeling were expected of them. In contrast, when Anthony Trollope's autobiography was published posthumously, in 1883, it harmed his reputation because he portrayed the novelist as a craftsman; as a shoemaker rather than as an artist. This was, no doubt, a defensive maneuver. Trollope was a sensitive man, prone to depression, who deliberately adopted a stiff upper lip and a bluff *persona*. But the image of himself which he chose to present was so out of line with the *Zeitgeist* that it was not until some forty years after his death that his imaginative gifts as a novelist again won critical recognition.

Although scientists may, like Archimedes, exclaim "Eureka!" when inspiration suggests a solution to a problem, they generally describe their experience in more prosaic terms than do musicians and poets. Newton, on being asked how he made his discoveries, replied, "I keep the subject constantly before me, and wait till the first dawnings open slowly by little and little into the full and clear light."[26] Gauss, describing the solution of a problem which had plagued him for years, wrote:

> Finally, two days ago I succeeded, not on account of my painful efforts, but by the Grace of God. Like a sudden flash of lightning, the riddle happened to be solved. I myself cannot say what was the conducting thread which connected what I previously knew with what made my success possible.[27]

So, although inspiration is clearly exciting and rewarding, whether or not it is accompanied by passionate emotion and excitable behavior depends upon the temperament of the person experiencing it, the circumstances in which he finds himself, and what he thinks is expected of him. It is quite

unjustified to link inspiration with instability or mental illness. Indeed, I believe that so-called "inspiration" is no more
than an extreme example of a process which constantly goes
on in the minds of all of us.

It is clear that inspiration is a different phenomenon from
the kind of rational thinking which we employ when planning a journey or deciding between alternative courses of
action. In Chapter 7, I criticized Freud's view that there are
two types of sharply contrasted mental functioning, the one
being rational thought directed toward external reality, the
other being fantasy unconnected with the real world and
governed by wish fulfillment. Although Freud was certainly
right in contrasting rational, directed thinking with daydreaming, he did not admit the possibility that unconscious
processes and fantasy also play an important part in the type
of creative thinking which is concerned with reality rather
than with wish fulfillment. Freud drew too sharp a distinction between rational and irrational. He linked together
play, fantasy, and the dream as being unrealistic, childish
forms of mental activity which were essentially escapist and
governed by the unconscious, while supposing that thinking
was a rational activity which was mainly controlled by the
ego. These are the two principles of mental functioning
which he named "primary process" and "secondary process." Freud believed primary process to be directed by the
pleasure principle, while secondary process was controlled
by the reality principle.

Such a view can be criticized on two counts. First, Freud
does not take into account the fact that even scientific thinking contains an element of play; what Einstein called "a free
play with concepts."[28] Second, Freud fails to give an explanation for the way in which solutions to problems may
suddenly appear without conscious deliberation. An example described by Gauss is quoted above. Because Freud
regarded the unconscious as essentially chaotic, a boiling
cauldron of primitive desires and impulses, he did not postulate any kind of ordering process as taking place uncon-

sciously. Yet, from Gauss's description and many similar reports, we know that there must be some kind of problem-solving, pattern-making process which goes on in the mind automatically, and which is certainly not directed consciously.

Graham Wallas has described a series of stages in the creative process which he calls preparation, incubation, illumination, and verification.[29]

Preparation is the stage in which a problem is investigated in all directions as thoroughly as possible. This investigation is consciously controlled and under the direction of the subject's will.

Incubation is a stage in which the problem is laid aside, often for a considerable period. We do not know exactly what takes place during this stage, but we may assume that some kind of scanning, sorting process is going on rather like that which modern theory supposes is taking place in dreams. Whether the problem under consideration is aesthetic or scientific, incubation seems to be an inescapable part of the creative process. Brahms, for example, described the germ of musical inspiration as a "gift" which must at first be left alone:

> At the time I must disregard this "gift" as completely as possible but ultimately I have to make it my own inalienable property by incessant labour. And that will not be quickly accomplished. The idea is like the seed-corn; it grows imperceptibly in secret. When I have invented or discovered the beginning of a song ... I shut up the book and go for a walk or take up something else; I think no more of it for perhaps half a year. Nothing is lost, though. When I come back to it again it has unconsciously taken a new shape, and is ready for me to begin working at it.[30]

The creative person must, at some point, cease conscious striving and passively allow these mysterious processes to take place. To be able to do this requires confidence; some degree of faith that, out of doing nothing, something new will emerge.

The term "inspiration" can be applied both to the sudden appearance of what Brahms calls a "gift" and to the later appearance of the "new shape" which manifests itself after a period of incubation. But it might be clearer if we reserved "inspiration" to describe the first phenomenon, and used Graham Wallas's term "illumination" for the second. Both phenomena are described by the mathematician Poincaré:

> For fifteen days I strove to prove that there could not be any functions like those I have since called Fuchsian functions. I was then very ignorant; every day I seated myself at my work table, stayed an hour or two, tried a great number of combinations and reached no results. One evening, contrary to my custom, I drank black coffee and could not sleep. Ideas rose in crowds; I felt them collide until pairs interlocked, so to speak, making a stable combination. By the next morning I had established the existence of a class of Fuchsian functions, those which come from the hypergeometric series; I had only to write out the results, which took but a few hours.

Later, Poincaré describes going on a journey which made him forget his mathematical work:

> Having reached Coutances, we entered an omnibus to go some place or other. At the moment when I put my foot on the step the idea came to me, without anything in my former thoughts seeming to have paved the way for it, that the transformations I had used to define the Fuchsian functions were identical with those of non-Euclidean geometry. I did not verify the idea; I should not have had time, as, upon taking my seat in the omnibus, I went on with a conversation already commenced, but I felt a perfect certainty. On my return to Caen, for conscience' sake I verified the result at my leisure.[31]

Inspiration, incubation, and illumination are all dependent upon mental processes which are not under the control of the will and which are far removed from Freud's notion of directed, "secondary process" thinking controlled by the reality principle. But this does not mean that such processes are escapist, childish, or unrealistic. Still less does it imply that these processes are in any way connected with mental instability. Although the "normal" person may not be capable of the creative achievements of a Brahms or a Poincaré, he is actually quite familiar with the processes of incubation and illumination at a humbler level. Most people know what it is to be tormented with anxiety about some problem or choice to which there appears to be no clear-cut answer. Often, after a night's rest, the solution appears obvious. "Sleeping on it" clearly gives time for some unconscious sorting process to take place which could be called short-term incubation.

Inspiration and illumination have, as we saw earlier, been associated with insanity because of the confusion between insanity and "divine madness." The link with insanity may also have been made because these phenomena are dependent upon unconscious processes which we do not fully understand and which therefore appear mysterious; as incomprehensible as delusions or hallucinations. Having disposed of the notion that there is any connection between insanity and inspiration, let us return to the original problem of whether or not there is any other possible link between genius and mental illness.

We have stated that creative people, when they do suffer from mental illness, usually cease production or at least show a decline in the quality of what they produce. On the other hand, we have also noted that what appears to be a rather large proportion of creative writers are either manic-depressives, or else subject to recurrent attacks of depression without mania or hypomania. In trying to reconcile these opposites, we may be able to throw some light upon the two opposing views of genius which were outlined at the beginning of this chapter.

One feature of the highly creative is the zeal with which they pursue their chosen avocation. Creative ability is not simply a question of being endowed by Nature with superior gifts. It is not rare to encounter people of extremely high intelligence who, nevertheless, are not creative. They seem to lack the driving force, the compulsive urge to discovery, which characterizes men and women of genius. Although some geniuses achieve immediate recognition, innovators are often reviled. Many creative people labor for years in obscurity, or are only recognized posthumously. Although the desire for fame and prosperity is certainly one motive impelling most creative endeavors, it is not the only motive, nor, I believe, the most important. The act of creation, whether in the arts or in the sciences, is self-rewarding, quite apart from any worldly success which it may bring.

The two opposing views about the nature of genius which have formed the main subject of this chapter can be reconciled if we assume that men and women who are creatively gifted are characterized by a susceptibility to mental illness which is greater than average, but which does not necessarily lead to actual breakdown because creative powers are to some extent protective against mental illness. Experimental psychology lends some support to this hypothesis. It has been demonstrated that creative people exhibit more neurotic traits than the average person, but are also better equipped than most people to deal with their neurotic problems. It has also been shown that some of the psychological characteristics which are inherited as part of the predisposition to schizophrenia are divergent, loosely associative styles of thinking which, when normal, are "creative," but which, when out of control, are transformed into the "thought disorder" typical of schizophrenia.

If it is true that creative work is protective against breakdown, we can understand why some talented people are motivated to employ their talents in creative endeavor, while others are not. Those who have inherited a predisposition to mental disorder will be internally driven by forces which do not operate in the well balanced. In the case of the creative writers who are subject to severe attacks of depression, it is not difficult to understand how creative work can stave off descent into the abyss. One of the main characteristics of persons who are particularly liable to depression is the fragility of their self-esteem. We all become temporarily depressed as a consequence of loss, failure, or bereavement. But most of us, because of a fortunate genetic endowment or a felicitous early childhood, possess inner sources of self-esteem which are sufficient to sustain us in the face of the normal hazards of existence. When fate assails us, we reel, but we recover. We know that, come what may, we shall live to fight another day. But those prone to severe depression have no such conviction. They seem to lack any inner sources of self-esteem. When faced with even a minor setback, a marital quarrel, a rejection slip, or a bad review, they are plunged into a state of melancholia from which they can envisage no escape. For such people, avoidance of this state becomes the major endeavor of their lives. Some, like Balzac, keep the devil at bay by manic overwork. Success and public recognition can, in some degree, compensate for inner emptiness by providing recurrent injections of self-esteem from external sources. Depressives are as dependent upon frequent "fixes" of recognition and success as are addicts on their drug. It is not difficult to understand that liability to depression is a powerful spur to creative achievement in those who are gifted enough to use this way of coping with their temperamental vulnerability.

But liability to depression is not the only variety of mental disability. There are also those whom psychiatrists call schizoid; people who, if they become mentally ill, are likely to develop some variety of schizophrenic illness. Kafka, who is the subject of Chapter 2, is an example of this type of personality, and a writer whose talent almost certainly protected him from becoming overtly mentally ill. Schizoid people have great difficulty in forming close relationships. They want intimacy, but also fear it. By keeping aloof, they are protecting what they feel to be a fragile ego from being damaged or submerged by close involvement. Newton, who is discussed in Chapter 3, is an extreme example. A particularly strong need for autonomy is characteristic of some philosophers. It is an odd and interesting fact that most of the world's greatest thinkers since the time of the Greeks have not married or formed close personal ties. The higher reaches of abstract thought require long periods of solitary concentration which are incompatible with married life. But those who are attracted to such intellectual pursuits are generally those who shun close involvement as threatening rather than treating it as life-enhancing. Independence of thought and emotional independence march hand in hand.

Leibniz attributed his autonomy as a thinker to the fact that he taught himself and did not cumber his brain with teachings accepted on authority. Spinoza believed that his own power of logical reasoning was the only instrument necessary to create a comprehensive philosophy. Kant stated that the autonomy of the will was the sole principle of all moral laws. Wittgenstein proclaimed that he was glad that he had not let himself be influenced. Nietzsche insisted on what he called independence of soul. None of these philosophers married. Most lived alone for the greater part of their lives.

Complete personal isolation is not a possibility for human beings who wish to retain their sanity. Those who are temperamentally incapable of close relationships and who are also gifted may use writing as an indirect way of communication. But there is another, more important function which creative endeavor performs which is particularly significant both in people who fear insanity, and in those who fear being overwhelmed or destroyed by intimate relationships. The creative act is essentially integrative. Opposites are united; disparate elements are reconciled. At least some of those who create their own, autonomous *Weltanschauung* are driven to do so by a need to prevent their own disintegration.

Although Lamb was right in affirming that the genius is not mad in that "he is not possessed by his subject, but has dominion over it," he was wrong in asserting that "the greatness of wit, by which the poetic talent is here chiefly to be understood, manifests itself in the admirable balance of all the faculties."

In the consideration of genius, imbalance, too, has its place. The motive force which impels a man or woman to embark upon the hazardous, often unrewarding task of endeavoring to make coherence out of the external world or out of their own inner selves often originates from alienation or despair. As Irvin Ehrenpreis once put it, "The power of the human mind to recompose painful ordeals as shapely and seductive music, as stories or poems—these resources are what keep us from going rigid with horror in the face of the grinding wretchedness that even the most placid existence must endure."[32]

NOTES

1. Charles Lamb, *Essays of Elia and Last Essays of Elia* (London: Everyman's Library, 1977), p. 219.

2. Jonathan Richardson, *An Essay on the Theory of Painting* (London: W. Bowyer for J. Churchill, 1715), pp. 34, 199, 201.

3. Giorgio Vasari, *Le vite de' piu eccelenti pittori scultori ed architetti*, 9 vols., ed. Gaetano Milanesi (Florence: G. C. Sansoni, 1878–85), 4:315–16.

4. Thomas Carlyle, *Frederick the Great*, bk. 4, ch. 3.

5. Francis Galton, *Hereditary Genius*, 2d ed. (London: Macmillan, 1892), p. ix.

6. Ibid.

7. Havelock Ellis, *A Study of British Genius* (London: Hurst and Blackett, 1904), p. 191.

8. J. H. Plokker, *Artistic Self-Expression in Mental Disease*, trans. Ian Finlay (London and The Hague: Mouton, 1964), p. 70.

9. Eliot Slater and Alfred Meyer, "Contributions to a Pathography of the Musicians: Robert Schumann," *Confinia Psychiatrica* 2 (1959):65–94.

10. Richard Osborne, *Rossini* (London: Dent, 1986).

11. Seneca, "De tranquillitate animi," in *Moral Essays*, ed. and trans. John W. Basore (London: Heinemann, 1932), 17.10–12.

12. John Dryden, *Absalom and Achitophel*, part 1, line 150.

13. Franz G. Alexander and Sheldon T. Selesnick, *The History of Psychiatry* (London: Allen and Unwin, 1967), p. 140.

14. Ibid., p. 174.

15. Wilhelm Lange-Eichbaum, *Genie, Irrsinn und Ruhm* (Munich and Basel, 1956).

16. *The Maxims of Marcel Proust*, ed. Justin O'Brien (New York: Columbia University Press, 1948).

17. Kay R. Jamison, "Mood Disorders and Seasonal Patterns in Top British Writers and Artists," unpublished data.

18. N. J. C. Andreasen and A. Canter, "The Creative Writer," *Comprehensive Psychiatry* 15 (1974):123–31.

19. James Boswell, *The Life of Samuel Johnson, LL.D.*, 3d ed., vol. 1, ed. G. Birkbeck Hill (Oxford: Oxford University Press, 1887), pp. 63–64.

20. R. B. Onians, *The Origins of European Thought* (Cambridge: Cambridge University Press, 1954), pp. 161–62.

21. Iris Murdoch, *The Fire and the Sun: Why Plato Banished the Artists* (Oxford: Oxford University Press, 1977), p. 2.

22. J. W. Cross, ed., *George Eliot's Life as Related in Her Letters and Journals*, vol. 3 (Edinburgh and London: W. Blackwood and Sons, 1885), pp. 421–25.

23. W. Jerrold, ed., *Roundabout Papers: The Works of William Makepeace Thackeray with Biographical Introductions by His Daughter, Anne Ritchie*, vol. 12 (London: Smith, Elder, 1903), pp. 374–75.

24. H. Treffry Dunn, *Recollections of Dante Gabriel Rossetti and His Circle* (London: E. Mathews, 1904), p. 64.

25. Quoted in Modeste Tchaikovsky, *The Life and Letters of Peter Ilich Tchaikovsky*, trans. Rosa Newmarch (London: J. Lane, 1906), pp. 274–75.

26. Quoted in Frank Manuel, *A Portrait of Isaac Newton* (Cambridge: Harvard University Press, 1968), p. 86.

27. Quoted in Jacques Hadamard, *The Psychology of Invention in the Mathematical Field* (Princeton: Princeton University Press, 1945), p. 15.

28. Jeremy Bernstein, *Einstein* (New York: Viking, 1973), p. 172.

29. Graham Wallas, *The Art of Thought* (London: Cape, 1926).

30. Quoted in J. A. Fuller-Maitland, *Brahms* (London: Methuen, 1911), pp. 69–70.

31. Henri Poincaré, "Mathematical Creation," in *The Foundations of Science*, trans. G. Bruce Halsted (New York: Science Press, 1913), pp. 383–94.

32. Irvin Ehrenpreis, *New York Review of Books*, 1984.

13
Why Human Beings
Become Violent

MEN WHO COMMIT violent crimes are not infrequently told by magistrates or judges that they have behaved like animals. This is grossly unfair to other species. Nature is red in tooth and claw when one species preys upon another in search of food: but destructive violence between members of the same species is comparatively rare, and usually only occurs under special circumstances of overcrowding or shortage of food. Man is uniquely violent and cruel. When murder or other violent behavior occurs, man is behaving only like man, and not at all like any other living creature. Deliberate cruelty seems peculiar to the human species. One might argue that a cat playing with a mouse is enjoying the exercise of power; but it is unlikely that the cat is capable of entering into the mouse's presumed feelings of terror and helplessness. Men, on the contrary, seem to enjoy subjecting their own kind to violence and cruelty, even when their victims are helpless and totally at their mercy.

I want to underline the distinction between aggression

and destructive violence. There is some degree of aggression between members of the same species in many varieties of animal, and this aggression serves useful biological functions. An animal has to be able to compete with others for whatever resources of food are available. Many species obtain and defend territories, which has the effect of spreading the animals out and ensuring that each will gain a fair share of what is going. Aggression is also employed in establishing a pecking order in animals which live in groups. Groups of animals need to have a hierarchy if peace is to be preserved; and nomadic groups, like baboons, need leaders who can give orders and be obeyed if the safety of the group from predators is to be preserved. Aggression between males often occurs during the breeding situation as part of sexual selection, and occasionally results in serious injury or death. But most contests of this kind are highly ritualized; and the defeated animal is generally allowed to slink away without deadly wounds being inflicted.

In man, aggression also serves some positive functions. We need to be able to stand up for ourselves, to compete with our fellows, to define ourselves as separate individuals, to give orders, and to exact obedience under certain circumstances. For all these functions, some degree of aggression is needed. These positive aspects of aggression are reflected in our language. For example, we speak of "attacking a problem," of "getting our teeth into a subject," of "mastering a difficulty." The idea that aggression is an innate drive like sex, which produces accumulated tension requiring discharge, cannot be maintained. But man is certainly endowed with a considerable potential for aggressive behavior which can be evoked by various external stimuli; and some might argue that we are preprogrammed with a greater potential for aggression than is appropriate to modern circumstances. Washburn, for example, writes:

> Throughout most of human evolution, man was
> adapted to ways of life radically different from those of

today and there has been neither the time nor the control of breeding to change the biology of human aggression from what was adaptive in the past to what is adaptive now. Throughout most of human history, society has depended on young adult males to hunt, to fight, and to maintain the social order with violence.[1]

Aggression, therefore, is a potential response which we share with other animals and which, at least at the dawn of history, if not today, was biologically adaptive. The same cannot be said of destructive violence and cruelty, which are not only blots upon the human escutcheon, but which serve no obvious biological purpose. Indeed, one might argue that violence and cruelty are actually maladaptive. Edward O. Wilson has argued that reciprocal altruism in human societies, and to some extent in animal societies also, is an adaptive device which is likely to promote the well-being of each participant.[2] Kindness to other human beings is likely to pay in terms of reproductive potential and survival; or, as a friend of mine used to put it, "Civility is cheap, but it pays rich dividends!" Violence and cruelty, therefore, are phenomena which are not only repulsive, but which demand explanation.

Regrettably, the violent behavior of human beings is far too common to be explicable in terms of psychiatric abnormality. Violence is potential in all of us. However, in all Western societies, there are a number of individuals who lack the normal degree of control over immediate impulse. These are the so-called aggressive psychopaths who commit violent offenses of various kinds, and who may show an almost complete disregard for the feelings of their victims. There is considerable overlap between the groups of individuals who commit dangerous driving offenses, sexual offenses, and violent offenses.

Some of these abnormals suffer from genetic defects; others show what appears to be delayed maturation of the central nervous system, as evidenced by the persistence of electrical brain-wave patterns which are characteristic of

childhood. Many psychopaths show a failure of socializa-
tion, in that they have never formed ties of mutual regard
with others, and thus live in a world which they assume to be
hostile or indifferent to themselves. Those who feel that
nobody cares for them, themselves care for nobody. The
development of conscience, that is, of an internal regulator
of behavior, depends much more upon the wish to preserve
love and the esteem of one's fellows than upon the fear of
punishment. Since many psychopaths come from homes in
which there has been little love and a good deal of physical
punishment, it is not surprising that they have not developed a normal conscience. A child cannot respond to the
withdrawal of something which he has never had. It is
understandable that those who have never felt themselves to
be loved or approved of are not affected by the withdrawal
of love or by disapproval. When we read of children being
ill-treated or of old ladies being beaten up or raped, it is
natural that we should wish to revenge ourselves by inflicting savage punishments upon the criminals. But the history
of penology amply demonstrates that savage punishments
have little deterrent effect and may increase resentment and
hatred in those who suffer them. The people whom we most
wish to punish are those least likely to respond to punishment.

Although many psychopaths show both a lack of control
of hostility and also an abnormal propensity to behave in
cruel ways toward their fellowmen, much of the cruelty
which they exhibit is casual rather than deliberate. Thus,
they may injure someone whom they are robbing or sexually
assaulting because they do not identify with their victim or
care what the victim feels; but this is obviously a different
matter from the deliberate exercise of cruelty for its own
sake. In Holland and elsewhere, criminologists have experi-
mented in bringing violent criminals face to face with their
victims. In some instances, this has brought home to the
offender for the first time the realization that his victim is a

human being like himself, with the consequence that he has wished to make reparation.

It is possible that we may be able partly to understand the psychopath's lack of control over immediate impulse in terms of physiology. Psychopaths are emotionally isolated, even if not physically so; and, in other species, isolation appears to produce heightened reactivity to dangerous stimuli, which can be demonstrated by measuring hormonal responses. Human beings who have not learned to mix with their fellows in early childhood often show inappropriate aggressive responses. Sometimes they exhibit too little aggression, and fail to stand up for themselves when this would be appropriate. Sometimes they overreact with excessive violence because they perceive threat where none exists.

However, the people whose personalities are so abnormal as to warrant the label "psychopath" constitute a small proportion of the human race. The human tendency toward violence and cruelty cannot possibly be blamed upon them alone, although studying such people can illuminate our understanding of similar behavior in normal people.

Chemical substances can so impair the functioning of the normal person's brain that he becomes temporarily like the psychopath in being unable to exercise adequate control. Alcohol plays a significant part not only in dangerous driving, but also in crimes of violence. Football games appeal to adolescent males because they provide opportunities for so-called macho displays which bolster feelings of developing masculinity. But such displays are apt to be converted into something far more dangerous if alcohol is available. Modern society provides too few opportunities for young adult males to express the aggressive feelings to which I referred when quoting Washburn's remarks. If I were home secretary, I would try to triple the price of alcohol. I am quite sure that there would be some decrease in violent crime as a result.

Alcohol is not the only chemical which can turn normal

aggression into dangerous violence. Increasingly, other drugs, like amphetamines, barbiturates, and heroin produce similar effects. This is partly because of their direct action upon the brain, and partly because those addicted to them are driven to robbery in order to get money to supply their need for drugs.

A second factor predisposing toward violence and cruelty is ill-treatment in childhood. Throughout human history, children have been treated abominably. In *The History of Childhood,* a book by ten American historians, Lloyd De-Mause writes: "The history of childhood is a nightmare from which we have only recently begun to awaken. The further back in history one goes, the lower the level of child care, and the more likely children are to be killed, abandoned, beaten, terrorized, and sexually abused."[3]

We know that parents who batter their babies have, in most instances, themselves been deprived children who have been made to feel inadequate and ineffectual. Such parents, faced with a child who will not instantly obey, or who persists in crying, perceive the child as a threat to their own self-esteem, and retaliate with violence. Some of these parents make demands on their children for the affection which was not given to them when they themselves were children, and react with resentment when the child is unable to fulfill their needs. Baby battering is one instance of how personal maladaptation can override the basic biological behavior patterns which usually ensure that the immature are protected. Helplessness generally inhibits violence in human beings as well as in other species. In the ritual contests referred to earlier, the losing animal will often signal his defeat by presenting a vulnerable part of his anatomy to the winner. This inhibits the winning animal from further attack. One of the most distasteful features of human violence is that it may persist even when the victim is entirely at the mercy of his attacker.

The fact that human beings who have been neglected or

ill-treated in childhood seem more prone to treat others violently argues that a good deal of human cruelty is revenge. I share the dislike which many psychologists exhibit for so-called hydraulic models of the mind; but clinical experience makes it difficult for me to conceive of any model which does not allow of resentment in some way being stored in the long-term memory. If one allows that the accumulated irritation of a working day can be abreacted by kicking the dog, which is surely a commonplace observation, I see no reason why resentment should not be stored for much longer, perhaps even for a lifetime. The fact that memories of past humiliation and ill-treatment tend to persist accounts for a number of cases in which a violent act seems disproportionately savage when compared with the provocation. The violent act is revenging a whole series of rejections, humiliations, and the like, none of which by itself would provoke extreme retaliation. A good deal of human violence can be described as the worm turning; the person who has for years felt himself to be at the mercy of others suddenly turning the tables upon them.

A good example of what I mean can be found in Muriel Gardiner's book *The Deadly Innocents*.[4] Tom was a rejected child whose mother banned him from mixing with the rest of the family. He was kept in a shed at the end of the garden, and whipped if he made any attempt to get in touch with his ten siblings. Eventually, he became delinquent. When the facts of his life became known to the juvenile court, he was removed from home and put in charge of an uncle and aunt. Unfortunately, the uncle turned out to be a violent alcoholic who resented Tom and who treated him almost as cruelly as had his mother. Tom found a stray kitten with a broken leg which he tended with great care and gentleness. The kitten was the first creature with which he established ties of affection. One afternoon the uncle came home early from work, and, in a fit of rage, strangled the kitten in front of Tom. When Tom attempted to bury it, the uncle trod the little cross he had made into the ground, destroying the grave. At this point, Tom seized one of his uncle's guns (for this took place in America) and shot his uncle, his aunt, and another woman who was living in the house.

In Tom's case, isolation had deprived him of the opportunity to learn how to handle aggression or to gain self-esteem from relationships with siblings or other companions. Repeated ill-treatment and humiliation had induced a sense of chronic resentment. The provocation he received was extreme; but his response of triple murder is only explicable if his whole history is taken into account. He had been made into a scapegoat by his mother; and scapegoats, whether single individuals or whole categories of persons, like blacks, untouchables, or other groups made into outcasts, deeply feel their lack of status and are rightly resentful as a consequence.

The connection of injured self-esteem with violence goes some way to explaining why it is that, in Britain, murder is overwhelmingly a domestic crime. It is our nearest and dearest who know us well enough to get under our skins and who have the power to humiliate and to provoke us. One way of making the inadequate feel more so is to be critical or contemptuous of their sexual attractiveness or performance. Men are particularly vulnerable in this respect, and it is not surprising that wives and mistresses are so often victims of homicide. As the criminologist Norval Morris has put it, "You are safer on the streets than at home; safer with a stranger than with a friend or relative."[5]

This is perhaps the place to make the point that the widespread misuse of the word "sadism" has given rise to the supposition that a great deal of human violence and cruelty is partially sexual in origin. I have argued elsewhere that most sadomasochism is not what it seems; that, to use the terminology employed both by Russell and Russell[6] and by Abraham Maslow,[7] sadomasochism is "pseudo-sex" rather than sex itself, using sexual behavior patterns to establish dominance relationships, as happens in other primates. So many human beings in Western culture show an interest in sadomasochistic literature or films that it is not possible to argue that such interests are abnormal. There are many people who are uncertain of themselves and ineffective in sexual relationships, and such people may need sadomasochistic fantasies or rituals in order to become fully aroused. Their fascination with sadomasochism springs from their need to establish dominance (or to have the other person establish dominance) before they can venture upon a sexual relationship.

There are a few instances of murderers combining sexual excitement with the act of killing, of whom the so-called Monster of Dusseldorf, Peter Kürten, is one. John Christie was a necrophilic who had intercourse with the corpses of his victims; but such cases are exceedingly rare. I do not believe that torturers usually become sexually aroused when inflicting pain upon their victims, nor do I think it likely that riot police have erections when wielding their whips and clubs. This is not to deny that such distasteful activities may facilitate a weak man's sense of his own dominance, and hence minister to his sexual potency in subsequent sexual situations; but this is not to say that the exercise of cruelty is itself sexually exciting.

A third factor predisposing the normal person to violence and cruelty is the human tendency toward obedience. The experiments of the American psychologist Stanley Milgram are so well known that I need refer to them only briefly. They are summarized in his book *Obedience to Authority*.[8] To Milgram's surprise, around two-thirds of normal people would deliver what they supposed to be extremely painful, possibly near-lethal electric shocks to a subject whom they were told was engaged in an experiment on the effect of punishment upon learning, simply because they were urged to do so by the scientist in charge of the experiment. Obedience to authority is clearly adaptive in human society, as it is in the societies of animals who live in groups, to which I have already referred. A stable dominance hierarchy promotes peace and order within a society, makes possible organized resistance or escape if danger threatens, and allows for instant decision-making by individuals in positions of authority. Human societies could not function if we did not have a built-in tendency to obey managers, chiefs, and policemen. But there is also a dark side to this tendency. The excuse that they were only obeying authority is the one most frequently offered by those arraigned for torture or the slaughter of prisoners, from Eichmann down.

The film *Your Neighbour's Son* is an accurate reconstruction of the methods used in Greece to train potential torturers when the colonels were in power. Young men, mostly from rural areas, were subjected to a regime in which they suffered extremes of physical punishment and humiliation, while at the same time being told that they belonged to an elite group for which they had been especially selected. Total loyalty to the regime and instant obedience to orders, however irrational, were demanded of the recruits. Thus, they were made to eat grass or a burning cigarette; crawl on their knees to the canteen; and were frequently beaten and made to perform exercises carrying a full load of equipment to the point of total exhaustion. One torturer said, "We were forced to learn to love pain."

Gradually they were introduced to torture; first by witnessing it, then by participating in beating prisoners. Any reluctance to take part was dismissed as "sissy"; and any attempt to help prisoners was severely punished. At the same time, recruits were given special uniforms and many privileges. They learned to think of themselves as part of a powerful military police corps which was both feared and esteemed by the ordinary public. The evidence is that recruits trained in this way come to regard torture as a duty; a job which has to be done, and which they are proud of doing as well as possible. There is no evidence that such men gained any especial pleasure from torture; that is, they cannot be regarded as sadists. Twenty-five Greek torturers who were interviewed after the fall of the junta were all leading perfectly normal lives. After periods of observation varying between six and ten years, only one of the torturers showed evidence of guilt and depression.

A fourth factor which makes violence more likely is the interposition of distance between perpetrator and victim. Distance can be either physical or psychological or a mixture of both. If all human fights were confined to fisticuffs, there would not only be fewer deaths, but fewer instances of cruelty. A pilot who drops napalm upon people he cannot see may do so without a qualm. If he were asked to pour petrol over a child and then ignite it, he might well recoil in horror. Yet the injuries inflicted would be closely similar. Konrad Lorenz has argued that human beings possess inhibitory mechanisms against injuring their own kind which are not well developed and which are easily overcome because they are not armed with dangerous natural weapons like tusks or claws.[9] Animals which possess such weapons habitually ritualize conflicts in such ways that serious injury and death are comparatively rare. Natural selection has not allowed for the invention of weapons which kill at a distance. The destruction and death which can be inflicted upon large populations by nuclear weapons is inconceivably great. In spite of the examples of Hiroshima and Nagasaki, the effects are so horrible that our imaginations cannot encompass them. Yet there are people who state publicly that they would not flinch from pressing the button if they thought that the situation required it.

By psychological distance I mean the human capacity for treating other human beings as less than human. Erik Erikson introduced the inelegant but useful term "pseudospeciation" for the psychological tendency to maintain one's own superiority by supposing that other groups of men are inferior.[10] It is easy to persuade ordinary human beings to regard those who profess a different religion, or who have a different skin color, or who belong to a different part of society, as alien. Many societies maintain out-groups which are treated with contempt and often with actual cruelty. In Japan, for example, the descendants of a pariah caste, the Burakumin, are still discriminated against, both socially and economically. They used to be referred to as filthy, four-legged, nonhuman. Pariah castes provide a group of people to whom even the humblest member of the legitimate society can feel superior, and are often regarded as disgusting and potentially polluting. Pariah castes act as scapegoats for tensions within a society, just as individuals sometimes act as scapegoats for tensions within a family. Harshly authoritarian and insecure societies have a particular need for scapegoats, just as do authoritarian and insecure individuals. Political leaders have not been slow to discover that blaming the troubles of a society upon a particular out-group has the effect of uniting the other members of the society by providing them with a common enemy.

The more easily human beings are relegated to a subhuman category, or perceived as alien, the easier it becomes to inflict violence upon them. In Nazi Germany, the S.S. deliberately degraded concentration camp prisoners, forcing them to live in filth, often covered with their own excrement. When the commandant of Treblinka was asked why such humiliation and cruelty was practiced, since the prisoners were going to be killed in any case, Franz Stangl replied, "To condition those who actually had to carry out the policies, to make it possible for them to do what they did."[11]

Although pariah castes are deprived of both status and power, they are nevertheless regarded as possessing sinister, underhand potential for damaging the society which has rejected them. As I have already suggested, there is good reason to suppose that the insulted and injured do resent their position and harbor impulses toward revenge; but pariah castes are habitually supposed to engage in malicious activities which can only be the product of paranoid fantasy. Paradoxically, the very people to whom the legitimate society has denied the possibility of conventional power are supposed to possess magical powers which they may use maliciously. They are thus both despised and feared at the same time.

This brings me to the fifth factor which I consider important in the genesis of violence and cruelty, which is that of fear. Fear is closely related to pseudo-speciation, and pseudo-speciation is related to myth, since out-groups have attributed to them qualities which can only be called mythological. Fear of being helpless in the hands of malignant persecutors is, unfortunately, realistic in authoritarian regimes which practice torture as part of a campaign of terror. However, there are certainly a large number of persons in our culture who produce evidence of having felt, as young children, that they were helplessly at the mercy of adults who were perceived as threatening. We have only to look at myths and fairy tales to discover many instances of violence emanating from dragons, giants, and other figures who are immensely powerful compared with human beings and who may be supposed to reflect something of the infant's experience of the world. It is very easy to persuade human beings that particular groups of other human beings are malignant, evil, and bent upon harm.

I am convinced that there is a paranoid potential in most human beings which is easily mobilized in conditions of stress. This may be an individual experience, or the experience of a whole society. As an individual example, I will quote the case of a middle-aged man who was being treated for various phobic anxieties. The ostensible origin of his symptoms was an experience at the dentist. He was lying prone on the dentist's couch, and at one point during the treatment found it somewhat difficult to breathe. He therefore attempted to sit up, but the dentist pushed him down, saying, "You're bloody well not getting up!" He had previously considered the dentist to be somewhat "trendy" and unprofessional; but at this point the dentist's face appeared to alter. He changed, as it were, into a malign persecutor, and the patient actually fainted. This same patient was an unusually courageous man. During the Second World War, he had survived three air crashes without developing symptoms of anxiety.

When societies go through periods of stress, they also tend to develop paranoid ideas. The disintegration which followed the Black Death in Europe, or which accompanied the hyperinflation in Germany between the two world wars tended to throw up leaders who were not only pathological themselves, but who also mobilized latent feelings of paranoia in whole communities. The historian Norman Cohn has made a particular study of this phenomenon, which is contained in three books: *The Pursuit of the Millennium, Warrant for Genocide,* and *Europe's Inner Demons.*[12] Cohn demonstrates that when normal patterns of life are disrupted, millenniary movements flourish. These are led by prophets who not only promise a New Jerusalem, but who also identify an anti-Christ or other devilish enemy who must be exterminated if the millennium is to come about.

The history of anti-Semitism is a case study of paranoia. The myth of an international Jewish conspiracy dedicated to the overthrow of the existing order in Europe and the establishment of world domination was, even between the two world wars, taken quite seriously. It can also be detected as an underlying theme in popular fiction; for instance, in the thrillers of John Buchan and Sapper. In Germany, even before the First World War, an occult tradition of so-called Ariosophists existed which advocated the establishment of a pan-German world empire, ruled by an Aryan elite which had been purged of the pollution caused by intermarriage. As Nicholas Goodrick-Clarke has shown in his book *The Occult Roots of Nazism,*[13] the writings of such men as Guido List, born in 1848, and Lanz von Liebenfels, born in 1874, postulated the previous existence of a pure Ario-German culture which had later been debased by intermarriage with inferior breeds. List pictured a millennium in which inferior races would be eliminated and a monolithic state established, with a divine force possessing the unconscious of the German people. He even named the year in which the divine force would take over: 1932, the year before Hitler came to power.

In *Warrant for Genocide,* Norman Cohn has examined the influence of the *Protocols of the Elders of Zion,* a document fabricated in France by a Russian author some time between 1894 and 1899. This spurious document was supposed to reveal the program of an international conspiracy of Jews aimed at world conquest. It gradually spread throughout the world. On May 8, 1920, the *Times* devoted an article to it: "Have we been struggling these tragic years to blow up and extirpate the secret organization of German world dominion only to find beneath it another, more dangerous because more secret? Have we, by straining every fibre of our national body, escaped a 'Pax Germanica' only to fall into a 'Pax Judaeica?' "[14] The Germans were not the only nation to take seriously the notion of the Jewish Peril!

In the Middle Ages Jews were seen as agents of Satan, worshippers of the Devil, and participants in diabolical rites which included erotic orgies and, more particularly, the ritual murder of Christian children, with subsequent drinking of the children's blood and cannibalism. As late as 1913, Mendel Beiliss, a Jewish clerk of Kiev, was tried for the ritual murder of a Christian boy. Jews were also supposed to be poisoners of wells. Very similar beliefs were held about witches. Witches were supposed to be able to fly so that they could engage in conspiratorial *sabbats* (itself a Jewish term) in which the devil was worshipped, perverse sexual rites were indulged in, and children were cooked and eaten. They were also seen as causing the death of animals and the ruination of crops by poisoning. A later variant of the poison theme was propagated by Hitler, who affirmed that sexual intercourse with a Jew poisoned the blood. Even schemes for mass inoculation have been suspected of being Jewish plots to inject whole populations with syphilis.

I have said enough to demonstrate that when societies create out-groups which act as scapegoats, outsiders are feared as well as hated. Fear is a potent instigator of violence and cruelty; and its presence partly accounts for the fact that, even when the members of such out-groups are helpless in the hands of their persecutors, they are both tortured and exterminated.

Under certain adverse circumstances, paranoid feelings can be aroused in most people. In my view, this paranoid potential takes origin from the fact that human beings are born into the world in a very helpless state, and remain dependent upon, and at the mercy of, those who are older, bigger, and stronger for a greater proportion of the total life-span than occurs in any other species. The psychoanalyst Thomas Szasz begins his book of aphorisms, *The Second Sin*, by stating, "Childhood is a prison sentence of twenty-one years."[15] Although we may hope that the majority of children do not regard their early years in quite such a negative light, we have all experienced being picked up or left to cry at the whim of others; and fears of once again being reduced to the condition of helpless pawns whose needs and wishes are disregarded are easily rearoused.

This brings me to a consideration of the sixth and last factor which I consider to be provocative of violence. Human beings who feel themselves to be disregarded by the society in which they live, even though they do not belong to a definable out-group, are naturally more prone to resentment and violence than those who feel themselves to be respected. The deprived, the unemployed, the unskilled, do not easily acquiesce in their status. It is not nice to be a gamma; and it is tempting to revenge oneself on the alphas whom one blames for organizing society ineffectively. And the larger the community in which such individuals live, the less likely are they to feel valued or accepted.

It does not surprise me that day-to-day violence is largely an urban problem. It is principally in big cities that the individual can easily feel that he is a mere cog; an expendable element in a vast machine which can easily do without him. In a village, hostile tensions between neighbors can be extreme. Gossip, backbiting, and malice flourish as much, if not more, in small communities as in large. But individuals are *recognized* in small communities. They at least feel that they exist; and, even if their place is no more than that of the village idiot, it is at least better than feeling one is nothing.

Although there has undoubtedly been an increase in urban violence in Britain during the last fifty years, the phenomenon is nothing new. The streets of London are still safer than they were at the turn of the century; while in the eighteenth century, gangs of hooligans known as Mohawks roamed the streets to the terror of the populace. The cry "Who goes home?" in Parliament dates from a time when it was not safe for a member of the House to attempt to reach his home alone. But, today, cities are bigger, population has increased, and the feeling that society is divinely ordered has disappeared.

Authoritarian societies, in which individuals "know their place" and are kept in it by a combination of threat, moral suasion, and an appeal to the Deity, do not have such overt problems with those at the bottom of the heap as we do. I once knew a cook who attributed the rise of Hitler to his disregard for social norms. If only he had remained in his proper station as a house painter, she affirmed, we should not have had all that trouble with him.

It has often been observed that revolutions do not occur when deprivation of those at the bottom of society is at its worst, and when no hope of improvement is visualized. It is rather when hopes have been aroused and then disappointed that violence erupts. In eighteenth-century France, conditions were actually improving, but this improvement came to an abrupt end in 1787, when a fiscal crisis, the threat of increased taxation, and a disastrous harvest combined to threaten many with starvation. The circumstances which instigate violence seem generally to be those which involve what has been called "the disappointment by illegitimate means of legitimate expectations."[16] Today, those of us who are relatively successful tend to feel guilty and less certain of our rights; while those who are unsuccessful feel ill-treated by those above them. We have not begun to solve the problem of how to make the less gifted and the less competent feel wanted or valuable. In urban, industrial societies, there are far too many people who feel humiliated, ineffective, inadequate, and of no account. It is from their ranks that the majority of those who commit acts of violence are drawn; and it is toward giving such people a sense of value and significance that more of our best efforts ought to be directed.

NOTES

1. S. L. Washburn, "Conflict in Primate Society," in *Conflict in Society,* ed. Anthony de Reuck (London: Churchill, 1966), p. 11.

2. Edward O. Wilson, *Sociobiology* (Cambridge: Harvard University Press, 1975), p. 120.

3. Lloyd DeMause, ed., *The History of Childhood: Evolution of Parent-Child Relationships as a Factor in History* (London: Souvenir, 1976), p. 1.

4. Muriel Gardiner, *The Deadly Innocents: Portraits of Children Who Kill* (London: Hogarth Press, 1977), pp. 95–128.

5. Norval Morris and Gordon Hawkins, *The Honest Politician's Guide to Crime Control* (Chicago: University of Chicago Press, 1970), p. 57.

6. Claire Russell and W. M. S. Russell, *Violence, Monkeys and Man* (London: Macmillan, 1968).

7. A. H. Maslow, H. Rand, and S. Newman, "Some Parallels Between Sexual and Dominance Behaviour of Infra-human Primates and the Fantaşies of Patients in Psychotherapy," *Journal of Nervous and Mental Disease* 131 (1960):202–12.

8. Stanley Milgram, *Obedience to Authority: An Experimental View* (New York: Harper and Row, 1974).

9. Konrad Lorenz, *On Aggression* (London: Methuen, 1966), p. 207.

10. Erik H. Erikson, *Identity* (London: Faber and Faber, 1968), p. 41.

11. Quoted in Gitta Sereny, *Into That Darkness: From Mercy Killing to Mass Murder* (New York: McGraw-Hill, 1974), p. 101.

12. Norman Cohn, *The Pursuit of the Millennium* (London: Secker and Warburg, 1957); *Warrant for Genocide: The Myth of the Jewish World-Conspiracy and the Protocols of the Elders of Zion* (London: Eyre and Spottiswoode, 1967); and *Europe's Inner Demons: An Enquiry Inspired by the Great Witch-Hunt* (New York: Basic Books, 1975).

13. N. Goodrick-Clarke, *The Occult Roots of Nazism* (Wellingborough: Aquarian Press, 1985).

14. Quoted in Cohn, *Warrant for Genocide*, p. 153.

15. Thomas Szasz, *The Second Sin* (London: Routledge and Kegan Paul, 1974), p. 1.

16. Roger Brown and Richard J. Herrnstein, *Psychology* (London: Methuen, 1975), p. 274.

14

Psychiatric Responsibility in the Open Society

FOR THE PURPOSE of this chapter, there is no need to define the term "open society" too closely. As Karl Popper delineates it, the open society is an ideal towards which men should strive, rather than an actuality.[1] But, however imperfectly realized, the open society is one in which personal freedom is highly valued, in which individuals are, to use Popper's phrase, "confronted with personal decisions," and in which decisions, both personal and collective, are based upon reason rather than upon authority or tradition. What part has the psychiatrist to play in such a society; and has he anything special to contribute to it?

A hundred years ago, the role of the psychiatrist in society was both limited and clearly defined. His job was to look after the insane; an occupation which was largely custodial, since the insane were mostly untreatable, or at any rate incurable. As cities grew in size, both in Great Britain and the United States, large institutions had to be constructed to accommodate the mentally ill from these urban populations.

These institutions, at first called lunatic asylums, and only recently named mental hospitals, were, at any rate in Britain, often placed at considerable distance from the community whose needs they were designed to serve, in order that the distasteful phenomena of insanity should impinge upon the ordinary citizen as little as possible. Psychiatry was a backwater specialty in which those out of mind were as far as possible put out of sight, while those who cared for them were similarly circumstanced.

Psychiatrists, therefore, tended to be men of little professional distinction. There were honorable exceptions: men like Tuke and Connolly in England or Pinel in France, who were responsible for replacing brutality with enlightened regimes for lunatics; but psychiatrists in the nineteenth century were all too often indolent failures content to carry out a perfunctory "round" of their charges once a day and to spend the rest of their time playing cricket. The idea that such men had a special role to play in society other than that of seeing that their patients were safely confined and treated with reasonable humanity would not have occurred to anyone.

The custodial role of the psychiatrist is still important. In England in 1978, the Department of Health and Social Security estimated that there were 79,165 patients resident in mental illness hospitals and units, representing a rate of 171 per 100,000 population; 26 percent of all hospital beds were occupied by patients with mental illness.[2] In 1975, 193,000 people were inpatients in the state and county mental hospitals of the United States. Another 75,000 were patients in private and federal hospitals.[3] These figures are not often appreciated by the general public. During the last twenty years, advances in the discovery of tranquilizing drugs and other physical methods of treatment have made it possible for a number of patients to live outside mental hospitals who would formerly have had to remain as inpatients. The news media have publicized this and given the public the false impression that the mental hospitals are rapidly emptying. The figures belie this hopeful supposition.

Although there is certainly a more rapid turnover of patients than there was, many of those discharged are readmitted and there remains a chronic core of patients who are unable to take their place in the ordinary community. How far this chronicity is the consequence of living in a hospital is as yet undetermined. On both sides of the Atlantic a great deal still requires to be done to transform mental hospitals from places of confinement into truly therapeutic institutions; to integrate these hospitals into the community; and to prevent the deterioration which inevitably occurs in persons deprived of liberty who are confined for any long period in any institution.

It is worth noting that, in England, four-fifths of those admitted to mental hospitals are "voluntary patients"; whereas, in America, four-fifths of admissions are involuntary. American psychiatrists working in public mental hospitals are, therefore, compelled to assume the distasteful role of jailers to an even greater extent than are their British counterparts.

That there is bound to be some conflict between the roles of therapist and jailer is obvious. What is not so generally realized is that society's greater appreciation of the possibilities of psychiatric treatment has resulted in an increased threat to personal liberty. We shall return to this topic at a later point.

Around the beginning of this century, society's attitude to psychiatrists began to change; very largely because of the rise of psychoanalysis. Psychiatrists started to emerge from their remote seclusion in mental hospitals to become, increasingly, the guides and mentors, not of the insane, but of those troubled people we call neurotic. The popular image of the psychiatrist changed from that of jailer to that of crank or eccentric; a label which has, with some justification, been attached to him ever since. However, as with other eccentrics in other societies, psychiatrists tended to become invested with special, almost magical powers, supposedly gained from dredging in psychic depths to which no ordinary person would care to descend. It was even assumed that their new knowledge of human nature could somehow come to embrace the whole range of human affairs and be used to transform society. Gradually these eccentrics began to be consulted by persons from the upper strata of society; partly because no one else could afford their fees, and partly because psychoanalysis and its offshoots had an intellectual appeal to which the less educated were unable to respond. This tendency was further underlined by the fact that the psychoses, to which psychoanalysis has but a limited application, occur more commonly in the underprivileged; while neurosis, though no respecter of class, is more often found among the sophisticated and complex. In Europe, and later in America, psychoanalysts began to be consulted by intellectuals; a social phenomenon to which, perhaps, too little attention has been paid. On the face of it, it is surprising that the highly educated and socially secure should have apparently demeaned themselves so far as to seek analytical help at a period when self-esteem, far more than today, depended upon position in society. It is, I think, no coincidence that this phenomenon should have been contemporaneous with the decline of belief in conventional Christianity and with the dissolution of a class structure based upon land and family in favor of a less secure hierarchy based more upon the acquisition of wealth. Nowadays, we take it for granted that psychoanalysts will be consulted by distinguished figures, from politicians to philosophers; but in the 1900s it must have seemed an odd thing to do to those who were brought up to think that they were the elite and that no one else was likely to know more than themselves about human nature and the conduct of human relationships and human affairs in general.

Moreover, the idea of progress, of a general tendency towards the improvement of society and the world in general as a result of increasing civilization, so dear to the Victorians, was still operative. Disillusion with Western civilization had not yet overtaken its protagonists, nor had anthropology revealed that so-called "savages" might be better adapted to their environment than we to ours. Psychoanalysis, as it gradually gained recognition, was regarded as a scientific discovery on a par with the discovery of radium or the like; a way of ameliorating man's lot by abolishing neurosis. Freud himself was no utopian. Indeed he became increasingly pessimistic about psychoanalysis as a therapeutic method, though remaining convinced of its scientific status. Many of his followers, however, both in the early days and even today, believed that psychoanalysis was far more than a therapy designed to relieve a few neurotic sufferers. Melanie Klein, for example, writes in one passage of her hope that child analysis will one day become universal.[4] Admittedly, she refers to this hope as "utopian"; but even to imagine that "child-analysis will become as much a part of every person's upbringing as school education is now" is an extraordinary flight of fancy.

This tendency towards utopianism has persisted to some extent among psychoanalysts, although it is probably rather less than it was. It is reinforced by the fact that many analysts lead isolated, dedicated lives, seeing few people other than patients and colleagues, and playing less part than most other professional men in public affairs. It is easier to sustain the belief that one has the answer to the universe if one has no idea how the universe works. Psychoanalysis is primarily an interpretative discipline; a method of making sense out of the previously incomprehensible, and a way of helping individuals to understand themselves better. Although Freud did apply psychoanalytic interpretation to social phenomena to some extent and, for example, conducted correspondence on the subject of war, he was never unrealistic enough to suppose that a method of individual treatment of neurosis could readily be transferred to solve all the problems of society.

That psychoanalysis has not proved to be a universal panacea, nor even the therapeutic success for which enthusiasts hoped, does not mean that psychiatrists and psychoanalysts have nothing to contribute to the study of society. It is a truism to say that society is composed of individuals and that political institutions are, or in an open society should be, designed to promote the well-being of society's members. What constitutes individual well-being and what best contributes to this end are both arguable matters. Whether the health and happiness of individuals is best achieved by material prosperity, by sexual fulfillment, through faith or through agnosticism, by being reared in a kibbutz or in a small family, by being encouraged to be, or discouraged from being, competitive; all these and many similar topics are themes to which the psychiatrist may legitimately address himself and upon which he is entitled to something of a special hearing because of his intimate knowledge of the emotional problems of individuals. It does not, however, follow that he should therefore be regarded as an expert upon education, the control of crime, the resolution of color prejudice or the abolition of war. To all these subjects, the psychiatrist has something to contribute, but it is a limited contribution, derived from his experience with comparatively few individuals.

The analytical treatment of neurotics takes a very long time; which is one reason why psychoanalysis has so far been available, with very few exceptions, only to the privileged rich. This state of affairs is bound to create the hope, however utopian, that if only greater resources of time, money, and trained personnel were provided, many of the misfits in society could be better fitted to take their place in it. Moreover, this hope contains the unspoken assumption that psychoanalysis, or some such psychotherapeutic method, is likely to be as effective a treatment for social deviants as it is for neurotics; and that, if only all criminals, drug addicts, sexual perverts, and the like were treated as patients rather than offenders, their problems and the problems they create would be solved. Hence, there is a strong tendency to exaggerate what psychiatric treatment can accomplish and to suggest that more facilities for treatment exist than is in fact the case. Readers of Popper's *The Open Society* will be familiar with his thesis that utopianism inevitably leads to tyranny. The present tendency in society to idealize the therapeutic approach to misfits is a good example. I do not mean to suggest that, were greater resources available, nothing further could be done for the mentally ill. There is an enormous amount which could and should be done but, as things are at present, the resources do not exist, and psychiatrists are being asked to undertake more than they can possibly accomplish and to direct their therapeutic efforts towards a clientele who are less likely to respond to their efforts than are neurotics who seek help voluntarily. This has led to a number of abuses, of which unnecessary deprivation of liberty is the most obvious. It has been demonstrated that, as one might expect, the majority of psychiatrists and psychoanalysts are mildly left-wing, liberal, and anti-authoritarian. It is perhaps paradoxical that the therapeutic approach to persons who would, in previous generations, have been considered wicked or feckless has resulted in a decline in liberty, but such is the case. In what follows I am heavily indebted to *The Right to Be Different* by Nicholas N. Kittrie.[5] It is significant that a professor of criminal law should be moved to write such a powerful indictment of what he calls the "therapeutic state."

In his book, Professor Kittrie demonstrates, with a wealth of examples, that misplaced therapeutic enthusiasm has led to many persons being confined for indefinite periods with few of the safeguards against wrongful confinement which are available to criminals being effectively operative. Thus, thirty-three U.S. states have laws allowing the indefinite commitment of drug addicts to therapeutic institutions from which they can only be released if "cured."[6] Since, even after extensive exposure to the best treatment programs, only about 3 percent of addicts remain abstinent after release, it is obvious that many persons are being confined indefinitely upon false premises.

It is surely the duty of the psychiatrist to society to point out that he has, as yet, no effective method of treating the personality disorder which, it is generally agreed, underlies the phenomenon of addiction to narcotics; and, while pursuing research which may lead to effective treatments, it is his duty to refuse to act as jailer for those he cannot as yet help. He might add that, in the recent exacerbation of anxiety about the taking of drugs, it is often forgotten that the legal control of narcotics is of very recent origin, as is the supposition that crime and addiction are necessarily linked. Before 1914, there were no laws in the United States regulating the traffic in narcotics, and there is little doubt that, in the U.S., the association of drug addiction with crime is the result of punitive legislation.

In Great Britain, the poet Crabbe took opium for over forty years; yet it did not interfere with his literary output and he died at the age of seventy-eight. Wilkie Collins took increasing doses of laudanum (tincture of opium) from 1862 to his death at the age of sixty-five in 1889. His novels may have deteriorated but he did not cease production. Addiction to even heroin and morphine does not cause as much physical damage as does addiction to alcohol; and it is often preferable, as the law allows in Britain, for addicts to be allowed to obtain a regular dose of narcotic upon prescription than to try and fail to forcibly wean them from it.

Similarly, in the mistaken belief that psychiatrists can cure large numbers of alcoholics of their addiction *against their will*, twenty-six U.S. states have laws which allow the commitment of alcoholics to institutions from which release is conditional upon cure.[7] Since the treatment facilities available fall far short of what is required, the effect of this compulsion, intended as a liberal, therapeutic device, is simply to extend the period during which an alcoholic offender is confined, without in fact improving his condition. This is, of course, not to argue that no alcoholics can be cured. Some can and are helped by psychiatric treatment to achieve and sustain total abstinence; but, in my limited experience, this is entirely dependent upon the *voluntary* cooperation of the alcoholic.

More dubious still are the laws determining the confinement of so-called "psychopaths"; a category of mental abnormality so hard to define that "a 1950 New Jersey report cited twenty-nine different definitions of the condition by twenty-nine medical authorities." At least twenty states have made use of statutes relating to psychopaths, with the result that mental institutions are overloaded with people for whom they have no effective treatment. Kittrie gives examples of offenders guilty of only trivial offenses—for example, indecent exposure—who have been committed to institutions for indefinite periods. I will add one example from Great Britain. The Mental Health Act of 1959 unfortunately included provision for the forcible confinement of psychopaths. In the words of the act, psychopathic disorder is defined as "a persistent disorder or disability of mind (whether or not including subnormality of intelligence) which results in abnormally aggressive or seriously irresponsible conduct on the part of the patient and requires or is susceptible to medical treatment."

In 1968, Eric Edward Wills, aged twenty-one, who had been charged with larceny and with obtaining money under false pretenses, was sent to a mental hospital for a report. He was there diagnosed as a psychopath. The medical report submitted to the magistrate revealed that he was a compulsive gambler and recommended that the operation of prefrontal lobotomy be performed upon him. The magistrate promptly ordered that this operation be carried out. Fortunately, the press heard of the case, realized the implications, and the decision was rescinded.

Deprivation of liberty on the grounds of insanity, whether or not accompanied by the intention of enforced therapy, is also open to abuse. In the Soviet Union, confinement in a mental hospital may be instituted if the "patient" is regarded as being a "public danger." More particularly, Soviet law allows for forcible commitment if an individual is said to suffer from a "hypochondriacal delusional condition, causing an irregular, aggressive attitude in the patient towards individuals, organizations or institutions." Even more sinisterly, the law recognizes that "externally correct behavior and dissimulation" may mask what is supposed to be the individual's true intention.

It is well known and amply documented that mental hospitals are used in the Soviet Union to confine persons who are thought to be hostile to the regime; and that psychiatrists have cooperated in this misuse of their medical function. Perhaps some psychiatrists are such dedicated Communists that they do in fact believe that anyone who does not share their faith must be insane. Others may well be threatened with dismissal and loss of livelihood if they do not agree to treat as patients those whom the government wishes to remove from society. As readers of *A Question of Madness* by Zhores and Roy Medvedev will know, whatever the reasons may be, it is clearly not difficult for the Soviet government to find psychiatrists who will cooperate.[8]

In the West, it is less likely that individuals are wrongly committed to mental hospitals on purely political grounds, although the cases of Earl Long, the governor of Louisiana, and, more especially, of May Kimbrough Jones, both quoted by Kittrie, must give rise to doubt. But it is very easy indeed for individuals to be judged insane upon dubious criteria; to be committed indefinitely to mental institutions where they will receive no treatment; and to be deprived of liberty, perhaps for life, in spite of the fact that they may be causing no harm to themselves or to anyone else.

In the United States, Thomas Szasz, a psychoanalyst, has propounded the thesis that the inmates of mental hospitals are the scapegoats of society, fulfilling the same function for society as did witches in the Middle Ages. He believes that any form of coercion applied to the so-called mentally ill is unjustifiable and that the psychiatrist's function should be confined to elucidating the "problems in living" of those who voluntarily seek his help.[9] This, to my mind, is oversimplifying the issue. There are a number of persons in any society who are, and should be, regarded as mentally ill and who may, unfortunately, require confinement against their will, at any rate temporarily. In his essay on liberty, John Stuart Mill wrote: "The only purpose for which power can be rightfully exercised over any member of a civilised community, against his will, is to prevent harm to others. His own good, either physical or moral, is not a sufficient warrant."[10] Although Mill admits of some modification of this principle in the case of juveniles, he does not really consider the case of the mentally ill, in spite of the fact that, in a footnote to a later passage of the essay, he has sharp observations to make about the inadequacy of the evidence as to insanity which is often accepted by jurors. According to Mill, it would obviously be right to certify and confine an individual who was suffering from paranoid schizophrenia and threatening to murder his imagined persecutors. (In this connection it is of interest to note that acute paranoid episodes, in which individuals go berserk and do in fact kill others, are among the few forms of mental illness common to all cultures and are universally recognized as calling for the forcible restraint of the sufferer.)

But how about the sufferer from melancholia who announces his intention of committing suicide? Although it is true that suicide does usually harm those nearest to the suicide, I doubt if Mill would have thought this kind of harm sufficient to come within the category he defines. Suicide is primarily a matter of the individual harming himself; and this, Mill considers, he should be left free to do. Yet every psychiatrist will have had many patients who have been actively suicidal and who may have made more than one attempt to kill themselves but who, on recovery from their disorder, have been extremely glad that they were restrained from doing so and grateful for any treatment which led to their recovery. Moreover, there are patients in a state of mania or hypomania who may undertake all kinds of ill-judged commitments, financial and otherwise, which result in harm to themselves and from which, upon recovery, they have been grateful for being restrained. Should one deny treatment to those suffering from these types of mental disorder on the grounds that it is an unwarrantable interference with their personal liberty to do so?

In Great Britain, it has been the practice to certify and confine against their will not only those who are obviously likely to harm others but also those who are likely to harm themselves, either by suicide or else by overreaching themselves while in that state of high excitement and overconfidence we designate as hypomania. I think it right that this should be so, and I can see no way in which psychiatrists can in conscience entirely avoid the distasteful role of acting as temporary jailers and exercising coercion over some patients, even though this may conflict with their function as therapists.

But I also think that psychiatrists have a special duty, in the open society, to see that this coercion is kept to an absolute minimum. So far as I can see, this involves two principles. First, no psychiatrist should be misled by his own therapeutic enthusiasm or by the well-meaning therapeutic hopes of others into promising treatment for social deviants which he cannot carry out. Thus, because he believes that a criminal or an alcoholic or a psychopath or a .psychotic might be helped by a full-scale analysis of fifty minutes five days a week, he should not agree to his confinement in a mental institution where he will get, if he is lucky, a ten-minute interview once a week. It is not disputed that some patients in these categories can be helped by analysis; or indeed by psychotherapies less drastic, although it must be admitted that the patients who benefit most from such treatment are generally those who are too inhibited to be social deviants, rather than the reverse. But there is no point in depriving people of liberty if one has no treatment to offer them. As Norval Morris of the University of Chicago has put it: "The rehabilitative ideal is seen to impart unfettered discretion. Whereas the treaters seem convinced of the benevolence of their treatment methods, those being treated take a different view, and we, the observers share their doubts. The jailer in a white coat and with a doctorate remains a jailer—but with larger power over his fellows."[11] So much is this the case that Professor Morris advises that no criminal should plead not guilty upon grounds of insanity.

Second, no psychiatrist should cooperate in coercion unless he is convinced that the person concerned is a danger to others or to himself. If we exclude the mentally defective, the intoxicated, the physically ill, and the senile, who raise problems beyond the scope of this paper, this will in practice involve only those individuals who are murderous, suicidal, or obviously manic. A few paranoid individuals may remain murderous throughout life, but they are very few. Manic depressives, whether manic or depressed, almost invariably recover from any given attack of their disorder. Therefore, by far the majority of those who are forcibly confined will need to be so for only short periods.

Twenty-five years ago, when I was a newly fledged psychiatrist, I should have been in favor of casting the coercive net far wider. It seemed obvious, for instance, that the schizophrenic with delusions and hallucinations and other clear-cut manifestations of mental illness should be in a mental hospital where, if he could not be cured, he would at least be treated with tolerance and understanding. If he had not the insight to see this, then reluctantly, he should be certified insane. Now I realize that our criteria of mental illness are sadly inadequate; that many harmless people have "delusional systems" by which they live; and I am against depriving anybody of liberty, however "mad" he may appear, unless he is a danger to others or to himself.

In the open society, the psychiatrist has a second duty which is equally important. That is, he must do his best to insure that techniques of psychiatric investigation and treatment are not misused for other purposes by governments or other agencies such as the police or military. I have already drawn attention to the misuse of mental hospitals as places of confinement for those whom society or government finds inconvenient. There are many other possibilities of abuse. Prefrontal lobotomy is an obvious example. The misuse of drugs which alter mood or which release inhibitions so that information can be obtained is another. The techniques of conditioning used in "behavior therapy" could easily be used for the convenience of society, rather than to promote the well-being of the individual. So could the new electronic techniques of modifying brain function by the implantation of electrodes into the brain substance. Such dangers, thanks to the publicity given to them by books and newspapers, are beginning to be widely appreciated. However, there is still a pressing need for vigilance. I shall end this chapter by giving an example of the misuse of psychiatric research by government in which I was personally involved in protest.

The history goes back a long way. In 1960, the late Professor Kennedy, then professor of psychiatry at the University of Edinburgh, was rash enough to reveal that he had been employed, during the last war, at an interrogation center in Cairo, in giving advice as to how methods of psychological pressure could be brought to bear upon prisoners from whom information was wanted. This disclosure created a certain amount of unease; more, I think, among the general public than among the medical profession. What, they asked, was a doctor doing in this context? Surely

a doctor's job was to heal the sick, not to instruct governments in how to break down prisoners mentally in such a
way that they would yield up information. I took this point
of view myself, although I knew that not all my psychiatric
colleagues shared it. At the time, there was considerable
interest in "brainwashing" techniques, as practiced by the
Russians and the Chinese. The Korean War, with its revelations as to how nearly a third of the Americans captured had
been persuaded to "collaborate," was still fresh in people's
minds. There was still a lingering feeling that the British
army did not behave like that, although, of course, no one
expected that they would invariably behave to prisoners
with saintly forbearance. The best I could do at the time was
to write an article, which was published in the *New Statesman,* entitled "Torture Without Violence." In it, I deplored
the fact that doctors should lend themselves to use by government in the way which Professor Kennedy had indicated,
and suggested that this conduct was contrary to the Hippocratic oath, as indeed it was. He made no riposte to the
article; perhaps because of ill health, since in fact he died
within a few months of its publication. There were various
repercussions to this article. One lawyer wrote from Cyprus
to say that he had knowledge of British methods of interrogation, and that these included what he called
"drug-induced hypnosis." It emerged that there was a special training center for interrogators—it still exists—at
Maresfield in Sussex: though what went on there proved
difficult to find out. Eventually, we got so far as to persuade
Mr. Francis Noel-Baker to ask a question in the House of
Commons of the Prime Minister, then Mr. Harold Macmillan. He evaded the issue, saying that it was not in the
public interest to reveal what methods of interrogation were
taught to British interrogators since such information might
be of use to potential enemies. He did, however, write, "I can
give an unequivocal assurance that in the training of British
interrogators the use of 'brain washing,' drugs or physical
violence is expressly and emphatically forbidden."

I gave up inquiry at this point. It seemed difficult to carry matters beyond the Prime Minister. From time to time, various rather disturbing allegations of brutal conduct on the part of the British forces emerged from Cyprus, Aden, and other trouble spots. Then came the revelations about Northern Ireland. We learned that men were being starved, deprived of sleep, made to assume uncomfortable postures standing spread-eagled against a wall for hours at a time; and, more sinisterly, that they were being hooded and exposed to continuous noise at the same time. These revelations shocked a great number of people, and, eventually, an inquiry was instituted under the chairmanship of the former ombudsman, Sir Edmund Compton. This resulted in a report[12] which, though deploring the use of "brutality," alleged that the methods of interrogation employed in Northern Ireland were not in fact brutal. The hooding, the posture on the wall, and the continuous noise were, so Compton alleged, designed primarily to stop internees communicating with each other. A secondary effect, the report went on, might be to render the men so treated more susceptible to interrogation: "It can also, in the case of some detainees, increase their sense of isolation and so be helpful to the interrogator thereafter."

I think that any uninformed person reading the Compton Report would have concluded that, although what was done to internees was not pleasant, there was little evidence of severe *physical* pressure being employed. Some men had complained of being knocked about, or being forced to do unaccustomed physical exercises, or being forced to stand up against the wall again when they had collapsed from fatigue and the effects of being given only one slice of bread and some water every six hours or so. But the tenor of the report was that although more supervision of interrogators was desirable—and it must be remembered that the interrogations were carried out primarily by the Royal Ulster Constabulary and not by British armed forces personnel—not much harm was being done, and possibly some unpleasant procedures were temporarily necessary if the IRA was to be stopped from pursuing its policy of terrorism.

It is at this point, I think, that specialized psychiatric knowledge became relevant. Anyone who had read the literature on sensory deprivation and its effects must have concluded that a variant of sensory deprivation was being used as a method of breaking down internees. The hooding and the continuous noise were designed, not to isolate men from each other, as the Compton Report alleged, but as a deliberate method of producing mental confusion and disorientation. I was no expert in the field of sensory deprivation: but I knew that the effects were so disturbing that, even among healthy volunteers who were acting as experimental guinea pigs and being paid for it, a high proportion pressed the "panic button" long before the experimental period was up. In mild sensory deprivation conditions, male volunteers endured only an average of twenty-nine hours; and in more rigorous conditions, only one man in ten endured more than ten hours. If no limit in time has been set to the termination of the experiment, fears of insanity and confusion may come on within as little as two hours. I knew that many people lost all sense of time; that others became hallucinated; that the experience could, at any rate for some people, be compared with a bad "trip" as a result of taking LSD. I knew, moreover, that an interesting fact had emerged from the Princeton experiments.[13] If the experimenters used Princeton students, a number became paranoid, thought the experimenter had abandoned them, and so on. But when the experimenters had run short of their own students, and had to seek volunteers from further afield, the proportion who became paranoid was much higher. If the very mild degree of distrust which one might feel at entrusting oneself to the care of university professors not of one's own university became so quickly magnified under sensory deprivation, what, one wondered, would be the effect of sensory deprivation upon men who knew themselves to be in the hands of actual enemies?

At the time of publication of the Compton Report I was asked if I would write an article on its psychiatric aspects for the *Sunday Times* and did so on the following day. In the article, I tried to make it clear that physical brutality was not the only kind of brutality which mattered; that sensory deprivation techniques could be used to produce what was equivalent to a temporary episode of insanity; that no one could possibly know what the long-term aftereffects of such procedures would be upon the men to whom they had been applied; and that the home secretary had no business to say that these methods had no serious sequelae, as he had been rash enough to do in the House of Commons. I thought it important to do this because I surmised that the general public would have no idea that any method of psychological pressure without actual physical torture could be expected to have serious effects. Psychiatrists who spend most of their time only in interchanges with other psychiatrists take for granted a number of things which it is actually rash to assume that non-psychiatrists have any idea of.

After various further protests in the House of Commons and elsewhere, a group of three privy councillors, Lord Parker, Lord Gardiner, and Mr. Boyd-Carpenter, were appointed to investigate the whole question of interrogation further, and I found myself giving evidence before them. I repeated to these distinguished men what I had said in the *Sunday Times* article, further reinforced by a study of the literature on sensory deprivation. I discovered that some of this literature is still not available, as it comes under the heading of "classified" information. It seems that government departments are quick off the mark in spotting what psychological and physiological techniques might be of use to them in war. A great deal of this research had, of course, been undertaken at the request of governments interested in the effect of isolation, weightlessness, and the like upon potential astronauts. What the Parker Committee was primarily interested in was whether the techniques of sensory deprivation employed in Northern Ireland could, as it were, be used in moderation without much risk of serious after-effects. They told me that it was undoubtedly true that much useful information had been obtained from internees by the use of these methods, and no doubt many lives had been saved as a result. I was, of course, unable to answer this question, since there was no literature available to me which could tell me whether sensory deprivation employed as an interrogation technique upon enemies had the dire effects which any psychiatrist must guess it would be likely to have. All I could say was that so-called "traumatic" neuroses had been known to result from traumas which were less severe; that producing psychotic symptoms in "normal" people by other methods, like the use of LSD, for instance, was fraught with risk; and that one could only tell what the effects would actually be after a long-term follow-up of the people concerned. In the event, the Parker Committee produced a report in which Lord Parker and Mr. Boyd-Carpenter thought that the methods employed in Ulster could continue to be used if subject to more stringent safeguards; while Lord Gardiner produced a minority report saying that these methods were wholly detestable, their results unpredictable, and that they were unworthy of British traditions in the treatment of prisoners. The Prime Minister, after the publication of the report, said in the House that these methods would henceforth be forbidden.

The moral of this story is not so much that it is possible for psychiatrists, on occasion, to participate effectively in protest, important though this is. It is to underline the fact that psychiatric techniques and research, designed originally to be helpful to disturbed individuals, can, in many instances, be extracted from their therapeutic setting and used for exactly the opposite purpose. It is the duty of the psychiatrist, in the open society, to be aware of this possibility, and to prevent it when he can. In my view, it is also his duty to refrain from giving professional advice or in any way participating in such abuse. "The condition upon which God hath given liberty to man is eternal vigilance; which condition if he break, servitude is at once the consequence of his crime and the punishment of his guilt."[14]

NOTES

1. Karl Popper, *The Open Society and Its Enemies*, 2 vols. (London: Routledge and Kegan Paul, 1945).

2. Jennifer Newton, *Preventing Mental Illness* (London: Routledge and Kegan Paul, 1988), p. 15.

3. Jonas Robitscher, *The Powers of Psychiatry* (Boston: Houghton Mifflin, 1980), p. 131.

4. Melanie Klein, *Contributions to Psycho-Analysis* (London: Hogarth Press/Institute of Psycho-Analysis, 1950), pp. 276–77.

5. Nicholas N. Kittrie, *The Right to Be Different* (Baltimore: Johns Hopkins Press, 1971).

6. Ibid., p. 236.

7. Ibid., p. 276.

8. Zhores A. Medvedev and Roy A. Medvedev, *A Question of Madness* (London: Macmillan, 1971).

9. Thomas Szasz, *The Myth of Mental Illness* (New York: Harper and Row, 1961).

10. John Stuart Mill, *On Liberty* (Harmondsworth: Penguin, 1974).

11. Norval Morris, "Impediments to Penal Reform," *University of Chicago Law Review* 33 (1966):627–37.

12. *Report of the Enquiry into Allegations Against the Security Forces of Physical Brutality in Northern Ireland Arising Out of Events on the 9th August, 1971,* Sir Edmund Compton, G.C.B., K.B.E., chairman (London: Her Majesty's Stationery Office, November 1971).

13. Jack Vernon, *Inside the Black Room* (London: Souvenir Press, 1963).

14. John Philpot Curran, "Speech on the Right of Election of Lord Mayor of Dublin," July 10, 1790.

Acknowledgments

I want especially to thank my editor at Grove Press, Fred Jordan, for his many helpful suggestions, and Joy Johannessen of Grove for her eagle-eyed, expert editing. Her emendations and suggestions have invariably improved both the text and the many references. Errors and omissions are mine alone.

"Churchill: The Man," from *Churchill Revised,* edited by A. J. P. Taylor, Robert Rhodes James, J. H. Plumb, Basil Liddell Hart, and Anthony Storr (New York: Dial Press, 1969). © 1969 by Doubleday, a division of Bantam, Doubleday, Dell Publishing Group, Inc. Reprinted by permission of the publisher.

"Kafka's Sense of Identity," first published in *Paths and Labyrinths,* edited by J. P. Stern and J. J. Whyte (London: Institute of Germanic Studies, University of London, 1985).

"Isaac Newton," first published in the *British Medical Journal* 291 (December 21–28, 1985): 1779–84. Reprinted by permission of the *British Medical Journal.*

"Psychoanalysis and Creativity," first published in *Psychoanalysis and the Humanities,* edited by Peregrine Horden (London: Duckworth, 1985).

"Intimations of Mystery," first published in *William Golding: The Man and His Books,* edited by John Carey (London: Faber and Faber, 1986).

"Jung's Conception of Personality," first published in *Persons and Personality,* edited by Arthur Peacocke and Grant Gillett (Oxford: Basil Blackwell, 1987).

"Why Psychoanalysis Is Not a Science," first published in *Mind-waves*, edited by Colin Blakemore (Oxford: Basil Blackwell, 1987). Reprinted by permission of the publisher.

"The Psychology of Symbols," first published in *Symbols in Life and Art*, edited by James Leith (Montreal: McGill-Queen's University Press, 1987). Reprinted by permission of the publisher.

"The Sanity of True Genius," first published in *The Virginia Quarterly Review* 61, no. 1 (Winter 1985). Reprinted by permission of *The Virginia Quarterly Review*.

"Psychiatric Responsibility in the Open Society," first published in *The Open Society in Theory and Practice*, edited by Dante Germino and Klaus von Beyme (The Hague: Martinus Nijhoff, 1974), pp. 276–90. © 1974 by Martinus Nijhoff Publishers, Dordrecht, Holland. Reprinted by permission of the publisher.

The other papers in this collection have not previously been published, although earlier versions of "Why Human Beings Become Violent" have appeared in various places. Several of these papers have been extensively revised for this collection. I am grateful to the editors and publishers who have given me permission to reprint those papers of which I did not retain the copyright.